Yeast

A Problem

by
Charles Kingsley

Yeast
A Problem
by Charles Kingsley

Copyright © 2024

All Rights reserved.

No part of this publication may be reproduced, stored in a retrieval system, or transmitted in any form or by any means, electronic, mechanical, photocopying or Otherwise, without the written permission of the publisher.
The author/editor asserts the moral right to be identified as the author/editor of this work.

ISBN: 978-93-68097-32-7

Published by

DOUBLE 9 BOOKS
2/13-B, Ansari Road
Daryaganj, New Delhi – 110002
info@double9books.com
www.double9books.com
Tel. 011-40042856

This book is under public domain

ABOUT THE AUTHOR

Charles Kingsley was a broad church priest of the Church of England, a university lecturer, a social reformer, a historian, a novelist, and a poet. He lived from 12 June 1819 to 23 January 1875. He is known for his involvement in Christian socialism, the working men's college, and the establishment of labor cooperatives, which were unsuccessful but inspired later labor reforms. He was Charles Darwin's friend and correspondent. The eldest child of the Reverend Charles Kingsley and his wife, Mary Lucas Kingsley, Kingsley was born in Holne, Devon. Both his sister Charlotte Chanter (1828-1882) and brother Henry Kingsley (1830-1876) were writers. He was the uncle of the explorer and scientist Mary Kingsley and the father of the novelist Lucas Malet (Mary St. Leger Kingsley, 1852–1931). (1862–1900). The early years of Charles Kingsley were spent in Barnack, Northamptonshire, and Clovelly, Devon, where his father served as Curate from 1826 to 1832 and Rector from 1832 to 1836. Before attending King's College London and the University of Cambridge, he received his education at Bristol Grammar School and Helston Grammar School. Charles enrolled in Cambridge's Magdalene College in 1838 and earned his degree there in 1842.

CONTENTS

PREFACE TO THE FOURTH EDITION 7
PREFACE TO THE FIRST EDITION 13

CHAPTER I
THE PHILOSOPHY OF FOX-HUNTING 15

CHAPTER II
SPRING YEARNINGS 26

CHAPTER III
NEW ACTORS, AND A NEW STAGE 38

CHAPTER IV
AN 'INGLORIOUS MILTON' 59

CHAPTER V
A SHAM IS WORSE THAN NOTHING 66

CHAPTER VI
VOGUE LA GALÈRE 72

CHAPTER VII
THE DRIVE HOME, AND WHAT CAME OF IT 85

CHAPTER VIII
WHITHER? 92

CHAPTER IX
HARRY VERNEY HEARS HIS LAST SHOT FIRED 104

CHAPTER X
'MURDER WILL OUT,' AND LOVE TOO 112

CHAPTER XI
    THUNDERSTORM THE FIRST 128

CHAPTER XII
    THUNDERSTORM THE SECOND 138

CHAPTER XIII
    THE VILLAGE REVEL 147

CHAPTER XIV
    WHAT'S TO BE DONE? 170

CHAPTER XV
    DEUS E MACHINÂ 183

CHAPTER XVI
    ONCE IN A WAY 201

CHAPTER XVII
    THE VALLEY OF THE SHADOW OF DEATH 209

EPILOGUE 226

PREFACE TO THE FOURTH EDITION

This book was written nearly twelve years ago; and so many things have changed since then, that it is hardly fair to send it into the world afresh, without some notice of the improvement—if such there be—which has taken place meanwhile in those southern counties of England, with which alone this book deals.

I believe that things are improved. Twelve years more of the new Poor Law have taught the labouring men greater self-help and independence; I hope that those virtues may not be destroyed in them once more, by the boundless and indiscriminate almsgiving which has become the fashion of the day, in most parishes where there are resident gentry. If half the money which is now given away in different forms to the agricultural poor could be spent in making their dwellings fit for honest men to live in, then life, morals, and poor-rates, would be saved to an immense amount. But as I do not see how to carry out such a plan, I have no right to complain of others for not seeing.

Meanwhile cottage improvement, and sanitary reform, throughout the country districts, are going on at a fearfully slow rate. Here and there high-hearted landlords, like the Duke of Bedford, are doing their duty like men; but in general, the apathy of the educated classes is most disgraceful.

But the labourers, during the last ten years, are altogether better off. Free trade has increased their food, without lessening their employment. The politician who wishes to know the effect on agricultural life of that wise and just measure, may find it in Mr. Grey of Dilston's answers to the queries of the French Government. The country parson will not need to seek so far. He will see it (if he be an observant man) in the faces and figures of his school-children. He will see a rosier, fatter, bigger-boned race growing up, which bids fair to surpass in bulk the puny and ill-fed generation of 1815-45, and equal, perhaps, in thew and sinew, to the men who saved Europe in the old French war.

If it should be so (as God grant it may), there is little fear but that the labouring men of England will find their aristocracy able to lead them in the battle-field, and to develop the agriculture of the land at home, even better than did their grandfathers of the old war time.

To a thoughtful man, no point of the social horizon is more full of light, than the altered temper of the young gentlemen. They have their faults and follies still—for when will young blood be other than hot blood? But when one finds, more and more, swearing banished from the hunting-field, foul songs from the universities, drunkenness and gambling from the barracks; when one finds everywhere, whether at college, in camp, or by the coverside, more and more, young men desirous to learn their duty as Englishmen, and if possible to do it; when one hears their altered tone toward the middle classes, and that word 'snob' (thanks very much to Mr. Thackeray) used by them in its true sense, without regard of rank; when one watches, as at Aldershott, the care and kindness of officers toward their men; and over and above all this, when one finds in every profession (in that of the soldier as much as any) young men who are not only 'in the world,' but (in religious phraseology) 'of the world,' living God-fearing, virtuous, and useful lives, as Christian men should: then indeed one looks forward with hope and confidence to the day when these men shall settle down in life, and become, as holders of the land, the leaders of agricultural progress, and the guides and guardians of the labouring man.

I am bound to speak of the farmer, as I know him in the South of England. In the North he is a man of altogether higher education and breeding: but he is, even in the South, a much better man than it is the fashion to believe him. No doubt, he has given heavy cause of complaint. He was demoralised, as surely, if not as deeply, as his own labourers, by the old Poor Law. He was bewildered—to use the mildest term—by promises of Protection from men who knew better. But his worst fault after all has been, that young or old, he has copied his landlord too closely, and acted on his maxims and example. And now that his landlord is growing wiser, he is growing wiser too. Experience of the new Poor Law, and experience of Free-trade, are helping him to show himself what he always was at heart, an honest Englishman. All his brave persistence and industry, his sturdy independence and self-help, and last, but not least, his strong sense of justice, and his vast good-nature, are coming out more and more, and working better and better upon the land and the labourer; while among his sons I see many growing up brave, manly, prudent young men, with a steadily increasing knowledge of what is required of them, both as manufacturers of food, and employers of human labour.

The country clergy, again, are steadily improving. I do not mean merely in morality—for public opinion now demands that as a sine quà non—but in actual efficiency. Every fresh appointment seems to me, on the whole, a better one than the last. They are gaining more and more the love and respect of their flocks; they are becoming more and more centres of civilisation and morality to their parishes; they are working, for the most part, very hard, each in his own way; indeed their great danger is, that they should trust too much in that outward 'business' work which they do so heartily; that they should fancy that the administration of schools and charities is their chief business, and literally leave the Word of God to serve tables. Would that we clergymen could learn (some of us are learning already) that influence over our people is not to be gained by perpetual interference in their private affairs, too often inquisitorial, irritating, and degrading to both parties, but by showing ourselves their personal friends, of like passions with them. Let a priest do that. Let us make our people feel that we speak to them, and feel to them, as men to men, and then the more cottages we enter the better. If we go into our neighbours' houses only as judges, inquisitors, or at best gossips, we are best—as too many are—at home in our studies. Would, too, that we would recollect this—that our duty is, among other things, to preach the Gospel; and consider firstly whether what we commonly preach be any Gospel or good news at all, and not rather the worst possible news; and secondly, whether we preach at all; whether our sermons are not utterly unintelligible (being delivered in an unknown tongue), and also of a dulness not to be surpassed; and whether, therefore, it might not be worth our while to spend a little time in studying the English tongue, and the art of touching human hearts and minds.

But to return: this improved tone (if the truth must be told) is owing, far more than people themselves are aware, to the triumphs of those liberal principles, for which the Whigs have fought for the last forty years, and of that sounder natural philosophy of which they have been the consistent patrons. England has become Whig; and the death of the Whig party is the best proof of its victory. It has ceased to exist, because it has done its work; because its principles are accepted by its ancient enemies; because the political economy and the physical science, which grew up under its patronage, are leavening the thoughts and acts of Anglican and of Evangelical alike, and supplying them with methods for carrying out their own schemes. Lord Shaftesbury's truly noble speech on Sanitary Reform at Liverpool is a striking proof of the extent to which the Evangelical leaders have given in their adherence to those scientific laws, the original preachers of which have been called by his Lordship's party heretics and infidels, materialists and rationalists. Be it so. Provided truth be preached, what matter who preaches it? Provided the leaven of sound inductive science leaven the whole lump, what matter who sets it working? Better, perhaps, because more likely to produce practical success, that these novel truths should be instilled into the minds of the educated classes by men who share somewhat in their prejudices and superstitions, and doled out to them in such measure as will not terrify or disgust them. The child will take its medicine from the nurse's hand trustfully enough, when it would scream itself into convulsions at the sight of the doctor, and so do itself more harm than the medicine would do it good. The doctor meanwhile (unless he be one of Hesiod's 'fools, who know not how much more half is than the whole') is content enough to see any part of his prescription got down, by any hands whatsoever.

But there is another cause for the improved tone of the Landlord class, and of the young men of what is commonly called the aristocracy; and that is, a growing moral earnestness; which is in great part owing (that justice may be done on all sides) to the Anglican movement. How much soever Neo-Anglicanism may have failed as an Ecclesiastical or Theological system; how much soever it may have proved itself, both by the national dislike of it, and by the defection of all its master-minds, to be radically un-English, it has at least awakened hundreds, perhaps thousands, of cultivated men and women to ask themselves whether God sent them into the world merely to eat, drink, and be merry, and to have 'their souls saved' upon the Spurgeon method, after they die; and has taught them an answer to that question not unworthy of English Christians.

The Anglican movement, when it dies out, will leave behind at least a legacy of grand old authors disinterred, of art, of music; of churches too, schools, cottages, and charitable institutions, which will form so many centres of future civilisation, and will entitle it to the respect, if not to the allegiance, of the future generation. And more than this; it has sown in the hearts of young gentlemen and young ladies seed which will not perish; which, though it may develop into forms little expected by those who sowed it, will develop at least into a virtue more stately and reverent, more chivalrous and self-sacrificing, more genial and human, than can be learnt from that religion of the Stock Exchange, which reigned triumphant—for a year and a day—in the popular pulpits.

I have said, that Neo-Anglicanism has proved a failure, as seventeenth-century Anglicanism did. The causes of that failure this book has tried to point out: and not one word which is spoken of it therein, but has been drawn from personal and too-intimate experience. But now—peace to its ashes. Is it so great a sin, to have been dazzled by the splendour of an impossible ideal? Is it so great a sin, to have had courage and conduct enough to attempt the enforcing of that ideal, in the face of the prejudices of a whole nation? And if that ideal was too narrow for the English nation, and for the modern needs of mankind, is that either so great a sin? Are other extant ideals, then, so very comprehensive? Does Mr. Spurgeon, then, take so much broader or nobler views of the capacities and destinies of his race, than that great genius, John Henry Newman? If the world cannot answer that question now, it will answer it promptly enough in another five-and-twenty years. And meanwhile let not the party and the system which has conquered boast itself too loudly. Let it take warning by the Whigs; and suspect (as many a looker-on more than suspects) that its triumph may be, as with the Whigs, its ruin; and that, having done the work for which it was sent into the world, there may only remain for it, to decay and die.

And die it surely will, if (as seems too probable) there succeeds to this late thirty years of peace a thirty years of storm.

For it has lost all hold upon the young, the active, the daring. It has sunk into a compromise between originally opposite dogmas. It has become a religion for Jacob the smooth man; adapted to the maxims of the market, and leaving him full liberty to supplant his brother by all methods lawful in that market. No longer can it embrace and explain all known facts of God and man, in heaven and earth, and satisfy utterly such minds and hearts as those of Cromwell's Ironsides, or the Scotch Covenanters, or even of a Newton and a Colonel Gardiner. Let it make the most of its Hedley Vicars and its Havelock, and sound its own trumpet as loudly as it can, in sounding theirs; for they are the last specimens of heroism which it is likely to beget—if indeed it did in any true sense beget them, and if their gallantry was really owing to their creed, and not to the simple fact of their being—like others—English gentlemen. Well may Jacob's chaplains cackle in delighted surprise over their noble memories, like geese who have unwittingly hatched a swan!

But on Esau in general:—on poor rough Esau, who sails Jacob's ships, digs Jacob's mines, founds Jacob's colonies, pours out his blood for him in those wars which Jacob himself has stirred up—while his sleek brother sits at home in his counting-house, enjoying at once 'the means of grace' and the produce of Esau's labour—on him Jacob's chaplains have less and less influence; for him they have less and less good news. He is afraid of them, and they of him; the two do not comprehend one another, sympathise with one another; they do not even understand one another's speech. The same social and moral gulf has opened between them, as parted the cultivated and wealthy Pharisee of Jerusalem from the rough fishers of the Galilæan Lake: and yet the Galilæan fishers (if we are to trust Josephus and the Gospels) were trusty, generous, affectionate—and it was not from among the Pharisees, it is said, that the Apostles were chosen.

Be that as it may, Esau has a birthright; and this book, like all books which I have ever written, is written to tell him so; and, I trust, has not been written in vain. But it is not this book, or any man's book, or any man at all, who can tell Esau the whole truth about himself, his powers, his duty, and his God. Woman must do it, and not man. His mother, his sister, the maid whom he may love; and failing all these (as they often will fail him, in the wild wandering life which he must live), those human angels of whom it is written—'The barren hath many more children than she who has an husband.' And such will not be wanting. As long as England can produce at once two such women as Florence Nightingale and Catherine Marsh, there is good hope that Esau will not be defrauded of his birthright; and that by the time that Jacob comes crouching to him, to defend him against the enemies who are near at hand, Esau, instead of borrowing Jacob's religion, may be able to teach Jacob his; and the two brothers face together the superstition and anarchy of Europe, in the strength of a lofty and enlightened Christianity, which shall be thoroughly human, and therefore thoroughly divine.

C. K.
February 17th, 1859.

PREFACE TO THE FIRST EDITION

This little tale was written between two and three years ago, in the hope that it might help to call the attention of wiser and better men than I am, to the questions which are now agitating the minds of the rising generation, and to the absolute necessity of solving them at once and earnestly, unless we would see the faith of our forefathers crumble away beneath the combined influence of new truths which are fancied to be incompatible with it, and new mistakes as to its real essence. That this can be done I believe and know: if I had not believed it, I would never have put pen to paper on the subject.

I believe that the ancient Creed, the Eternal Gospel, will stand, and conquer, and prove its might in this age, as it has in every other for eighteen hundred years, by claiming, and subduing, and organising those young anarchic forces, which now, unconscious of their parentage, rebel against Him to whom they owe their being.

But for the time being, the young men and women of our day are fast parting from their parents and each other; the more thoughtful are wandering either towards Rome, towards sheer materialism, or towards an unchristian and unphilosophic spiritualism. Epicurism which, in my eyes, is the worst evil spirit of the three, precisely because it looks at first sight most like an angel of light. The mass, again, are fancying that they are still adhering to the old creeds, the old church, to the honoured patriarchs of English Protestantism. I wish I could agree with them in their belief about themselves. To me they seem—with a small sprinkling of those noble and cheering exceptions to popular error which are to be found in every age of Christ's church—to be losing most fearfully and rapidly the living spirit of Christianity, and to be, for that very reason, clinging all the more convulsively—and who can blame them?—to the outward letter of it, whether High Church or Evangelical; unconscious, all the while, that they are sinking out of real living belief, into that dead self-deceiving belief-in-believing, which has been always heretofore, and is becoming in England now, the parent of the most blind, dishonest, and pitiless bigotry.

In the following pages I have attempted to show what some at least of the young in these days are really thinking and feeling. I know well that my sketch is inadequate and partial: I have every reason to believe, from the criticisms which I have received since its first publication, that it is, as far as it goes, correct. I put it as a problem. It would be the height of arrogance in me to do more than indicate the direction in which I think a solution may be found. I fear that my elder readers may complain that I have no right to start doubts without answering them. I can only answer,—Would that I had started them! would that I was not seeing them daily around me, under some form or other, in just the very hearts for whom one would most wish the peace and strength of a fixed and healthy faith. To the young, this book can do no harm; for it will put into their minds little but what is there already. To the elder, it may do good; for it may teach some of them, as I earnestly hope, something of the real, but too often utterly unsuspected, state of their own children's minds; something of the reasons of that calamitous estrangement between themselves and those who will succeed them, which is often too painful and oppressive to be confessed to their own hearts! Whatever amount of obloquy this book may bring upon me, I shall think that a light price to pay, if by it I shall have helped, even in a single case, to 'turn the hearts of the parents to the children, and the hearts of the children to the parents, before the great and terrible day of the Lord come,'—as come it surely will, if we persist much longer in substituting denunciation for sympathy, instruction for education, and Pharisaism for the Good News of the Kingdom of God.

1851.

CHAPTER I
THE PHILOSOPHY OF FOX-HUNTING

As this my story will probably run counter to more than one fashion of the day, literary and other, it is prudent to bow to those fashions wherever I honestly can; and therefore to begin with a scrap of description.

The edge of a great fox-cover; a flat wilderness of low leafless oaks fortified by a long, dreary, thorn capped clay ditch, with sour red water oozing out at every yard; a broken gate leading into a straight wood ride, ragged with dead grasses and black with fallen leaves, the centre mashed into a quagmire by innumerable horsehoofs; some forty red coats and some four black; a sprinkling of young-farmers, resplendent in gold buttons and green; a pair of sleek drab stable-keepers, showing off horses for sale; the surgeon of the union, in Mackintosh and antigropelos; two holiday schoolboys with trousers strapped down to bursting point, like a penny steamer's safety-valve; a midshipman, the only merry one in the field, bumping about on a fretting, sweating hack, with its nose a foot above its ears; and Lancelot Smith, who then kept two good horses, and 'rode forward' as a fine young fellow of three-and-twenty who can afford it, and 'has nothing else to do,' has a very good right to ride.

But what is a description, without a sketch of the weather?—In these Pantheist days especially, when a hero or heroine's moral state must entirely depend on the barometer, and authors talk as if Christians were cabbages, and a man's soul as well as his lungs might be saved by sea-breezes and sunshine; or his character developed by wearing guano in his shoes, and training himself against a south wall—we must have a weather description, though, as I shall presently show, one in flat contradiction of the popular theory. Luckily for our information, Lancelot was very much given to watch both the weather and himself, and had indeed, while in his teens, combined the two in a sort of a soul-almanack on the principles just mentioned—somewhat in this style:—

'*Monday*, 21*st*.—Wind S.W., bright sun, mercury at 30½ inches. Felt my heart expanded towards the universe. Organs of veneration and benevolence pleasingly excited; and gave a shilling to a tramp. An inexpressible joy bounded through every vein, and the soft air breathed purity and self-sacrifice through my soul. As I watched the beetles, those children of the sun, who, as divine Shelley says, "laden with light and odour, pass over the gleam of the living grass," I gained an Eden-glimpse of the pleasures of virtue.

'N.B. Found the tramp drunk in a ditch. I could not have degraded myself on such a day—ah! how could he?

'Tuesday, 22d.—Barometer rapidly falling. Heavy clouds in the south-east. My heart sank into gloomy forebodings. Read *Manfred*, and doubted whether I should live long. The laden weight of destiny seemed to crush down my aching forehead, till the thunderstorm burst, and peace was restored to my troubled soul.'

This was very bad; but to do justice to Lancelot, he had grown out of it at the time when my story begins. He was now in the fifth act of his 'Werterean' stage; that sentimental measles, which all clever men must catch once in their lives, and which, generally, like the physical measles, if taken early, settles their constitution for good or evil; if taken late, goes far towards killing them. Lancelot had found Byron and Shelley pall on his taste and commenced devouring Bulwer and worshipping *Ernest Maltravers*. He had left Bulwer for old ballads and romances, and Mr. Carlyle's reviews; was next alternately chivalry-mad; and Germany-mad; was now reading hard at physical science; and on the whole, trying to become a great man, without any very clear notion of what a great man ought to be. Real education he never had had. Bred up at home under his father, a rich merchant, he had gone to college with a large stock of general information, and a particular mania for dried plants, fossils, butterflies, and sketching, and some such creed as this:—

That he was very clever.

That he ought to make his fortune.

That a great many things were very pleasant—beautiful things among the rest.

That it was a fine thing to be 'superior,' gentleman-like, generous, and courageous.

That a man ought to be religious.

And left college with a good smattering of classics and mathematics, picked up in the intervals of boat-racing and hunting, and much the same creed as he brought with him, except in regard to the last article. The scenery-and-natural-history mania was now somewhat at a discount. He had discovered a new natural object, including in itself all—more than all—yet found beauties and wonders—woman!

Draw, draw the veil and weep, guardian angel! if such there be. What was to be expected? Pleasant things were pleasant—there was no doubt of that, whatever else might be doubtful. He had read Byron by stealth; he had been flogged into reading Ovid and Tibullus; and commanded by his private tutor to read Martial and Juvenal 'for the improvement of his style.' All conversation on the subject of love had been prudishly avoided, as usual, by his parents and teacher. The parts of the Bible which spoke of it had been always kept out of his sight. Love had been to him, practically, ground tabooed and 'carnal.' What was to be expected? Just what happened—if woman's beauty had nothing holy in it, why should his fondness for it? Just what happens every day—that he had to sow his wild oats for himself, and eat the fruit thereof, and the dirt thereof also.

O fathers! fathers! and you, clergymen, who monopolise education! either tell boys the truth about love, or do not put into their hands, without note or comment, the foul devil's lies about it, which make up the mass of the Latin poets—and then go, fresh from teaching Juvenal and Ovid, to declaim at Exeter Hall against poor Peter Dens's well-meaning prurience! Had we not better take the beam out of our own eye before we meddle with the mote in the Jesuit's?

But where is my description of the weather all this time?

I cannot, I am sorry to say, give any very cheerful account of the weather that day. But what matter? Are Englishmen hedge-gnats, who only take their sport when the sun shines? Is it not, on the contrary, symbolical of our national character, that almost all our field amusements are wintry ones? Our fowling, our hunting, our punt-shooting (pastime for Hymir himself and the frost giants)—our golf and skating,—our very cricket, and boat-racing, and jack and grayling fishing, carried on till we are fairly frozen out. We are a stern people, and winter suits us. Nature then retires modestly into the background, and spares us the obtrusive glitter of summer, leaving us to think and work; and therefore it happens that in England, it may be taken as a general rule, that whenever all the rest of the world is in-doors, we are out and busy, and on the whole, the worse the day, the better the deed.

The weather that day, the first day Lancelot ever saw his beloved, was truly national. A silent, dim, distanceless, steaming, rotting day in March. The last brown oak-leaf which had stood out the winter's frost, spun and quivered plump down, and then lay; as if ashamed to have broken for a moment the ghastly stillness, like an awkward guest at a great dumb dinner-party. A cold suck of wind just proved its existence, by toothaches on the north side of all faces. The spiders having been weather-bewitched the night before, had unanimously agreed to cover every brake and brier with gossamer-cradles, and never a fly to be caught in them; like Manchester cotton-spinners madly glutting the markets in the teeth of 'no demand.' The steam crawled out of the dank turf, and reeked off the flanks and nostrils of the shivering horses, and clung with clammy paws to frosted hats and dripping boughs. A soulless, skyless, catarrhal day, as if that bustling dowager, old mother Earth—what with match-making in spring, and *fêtes champêtres* in summer, and dinner-giving in autumn—was fairly worn out, and put to bed with the influenza, under wet blankets and the cold-water cure.

There sat Lancelot by the cover-side, his knees aching with cold and wet, thanking his stars that he was not one of the whippers-in who were lashing about in the dripping cover, laying up for themselves, in catering for the amusement of their betters, a probable old age of bed-ridden torture, in the form of rheumatic gout. Not that he was at all happy—indeed, he had no reason to be so; for, first, the hounds would not find; next, he had left half-finished at home a review article on the Silurian System, which he had solemnly promised an abject and beseeching editor to send to post that night; next, he was on the windward side of the cover, and dare not light a cigar; and lastly, his mucous membrane in general was not in the happiest condition, seeing that he had been dining the evening before with Mr. Vaurien of Rottenpalings, a young gentleman of a convivial and melodious turn of mind, who sang—and played also—as singing men are wont—in more senses than one, and had 'ladies and gentlemen' down from town to stay with him; and they sang and played too; and so somehow between vingt-un and champagne-punch, Lancelot had not arrived at home till seven o'clock that morning, and was in a fit state to appreciate the feelings of our grandfathers, when, after the third bottle of port, they used to put the black silk tights into their pockets, slip on the leathers and boots, and ride the crop-tailed hack thirty miles on a winter's night, to meet the hounds in the next county by ten in the morning. They are 'gone down to Hades, even many stalwart souls of heroes,' with John Warde of Squerries at their head—the fathers of the men who conquered at Waterloo; and we their degenerate grandsons are left instead, with puny arms, and polished leather boots, and a considerable taint of hereditary disease, to sit in club-houses, and celebrate the progress of the species.

Whether Lancelot or his horse, under these depressing circumstances, fell asleep; or whether thoughts pertaining to such a life, and its fitness for a clever and ardent young fellow in the nineteenth century, became gradually too painful, and had to be peremptorily shaken off, this deponent sayeth not; but certainly, after five-and-thirty minutes of idleness and shivering, Lancelot opened his eyes with a sudden start, and struck spurs into his hunter without due cause shown; whereat Shiver-the-timbers, who was no Griselda in temper—(Lancelot had bought him out of the Pytchley for half his value, as unrideably vicious, when he had killed a groom, and fallen backwards on a rough-rider, the first season after he came up from Horncastle)—responded by a furious kick or two, threw his head up, put his foot into a drain, and sprawled down all but on his nose, pitching Lancelot unawares shamefully on the pommel of his saddle. A certain fatality, by the bye, had lately attended all Lancelot's efforts to shine; he never bought a new coat without tearing it mysteriously next day, or tried to make a joke without bursting out coughing in the middle . . . and now the whole field were looking on at his mishap; between disgust and the start he turned almost sick, and felt the blood rush into his cheeks and forehead as he heard a shout of coarse jovial laughter burst out close to him, and the old master of the hounds, Squire Lavington, roared aloud—

'A pretty sportsman you are, Mr. Smith, to fall asleep by the cover-side and let your horse down—and your pockets, too! What's that book on the ground? Sapping and studying still? I let nobody come out with my hounds with their pocket full of learning. Hand it up here, Tom; we'll see what it is. French, as I am no scholar! Translate for us, Colonel Bracebridge!'

And, amid shouts of laughter, the gay Guardsman read out,—

'St. Francis de Sales: Introduction to a Devout Life.'

Poor Lancelot! Wishing himself fathoms under-ground, ashamed of his book, still more ashamed of himself for his shame, he had to sit there ten physical seconds, or spiritual years, while the colonel solemnly returned him the book, complimenting him on the proofs of its purifying influence which he had given the night before, in helping to throw the turnpike-gate into the river.

But 'all things do end,' and so did this; and the silence of the hounds also; and a faint but knowing whimper drove St. Francis out of all heads, and Lancelot began to stalk slowly with a dozen horsemen up the wood-ride, to a fitful accompaniment of wandering hound-music, where the choristers were as invisible as nightingales among the thick cover. And hark! just as the book was returned to his pocket, the sweet hubbub suddenly crashed out into one jubilant shriek, and then swept away fainter and fainter among the trees. The walk became a trot—the trot a canter. Then a faint melancholy shout at a distance, answered by a 'Stole away!' from the fields; a doleful 'toot!' of the horn; the dull thunder of many horsehoofs rolling along the farther woodside. Then red coats, flashing like sparks of fire across the gray gap of mist at the ride's-mouth, then a whipper-in, bringing up a belated hound, burst into the pathway, smashing and plunging, with shut eyes, through ash-saplings and hassock-grass; then a fat farmer, sedulously pounding through the mud, was overtaken and bespattered in spite of all his struggles;—until the line streamed out into the wide rushy pasture, startling up pewits and curlews, as horsemen poured in from every side, and cunning old farmers rode off at inexplicable angles to some well-known haunts of pug: and right ahead, chiming and jangling sweet madness, the dappled pack glanced and wavered through the veil of soft grey mist. 'What's the use of this hurry?' growled Lancelot. 'They will all be back again. I never have the luck to see a run.'

But no; on and on—down the wind and down the vale; and the canter became a gallop, and the gallop a long straining stride; and a hundred horsehoofs crackled like flame among the stubbles, and thundered fetlock-deep along the heavy meadows; and every fence thinned the cavalcade, till the madness began to stir all bloods, and with grim earnest silent faces, the initiated few settled themselves to their work, and with the colonel and Lancelot at their head, 'took their pleasure sadly, after the manner of their nation,' as old Froissart has it.

'Thorough bush, through brier,
Thorough park, through pale;'

till the rolling grass-lands spread out into flat black open fallows, crossed with grassy baulks, and here and there a long melancholy line of tall elms, while before them the high chalk ranges gleamed above the mist like a vast wall of emerald enamelled with snow, and the winding river glittering at their feet.

'A polite fox!' observed the colonel. 'He's leading the squire straight home to Whitford, just in time for dinner.'

They were in the last meadow, with the stream before them. A line of struggling heads in the swollen and milky current showed the hounds' opinion of Reynard's course. The sportsmen galloped off towards the nearest bridge. Bracebridge looked back at Lancelot, who had been keeping by his side in sulky rivalry, following him successfully through all manner of desperate places, and more and more angry with himself and the guiltless colonel, because he only followed, while the colonel's quicker and unembarrassed wit, which lived wholly in the present moment, saw long before Lancelot, 'how to cut out his work,' in every field.

'I shan't go round,' quietly observed the colonel.

'Do you fancy I shall?' growled Lancelot, who took for granted—poor thin-skinned soul! that the words were meant as a hit at himself.

'You're a brace of geese,' politely observed the old squire; 'and you'll find it out in rheumatic fever. There—"one fool makes many!" You'll kill Smith before you're done, colonel!' and the old man wheeled away up the meadow, as Bracebridge shouted after him,—

'Oh, he'll make a fine rider—in time!'

'In time!' Lancelot could have knocked the unsuspecting colonel down for the word. It just expressed the contrast, which had fretted him ever since he began to hunt with the Whitford Priors hounds. The colonel's long practice and consummate skill in all he took in hand,—his experience of all society, from the prairie Indian to Crockford's, from the prize-ring to the continental courts,—his varied and ready store of information and anecdote,—the harmony and completeness of the man,—his consistency with his own small ideal, and his consequent apparent superiority everywhere and in everything to the huge awkward Titan-cub, who, though immeasurably beyond Bracebridge in intellect and heart, was still in a state of convulsive dyspepsia, 'swallowing formulæ,' and daily well-nigh choked; diseased throughout with that morbid self-consciousness and lust of praise, for which God prepares, with His elect, a bitter cure. Alas! poor Lancelot! an unlicked bear, 'with all his sorrows before him!'—

'Come along,' quoth Bracebridge, between snatches of a tune, his coolness maddening Lancelot. 'Old Lavington will find us dry clothes, a bottle of port, and a brace of charming daughters, at the Priory. In with you, little Mustang of the prairie! Neck or nothing!'—

And in an instant the small wiry American, and the huge Horncastle-bred hunter, were wallowing and staggering in the yeasty stream, till they floated into a deep reach, and swam steadily down to a low place in the bank. They crossed the stream, passed the Priory Shrubberies, leapt the gate into the park, and then on and upward, called by the unseen Ariel's music before them.—Up, into the hills; past white crumbling chalk-pits, fringed with feathered juniper and tottering ashes, their floors strewed with knolls of fallen soil and vegetation, like wooded islets in a sea of milk.—Up, between steep ridges of tuft crested with black fir-woods and silver beech, and here and there a huge yew standing out alone, the advanced sentry of the forest, with its luscious fretwork of green velvet, like a mountain of Gothic spires and pinnacles, all glittering and steaming as the sun drank up the dew-drops. The lark sprang upward into song, and called merrily to the new-opened sunbeams, while the wreaths and flakes of mist lingered reluctantly about the hollows, and clung with dewy fingers to every knoll and belt of pine.—Up into the labyrinthine bosom of the hills,—but who can describe them? Is not all nature indescribable? every leaf infinite and transcendental? How much more those mighty downs, with their enormous sheets of spotless turf, where the dizzy eye loses all standard of size and distance before the awful simplicity, the delicate vastness, of those grand curves and swells, soft as the outlines of a Greek Venus, as if the great goddess-mother Hertha had laid herself down among the hills to sleep, her Titan limbs wrapt in a thin veil of silvery green.

Up, into a vast amphitheatre of sward, whose walls banked out the narrow sky above. And here, in the focus of the huge ring, an object appeared which stirred strange melancholy in Lancelot,—a little chapel, ivy-grown, girded with a few yews, and elders, and grassy graves. A climbing rose over the porch, and iron railings round the churchyard, told of human care; and from the graveyard itself burst up one of those noble springs known as winter-bournes in the chalk ranges, which, awakened in autumn from the abysses to which it had shrunk during the summer's drought, was hurrying down upon its six months' course, a broad sheet of oily silver over a temporary channel of smooth greensward.

The hounds had checked in the woods behind; now they poured down the hillside, so close together 'that you might have covered them with a sheet,' straight for the little chapel.

A saddened tone of feeling spread itself through Lancelot's heart. There were the everlasting hills around, even as they had grown and grown for countless ages, beneath the still depths of the primeval chalk ocean, in the milky youth of this great English land. And here was he, the insect of a day, fox-hunting upon *them*! He felt ashamed, and more ashamed when the inner voice whispered—'Fox-hunting is not the shame—thou art the shame. If thou art the insect of a day, it is thy sin that thou art one.'

And his sadness, foolish as it may seem, grew as he watched a brown speck fleet rapidly up the opposite hill, and heard a gay view-halloo burst from the colonel at his side. The chase lost its charm for him the moment the game was seen. Then vanished that mysterious delight of pursuing an invisible object, which gives to hunting and fishing their unutterable and almost spiritual charm; which made Shakespeare a nightly poacher; Davy and Chantrey the patriarchs of fly-fishing; by which the twelve-foot rod is transfigured into an enchanter's wand, potent over the unseen wonders of the water-world, to 'call up spirits from the vasty deep,' which will really 'come if you do call for them'—at least if the conjuration be orthodox—and they there. That spell was broken by the sight of poor wearied pug, his once gracefully-floating brush all draggled and drooping, as he toiled up the sheep-paths towards the open down above.

But Lancelot's sadness reached its crisis, as he met the hounds just outside the churchyard. Another moment—they had leaped the rails; and there they swept round under the gray wall, leaping and yelling, like Berserk fiends among the frowning tombstones, over the cradles of the quiet dead.

Lancelot shuddered—the thing was not wrong—'it was no one's fault,'—but there was a ghastly discord in it. Peace and strife, time and eternity—the mad noisy flesh, and the silent immortal spirit,—the frivolous game of life's outside show, and the terrible earnest of its inward abysses, jarred together without and within him. He pulled his horse up violently, and stood as if rooted to the place, gazing at he knew not what.

The hounds caught sight of the fox, burst into one frantic shriek of joy—and then a sudden and ghastly stillness, as, mute and breathless, they toiled up the hillside, gaining on their victim at every stride. The patter of the horsehoofs and the rattle of rolling flints died away above. Lancelot looked up, startled at the silence; laughed aloud, he knew not why, and sat, regardless of his pawing and straining horse, still staring at the chapel and the graves.

On a sudden the chapel-door opened, and a figure, timidly yet loftily stepped out without observing him, and suddenly turning round, met him full, face to face, and stood fixed with surprise as completely as Lancelot himself.

That face and figure, and the spirit which spoke through them, entered his heart at once, never again to leave it. Her features were aquiline and grand, without a shade of harshness; her eyes shone out like twain lakes of still azure, beneath a broad marble cliff of polished forehead; her rich chestnut hair rippled downward round the towering neck. With her perfect masque and queenly figure, and earnest, upward gaze, she might have been the very model from which Raphael conceived his glorious St. Catherine— the ideal of the highest womanly genius, softened into self-forgetfulness by girlish devotion. She was simply, almost coarsely dressed; but a glance told him that she was a lady, by the courtesy of man as well as by the will of God.

They gazed one moment more at each other—but what is time to spirits? With them, as with their Father, 'one day is as a thousand years.' But that eye-wedlock was cut short the next instant by the decided interference of the horse, who, thoroughly disgusted at his master's whole conduct, gave a significant shake of his head, and shamming frightened (as both women and horses will do when only cross), commenced a war-dance, which drove

Argemone Lavington into the porch, and gave the bewildered Lancelot an excuse for dashing madly up the hill after his companions.

'What a horrible ugly face!' said Argemone to herself, 'but so clever, and so unhappy!'

Blest pity! true mother of that graceless scamp, young Love, who is ashamed of his real pedigree, and swears to this day that he is the child of Venus!—the coxcomb!

[Here, for the sake of the reader, we omit, or rather postpone a long dissertation on the famous Erototheogonic chorus of Aristophanes's Birds, with illustrations taken from all earth and heaven, from the Vedas and Proclus to Jacob Boëhmen and Saint Theresa.]

'The dichotomy of Lancelot's personality,' as the Germans would call it, returned as he dashed on. His understanding was trying to ride, while his spirit was left behind with Argemone. Hence loose reins and a looser seat. He rolled about like a tipsy man, holding on, in fact, far more by his spurs than by his knees, to the utter infuriation of Shiver-the-timbers, who kicked and snorted over the down like one of Mephistopheles's Demon-steeds. They had mounted the hill—the deer fled before them in terror—they neared the park palings. In the road beyond them the hounds were just killing their fox, struggling and growling in fierce groups for the red gobbets of fur, a panting, steaming ring of horses round them. Half a dozen voices hailed him as he came up.

'Where have you been?' 'He'll tumble off!' 'He's had a fall!' 'No he hasn't!' ''Ware hounds, man alive!' 'He'll break his neck!'

'He has broken it, at last!' shouted the colonel, as Shiver-the-timbers rushed at the high pales, out of breath, and blind with rage. Lancelot saw and heard nothing till he was awakened from his dream by the long heave of the huge brute's shoulder, and the maddening sensation of sweeping through the air over the fence. He started, checked the curb, the horse threw up his head, fulfilling his name by driving his knees like a battering-ram against the pales—the top-bar bent like a withe, flew out into a hundred splinters, and man and horse rolled over headlong into the hard flint-road.

For one long sickening second Lancelot watched the blue sky between his own knees. Then a crash as if a shell had burst in his face—a horrible grind—a sheet of flame—and the blackness of night. Did you ever feel it, reader?

When he awoke, he found himself lying in bed, with Squire Lavington sitting by him. There was real sorrow in the old man's face, 'Come to himself!' and a great joyful oath rolled out. 'The boldest rider of them all! I wouldn't have lost him for a dozen ready-made spick and span Colonel Bracebridges!'

'Quite right, squire!' answered a laughing voice from behind the curtain. 'Smith has a clear two thousand a year, and I live by my wits!'

CHAPTER II
SPRING YEARNINGS

I heard a story the other day of our most earnest and genial humorist, who is just now proving himself also our most earnest and genial novelist. 'I like your novel exceedingly,' said a lady; 'the characters are so natural—all but the baronet, and he surely is overdrawn: it is impossible to find such coarseness in his rank of life!'

The artist laughed. 'And that character,' said he, 'is almost the only exact portrait in the whole book.'

So it is. People do not see the strange things which pass them every day. 'The romance of real life' is only one to the romantic spirit. And then they set up for critics, instead of pupils; as if the artist's business was not just to see what they cannot see—to open their eyes to the harmonies and the discords, the miracles and the absurdities, which seem to them one uniform gray fog of commonplaces.

Then let the reader believe, that whatsoever is commonplace in my story is my own invention. Whatsoever may seem extravagant or startling is most likely to be historic fact, else I should not have dared to write it down, finding God's actual dealings here much too wonderful to dare to invent many fresh ones for myself.

Lancelot, who had had a severe concussion of the brain and a broken leg, kept his bed for a few weeks, and his room for a few more. Colonel Bracebridge installed himself at the Priory, and nursed him with indefatigable good-humour and few thanks. He brought Lancelot his breakfast before hunting, described the run to him when he returned, read him to sleep, told him stories of grizzly bear and buffalo-hunts, made him laugh in spite of himself at extempore comic medleys, kept his tables covered with flowers from the conservatory, warmed his chocolate, and even his bed. Nothing came amiss to him, and he to nothing. Lancelot longed at first every hour to be rid of him, and eyed him about the room as a bulldog does the monkey who rides him. In his dreams he was Sinbad the Sailor, and Bracebridge the Old Man of the Sea; but he could not hold out against the colonel's merry bustling kindliness, and the almost womanish tenderness of his nursing. The ice thawed rapidly; and one evening it split up altogether, when Bracebridge, who was sitting drawing by Lancelot's sofa, instead of amusing himself with the ladies below, suddenly threw his pencil into the fire, and broke out, *à propos de rien*—

'What a strange pair we are, Smith! I think you just the best fellow I ever met, and you hate me like poison—you can't deny it.'

There was something in the colonel's tone so utterly different from his usual courtly and measured speech, that Lancelot was taken completely by surprise, and stammered out,—

'I—I—I—no—no. I know I am very foolish—ungrateful. But I do hate you,' he said, with a sudden impulse, 'and I'll tell you why.'

'Give me your hand,' quoth the colonel: 'I like that. Now we shall see our way with each other, at least.'

'Because,' said Lancelot slowly, 'because you are cleverer than I, readier than I, superior to me in every point.'

The colonel laughed, not quite merrily. Lancelot went on, holding down his shaggy brows.

'I am a brute and an ass!—And yet I do not like to tell you so. For if I am an ass, what are you?'

'Heyday!'

'Look here.—I am wasting my time and brains on ribaldry, but I am worth nothing better—at least, I think so at times; but you, who can do anything you put your hand to, what business have you, in the devil's name, to be throwing yourself away on gimcracks and fox-hunting foolery? Heavens! If I had your talents, I'd be—I'd make a name for myself before I died, if I died to make it.' The colonel griped his hand hard, rose, and looked out of the window for a few minutes. There was a dead, brooding silence, till he turned to Lancelot,—

'Mr. Smith, I thank you for your honesty, but good advice may come too late. I am no saint, and God only knows how much less of one I may become; but mark my words,—if you are ever tempted by passion, and vanity, and fine ladies, to form *liaisons*, as the Jezebels call them, snares, and nets, and labyrinths of blind ditches, to keep you down through life, stumbling and grovelling, hating yourself and hating the chain to which you cling—in that hour pray—pray as if the devil had you by the throat,—to Almighty God, to help you out of that cursed slough! There is nothing else for it!—pray, I tell you!'

There was a terrible earnestness about the guardsman's face which could not be mistaken. Lancelot looked at him for a moment, and then dropped his eyes ashamed, as if he had intruded on the speaker's confidence by witnessing his emotion.

In a moment the colonel had returned to his smile and his polish.

'And now, my dear invalid, I must beg your pardon for sermonising. What do you say to a game of *écarté*? We must play for love, or we shall excite ourselves, and scandalise Mrs. Lavington's piety.' And the colonel pulled a pack of cards out of his pocket, and seeing that Lancelot was too thoughtful for play, commenced all manner of juggler's tricks, and chuckled over them like any schoolboy.

'Happy man!' thought Lancelot, 'to have the strength of will which can thrust its thoughts away once and for all.' No, Lancelot! more happy are they whom God will not allow to thrust their thoughts from them till the bitter draught has done its work.

From that day, however, there was a cordial understanding between the two. They never alluded to the subject; but they had known the bottom of each other's heart. Lancelot's sick-room was now pleasant enough, and he drank in daily his new friend's perpetual stream of anecdote, till March and hunting were past, and April was half over. The old squire came up after dinner regularly (during March he had hunted every day, and slept every evening); and the trio chatted along merrily enough, by the help of whist and backgammon, upon the surface of this little island of life,—which is, like Sinbad's, after all only the back of a floating whale, ready to dive at any moment.—And then?—

But what was Argemone doing all this time? Argemone was busy in her boudoir (too often a true boudoir to her) among books and statuettes, and dried flowers, fancying herself, and not unfairly, very intellectual. She had four new manias every year; her last winter's one had been that bottle-and-squirt mania, miscalled chemistry; her spring madness was for the Greek drama. She had devoured Schlegel's lectures, and thought them divine; and now she was hard at work on Sophocles, with a little help from translations, and thought she understood him every word. Then she was somewhat High-Church in her notions, and used to go up every Wednesday and Friday to the chapel in the hills, where Lancelot had met her, for an hour's mystic devotion, set off by a little graceful asceticism. As for Lancelot, she never thought of him but as an empty-headed fox-hunter who had met with his deserts; and the brilliant accounts which the all smoothing colonel gave at dinner of Lancelot's physical well doing and agreeable conversation only made her set him down the sooner as a twin clever-do-nothing to the despised Bracebridge, whom she hated for keeping her father in a roar of laughter.

But her sister, little Honoria, had all the while been busy messing and cooking with her own hands for the invalid; and almost fell in love with the colonel for his watchful kindness. And here a word about Honoria, to whom Nature, according to her wont with sisters, had given almost everything which Argemone wanted, and denied almost everything which Argemone had, except beauty. And even in that, the many-sided mother had made her a perfect contrast to her sister,—tiny and luscious, dark-eyed and dark-haired; as full of wild simple passion as an Italian, thinking little, except where she felt much—which was, indeed, everywhere; for she lived in a perpetual April-shower of exaggerated sympathy for all suffering, whether in novels or in life; and daily gave the lie to that shallow old calumny, that 'fictitious sorrows harden the heart to real ones.'

Argemone was almost angry with her sometimes, when she trotted whole days about the village from school to sick-room: perhaps conscience hinted to her that her duty, too, lay rather there than among her luxurious day-dreams. But, alas! though she would have indignantly repelled the accusation of selfishness, yet in self and for self alone she lived; and while she had force of will for any so-called 'self-denial,' and would fast herself cross and stupefied, and quite enjoy kneeling thinly clad and barefoot on the freezing chapel-floor on a winter's morning, yet her fastidious delicacy revolted at sitting, like Honoria, beside the bed of the ploughman's consumptive daughter, in a reeking, stifling, lean-to garret, in which had slept the night before, the father, mother, and two grown-up boys, not to mention a new-married couple, the sick girl, and, alas! her baby. And of such bedchambers there were too many in Whitford Priors.

The first evening that Lancelot came downstairs, Honoria clapped her hands outright for joy as he entered, and ran up and down for ten minutes, fetching and carrying endless unnecessary cushions and footstools; while Argemone greeted him with a cold distant bow, and a fine-lady drawl of carefully commonplace congratulations. Her heart smote her though, as she saw the wan face and the wild, melancholy, moonstruck eyes once more glaring through and through her; she found a comfort in thinking his stare impertinent, drew herself up, and turned away; once, indeed, she could not help listening, as Lancelot thanked Mrs. Lavington for all the pious and edifying books with which the good lady had kept his room rather than his brain furnished for the last six weeks; he was going to say more, but he saw the colonel's quaint foxy eye peering at him, remembered St. Francis de Sales, and held his tongue.

But, as her destiny was, Argemone found herself, in the course of the evening, alone with Lancelot, at the open window. It was a still, hot, heavy night, after long easterly drought; sheet-lightning glimmered on the far horizon over the dark woodlands; the coming shower had sent forward as his herald a whispering draught of fragrant air.

'What a delicious shiver is creeping over those limes!' said Lancelot, half to himself.

The expression struck Argemone: it was the right one, and it seemed to open vistas of feeling and observation in the speaker which she had not suspected. There was a rich melancholy in the voice;—she turned to look at him.

'Ay,' he went on; 'and the same heat which crisps those thirsty leaves must breed the thunder-shower which cools them? But so it is throughout the universe: every yearning proves the existence of an object meant to satisfy it; the same law creates both the giver and the receiver, the longing and its home.'

'If one could but know sometimes what it is for which one is longing!' said Argemone, without knowing that she was speaking from her inmost heart: but thus does the soul involuntarily lay bare its most unspoken depths in the presence of its yet unknown mate, and then shudders at its own *abandon* as it first tries on the wedding garment of Paradise.

Lancelot was not yet past the era at which young geniuses are apt to 'talk book' at little.

'For what?' he answered, flashing up according to his fashion. 'To be;— to be great; to have done one mighty work before we die, and live, unloved or loved, upon the lips of men. For this all long who are not mere apes and wall-flies.'

'So longed the founders of Babel,' answered Argemone, carelessly, to this tirade. She had risen a strange fish, the cunning beauty, and now she was trying her fancy flies over him one by one.

'And were they so far wrong?' answered he. 'From the Babel society sprung our architecture, our astronomy, politics, and colonisation. No doubt the old Hebrew sheiks thought them impious enough, for daring to build brick walls instead of keeping to the good old-fashioned tents, and gathering themselves into a nation instead of remaining a mere family horde; and gave their own account of the myth, just as the antediluvian savages gave theirs of that strange Eden scene, by the common interpretation of which the devil is made the first inventor of modesty. Men are all conservatives; everything new is impious, till we get accustomed to it; and if it fails, the mob piously discover a divine vengeance in the mischance, from Babel to Catholic Emancipation.'

Lancelot had stuttered horribly during the latter part of this most heterodox outburst, for he had begun to think about himself, and try to say a fine thing, suspecting all the while that it might not be true. But Argemone did not remark the stammering: the new thoughts startled and pained her; but there was a daring grace about them. She tried, as women will, to answer him with arguments, and failed, as women will fail. She was accustomed to lay down the law *à la* Madame de Staël, to *savants* and *non-savants* and be heard with reverence, as a woman should be. But poor truth-seeking Lancelot did not see what sex had to do with logic; he flew at her as if she had been a very barrister, and hunted her mercilessly up and down through all sorts of charming sophisms, as she begged the question, and shifted her ground, as thoroughly right in her conclusion as she was wrong in her reasoning, till she grew quite confused and pettish.—And then Lancelot suddenly shrank into his shell, claws and all, like an affrighted soldier-crab, hung down his head, and stammered out some incoherencies,—'N-n-not accustomed to talk to women—ladies, I mean. F-forgot myself.—Pray forgive me!' And he looked up, and her eyes, half-amused, met his, and she saw that they were filled with tears.

'What have I to forgive?' she said, more gently, wondering on what sort of strange sportsman she had fallen. 'You treat me like an equal; you will deign to argue with me. But men in general—oh, they hide their contempt for us, if not their own ignorance, under that mask of chivalrous deference!' and then in the nasal fine ladies' key, which was her shell, as bitter *brusquerie* was his, she added, with an Amazon queen's toss of the head,—'You must come and see us often. We shall suit each other, I see, better than most whom we see here.'

A sneer and a blush passed together over Lancelot's ugliness.

'What, better than the glib Colonel Bracebridge yonder?'

'Oh, he is witty enough, but he lives on the surface of everything! He is altogether shallow and *blasé*. His good-nature is the fruit of want of feeling; between his gracefulness and his sneering persiflage he is a perfect Mephistopheles-Apollo.'

What a snare a decently good nickname is! Out it must come, though it carry a lie on its back. But the truth was, Argemone thought herself infinitely superior to the colonel, for which simple reason she could not in the least understand him.

[By the bye, how subtly Mr. Tennyson has embodied all this in *The Princess*. How he shows us the woman, when she takes her stand on the false masculine ground of intellect, working out her own moral punishment, by destroying in herself the tender heart of flesh, which is either woman's highest blessing or her bitterest curse; how she loses all feminine sensibility to the under-current of feeling in us poor world-worn, case-hardened men, and falls from pride to sternness, from sternness to sheer inhumanity. I should have honoured myself by pleading guilty to stealing much of Argemone's character from *The Princess*, had not the idea been conceived, and fairly worked out, long before the appearance of that noble poem.]

They said no more to each other that evening. Argemone was called to the piano; and Lancelot took up the Sporting Magazine, and read himself to sleep till the party separated for the night.

Argemone went up thoughtfully to her own room. The shower had fallen, and the moon was shining bright, while every budding leaf and knot of mould steamed up cool perfume, borrowed from the treasures of the thundercloud. All around was working the infinite mystery of birth and growth, of giving and taking, of beauty and use. All things were harmonious—all things reciprocal without. Argemone felt herself needless, lonely, and out of tune with herself and nature.

She sat in the window, and listlessly read over to herself a fragment of her own poetry:—

SAPPHO

> She lay among the myrtles on the cliff;
> Above her glared the moon; beneath, the sea.
> Upon the white horizon Athos' peak
> Weltered in burning haze; all airs were dead;
> The sicale slept among the tamarisk's hair;
> The birds sat dumb and drooping. Far below
> The lazy sea-weed glistened in the sun:
> The lazy sea-fowl dried their steaming wings;
> The lazy swell crept whispering up the ledge,
> And sank again. Great Pan was laid to rest;
> And mother Earth watched by him as he slept,
> And hushed her myriad children for awhile.
>
> She lay among the myrtles on the cliff;
> And sighed for sleep, for sleep that would not hear,
> But left her tossing still: for night and day

A mighty hunger yearned within her heart,
Till all her veins ran fever, and her cheek,
Her long thin hands, and ivory-channell'd feet,
Were wasted with the wasting of her soul.
Then peevishly she flung her on her face,
And hid her eyeballs from the blinding glare,
And fingered at the grass, and tried to cool
Her crisp hot lips against the crisp hot sward:
And then she raised her head, and upward cast
Wild looks from homeless eyes, whose liquid light
Gleamed out between deep folds of blue-black hair,
As gleam twin lakes between the purple peaks
Of deep Parnassus, at the mournful moon.
Beside her lay a lyre. She snatched the shell,
And waked wild music from its silver strings;
Then tossed it sadly by,—'Ah, hush!' she cries,
'Dead offspring of the tortoise and the mine!
Why mock my discords with thine harmonies?
'Although a thrice-Olympian lot be thine,
Only to echo back in every tone,
The moods of nobler natures than thine own.'

'No!' she said. 'That soft and rounded rhyme suits ill with Sappho's fitful and wayward agonies. She should burst out at once into wild passionate life-weariness, and disgust at that universe, with whose beauty she has filled her eyes in vain, to find it always a dead picture, unsatisfying, unloving—as I have found it.'

Sweet self-deceiver! had you no other reason for choosing as your heroine Sappho, the victim of the idolatry of intellect—trying in vain to fill her heart with the friendship of her own sex, and then sinking into mere passion for a handsome boy, and so down into self-contempt and suicide?

She was conscious, I do believe, of no other reason than that she gave; but consciousness is a dim candle—over a deep mine.

'After all,' she said pettishly, 'people will call it a mere imitation of Shelley's *Alastor*. And what harm if it is? Is there to be no female Alastor? Has not the woman as good a right as the man to long after ideal beauty—to pine and die if she cannot find it; and regenerate herself in its light?'

'Yo-hoo-oo-oo! Youp, youp! Oh-hooo!' arose doleful through the echoing shrubbery.

Argemone started and looked out. It was not a banshee, but a forgotten fox-hound puppy, sitting mournfully on the gravel-walk beneath, staring at the clear ghastly moon.

She laughed and blushed—there was a rebuke in it. She turned to go to rest; and as she knelt and prayed at her velvet faldstool, among all the nicknacks which now-a-days make a luxury of devotion, was it strange if, after she had prayed for the fate of nations and churches, and for those who, as she thought, were fighting at Oxford the cause of universal truth and reverend antiquity, she remembered in her petitions the poor godless youth, with his troubled and troubling eloquence? But it was strange that she blushed when she mentioned his name—why should she not pray for him as she prayed for others?

Perhaps she felt that she did not pray for him as she prayed for others.

She left the Æolian harp in the window, as a luxury if she should wake, and coiled herself up among lace pillows and eider blemos; and the hound coiled himself up on the gravel-walk, after a solemn vesper-ceremony of three turns round in his own length, looking vainly for a 'soft stone.' The finest of us are animals after all, and live by eating and sleeping: and, taken as animals, not so badly off either—unless we happen to be Dorsetshire labourers—or Spitalfields weavers—or colliery children—or marching soldiers—or, I am afraid, one half of English souls this day.

And Argemone dreamed;—that she was a fox, flying for her life through a churchyard—and Lancelot was a hound, yelling and leaping, in a red coat and white buckskins, close upon her—and she felt his hot breath, and saw his white teeth glare. . . . And then her father was there: and he was an Italian boy, and played the organ—and Lancelot was a dancing dog, and stood up and danced to the tune of *'C'est l'amour, l'amour, l'amour,'* pitifully enough, in his red coat—and she stood up and danced too; but she found her fox-fur dress insufficient, and begged hard for a paper frill—which was denied her: whereat she cried bitterly and woke; and saw the Night peeping in with her bright diamond eyes, and blushed, and hid her beautiful face in the pillows, and fell asleep again.

What the little imp, who managed this puppet-show on Argemone's brain-stage, may have intended to symbolise thereby, and whence he stole his actors and stage-properties, and whether he got up the interlude for his own private fun, or for that of a choir of brother Eulenspiegels, or, finally, for the edification of Argemone as to her own history, past, present, or future, are questions which we must leave unanswered, till physicians have become a little more of metaphysicians, and have given up their present plan of ignoring for nine hundred and ninety-nine pages that most awful and significant custom of dreaming, and then in the thousandth page talking the boldest materialist twaddle about it.

In the meantime, Lancelot, contrary to the colonel's express commands, was sitting up to indite the following letter to his cousin, the Tractarian curate:—

'You complain that I waste my time in field-sports: how do you know that I waste my time? I find within myself certain appetites; and I suppose that the God whom you say made me, made those appetites as a part of me. Why are they to be crushed any more than any other part of me? I am the whole of what I find in myself—am I to pick and choose myself out of myself? And besides, I feel that the exercise of freedom, activity, foresight, daring, independent self-determination, even in a few minutes' burst across country, strengthens me in mind as well as in body. It might not do so to you; but you are of a different constitution, and, from all I see, the power of a man's muscles, the excitability of his nerves, the shape and balance of his brain, make him what he is. Else what is the meaning of physiognomy? Every man's destiny, as the Turks say, stands written on his forehead. One does not need two glances at your face to know that you would not enjoy fox-hunting, that you would enjoy book-learning and "refined repose," as they are pleased to call it. Every man carries his character in his brain. You all know that, and act upon it when you have to deal with a man for sixpence; but your religious dogmas, which make out that everyman comes into the world equally brutish and fiendish, make you afraid to confess it. I don't quarrel with a "douce" man like you, with a large organ of veneration, for following your bent. But if I am fiery, with a huge cerebellum, why am I not to follow mine?—For that is what you do, after all—what you like best. It is all very easy for a man to talk of conquering his appetites, when he has none to conquer. Try and conquer your organ of veneration, or of benevolence, or of calculation—then I will call you an ascetic. Why not!—The same Power which made the front of one's head made the back, I suppose?

'And, I tell you, hunting does me good. It awakens me out of my dreary mill-round of metaphysics. It sweeps away that infernal web of self-consciousness, and absorbs me in outward objects; and my red-hot Perillus's bull cools in proportion as my horse warms. I tell you, I never saw a man who could cut out his way across country who could not cut his way through better things when his turn came. The cleverest and noblest fellows are sure to be the best riders in the long run. And as for bad company and "the world," when you take to going in the first-class carriages for fear of meeting a swearing sailor in the second-class—when those who have "renounced the world" give up buying and selling in the funds—when my uncle, the pious banker, who will only "associate" with the truly religious, gives up dealing with any scoundrel or heathen who can "do business" with him—then you may quote pious people's opinions to me. In God's name, if the Stock Exchange, and railway stagging, and the advertisements in the Protestant Hue-and-Cry, and the frantic Mammon-hunting which has been for the last fifty years the peculiar pursuit of the majority of Quakers, Dissenters, and Religious Churchmen, are not *The World*, what is? I don't complain of them, though; Puritanism has interdicted to them all art, all excitement, all amusement—except money-making. It is their *dernier ressort*, poor souls!

'But you must explain to us naughty fox-hunters how all this agrees with the good book. We see plainly enough, in the meantime, how it agrees with "poor human nature." We see that the "religious world," like the "great world," and the "sporting world," and the "literary world,"

"Compounds for sins she is inclined to,
By damning those she has no mind to;"

and that because England is a money-making country, and money-making is an effeminate pursuit, therefore all sedentary and spoony sins, like covetousness, slander, bigotry, and self-conceit, are to be cockered and plastered over, while the more masculine vices, and no-vices also, are mercilessly hunted down by your cold-blooded, soft-handed religionists.

'This is a more quiet letter than usual from me, my dear coz, for many of your reproofs cut me home: they angered me at the time; but I deserve them. I am miserable, self-disgusted, self-helpless, craving for freedom, and yet crying aloud for some one to come and guide me, and teach me; and *who is there in these days who could teach a fast man, even if he would try*? Be sure, that as long as you and yours make piety a synonym for unmanliness, you will never convert either me or any other good sportsman.

'By the bye, my dear fellow, was I asleep or awake when I seemed to read in the postscript of your last letter, something about "being driven to Rome after all"? . . . Why thither, of all places in heaven or earth? You know, I have no party interest in the question. All creeds are very much alike to me just now. But allow me to ask, in a spirit of the most tolerant curiosity, what possible celestial bait, either of the useful or the agreeable kind, can the present excellent Pope, or his adherents, hold out to you in compensation for the solid earthly pudding which you would have to desert? . . . I daresay, though, that I shall not comprehend your answer when it comes. I am, you know, utterly deficient in that sixth sense of the angelic or supralunar beautiful, which fills your soul with ecstasy. You, I know, expect and long to become an angel after death: I am under the strange hallucination that my body is part of me, and in spite of old Plotinus, look with horror at a disembodiment till the giving of that new body, the great perfection of which, in your eyes, and those of every one else, seems to be, that it will be less, and not more of a body, than our present one. . . . Is this hope, to me at once inconceivable and contradictory, palpable and valuable enough to you to send you to that Italian Avernus, to get it made a little more certain? If so, I despair of your making your meaning intelligible to a poor fellow wallowing, like me, in the Hylic Borboros—or whatever else you may choose to call the unfortunate fact of being flesh and blood. . . . Still, write.'

CHAPTER III
NEW ACTORS, AND A NEW STAGE

When Argemone rose in the morning, her first thought was of Lancelot. His face haunted her. The wild brilliance of his intellect struggling through foul smoke-clouds, had haunted her still more. She had heard of his profligacy, his bursts of fierce Berserk-madness; and yet now these very faults, instead of repelling, seemed to attract her, and intensify her longing to save him. She would convert him; purify him; harmonise his discords. And that very wish gave her a peace she had never felt before. She had formed her idea; she had now a purpose for which to live, and she determined to concentrate herself for the work, and longed for the moment when she should meet Lancelot, and begin—how, she did not very clearly see.

It is an old jest—the fair devotee trying to convert the young rake. Men of the world laugh heartily at it; and so does the devil, no doubt. If any readers wish to be fellow-jesters with that personage, they may; but, as sure as old Saxon women-worship remains for ever a blessed and healing law of life, the devotee may yet convert the rake—and, perhaps, herself into the bargain.

Argemone looked almost angrily round at her beloved books and drawings; for they spoke a message to her which they had never spoken before, of self-centred ambition. 'Yes,' she said aloud to herself, 'I have been selfish, utterly! Art, poetry, science—I believe, after all, that I have only loved them for my own sake, not for theirs, because they would make me something, feed my conceit of my own talents. How infinitely more glorious to find my work-field and my prize, not in dead forms and colours, or ink-and-paper theories, but in a living, immortal, human spirit! I will study no more, except the human heart, and only that to purify and ennoble it.'

True, Argemone; and yet, like all resolutions, somewhat less than the truth. That morning, indeed, her purpose was simple as God's own light. She never dreamed of exciting Lancelot's admiration, even his friendship for herself. She would have started as from a snake, from the issue which the reader very clearly foresees, that Lancelot would fall in love, not with Young Englandism, but with Argemone Lavington. But yet self is not eradicated even from a woman's heart in one morning before breakfast. Besides, it is not 'benevolence,' but love—the real Cupid of flesh and blood, who can first

'Touch the chord of self which, trembling,
Passes in music out of sight.'

But a time for all things; and it is now time for Argemone to go down to breakfast, having prepared some dozen imaginary dialogues between herself and Lancelot, in which, of course, her eloquence always had the victory. She had yet to learn, that it is better sometimes not to settle in one's heart what we shall speak, for the Everlasting Will has good works ready prepared for us to walk in, by what we call fortunate accident; and it shall be given us in that day and that hour what we shall speak.

Lancelot, in the meantime, shrank from meeting Argemone; and was quite glad of the weakness which kept him upstairs. Whether he was afraid of her—whether he was ashamed of himself or of his crutches, I cannot tell, but I daresay, reader, you are getting tired of all this soul-dissecting. So we will have a bit of action again, for the sake of variety, if for nothing better.

Of all the species of lovely scenery which England holds, none, perhaps, is more exquisite than the banks of the chalk-rivers—the perfect limpidity of the water, the gay and luxuriant vegetation of the banks and ditches, the masses of noble wood embosoming the villages, the unique beauty of the water-meadows, living sheets of emerald and silver, tinkling and sparkling, cool under the fiercest sun, brilliant under the blackest clouds.—There, if anywhere, one would have expected to find Arcadia among fertility, loveliness, industry, and wealth. But, alas for the sad reality! the cool breath of those glittering water-meadows too often floats laden with poisonous miasma. Those picturesque villages are generally the perennial hotbeds of fever and ague, of squalid penury, sottish profligacy, dull discontent too stale for words. There is luxury in the park, wealth in the huge farm-steadings, knowledge in the parsonage: but the poor? those by whose dull labour all that luxury and wealth, ay, even that knowledge, is made possible—what are they? We shall see, please God, ere the story's end.

But of all this Lancelot as yet thought nothing. He, too, had to be emancipated, as much as Argemone, from selfish dreams; to learn to work trustfully in the living Present, not to gloat sentimentally over the unreturning Past. But his time was not yet come; and little he thought of all the work which lay ready for him within a mile of the Priory, as he watched the ladies go out for the afternoon, and slipped down to the Nun's-pool on his crutches to smoke and fish, and build castles in the air.

The Priory, with its rambling courts and gardens, stood on an island in the river. The upper stream flowed in a straight artificial channel through the garden, still and broad, towards the Priory mill; while just above the Priory wall half the river fell over a high weir, with all its appendages of bucks and hatchways, and eel-baskets, into the Nun's-pool, and then swept round under the ivied walls, with their fantastic turrets and gables, and little loopholed windows, peering out over the stream, as it hurried down over the shallows to join the race below the mill. A postern door in the walls opened on an ornamental wooden bridge across the weir-head—a favourite haunt of all fishers and sketchers who were admitted to the dragon-guarded Elysium of Whitford Priors. Thither Lancelot went, congratulating himself, strange to say, in having escaped the only human being whom he loved on earth.

He found on the weir-bridge two of the keepers. The younger one, Tregarva, was a stately, thoughtful-looking Cornishman, some six feet three in height, with thews and sinews in proportion. He was sitting on the bridge looking over a basket of eel-lines, and listening silently to the chat of his companion.

Old Harry Verney, the other keeper, was a character in his way, and a very bad character too, though he was a patriarch among all the gamekeepers of the vale. He was a short, wiry, bandy-legged, ferret-visaged old man, with grizzled hair, and a wizened face tanned brown and purple by constant exposure. Between rheumatism and constant handling the rod and gun, his fingers were crooked like a hawk's claws. He kept his left eye always shut, apparently to save trouble in shooting; and squinted, and sniffed, and peered, with a stooping back and protruded chin, as if he were perpetually on the watch for fish, flesh, and fowl, vermin and Christian. The friendship between himself and the Scotch terrier at his heels would have been easily explained by Lessing, for in the transmigration of souls the spirit of Harry Verney had evidently once animated a dog of that breed. He was dressed in a huge thick fustian jacket, scratched, stained, and patched, with bulging, greasy pockets; a cast of flies round a battered hat, riddled with shot-holes, a dog-whistle at his button-hole, and an old gun cut short over his arm, bespoke his business.

'I seed that 'ere Crawy against Ashy Down Plantations last night, I'll be sworn,' said he, in a squeaking, sneaking tone.

'Well, what harm was the man doing?'

'Oh, ay, that's the way you young 'uns talk. If he warn't doing mischief, he'd a been glad to have been doing it, I'll warrant. If I'd been as young as you, I'd have picked a quarrel with him soon enough, and found a cause for tackling him. It's worth a brace of sovereigns with the squire to haul him up. Eh? eh? Ain't old Harry right now?'

'Humph!' growled the younger man.

'There, then, you get me a snare and a hare by to-morrow night,' went on old Harry, 'and see if I don't nab him. It won't lay long under the plantation afore he picks it up. You mind to snare me a hare to-night, now!'

'I'll do no such thing, nor help to bring fake accusations against any man!'

'False accusations!' answered Harry, in his cringing way. 'Look at that now, for a keeper to say! Why, if he don't happen to have a snare just there, he has somewhere else, you know. Eh? Ain't old Harry right now, eh?'

'Maybe.'

'There, don't say I don't know nothing then. Eh? What matter who put the snare down, or the hare in, perwided he takes it up, man? If 'twas his'n he'd be all the better pleased. The most notoriousest poacher as walks unhung!' And old Harry lifted up his crooked hands in pious indignation.

'I'll have no more gamekeeping, Harry. What with hunting down Christians as if they were vermin, all night, and being cursed by the squire all day, I'd sooner be a sheriff's runner, or a negro slave.'

'Ay, ay! that's the way the young dogs always bark afore they're broke in, and gets to like it, as the eels does skinning. Haven't I bounced pretty near out of my skin many a time afore now, on this here very bridge, with "Harry, jump in, you stupid hound!" and "Harry, get out, you one-eyed tailor!" And then, if one of the gentlemen lost a fish with their clumsiness — Oh, Father! to hear 'em let out at me and my landing-net, and curse fit to fright the devil! Dash their sarcy tongues! Eh! Don't old Harry know their ways? Don't he know 'em, now?'

'Ay,' said the young man, bitterly. 'We break the dogs, and we load the guns, and we find the game, and mark the game, — and then they call themselves sportsmen; we choose the flies, and we bait the spinning-hooks, and we show them where the fish lie, and then when they've hooked them, they can't get them out without us and the spoonnet; and then they go home to the ladies and boast of the lot of fish they killed — and who thinks of the keeper?'

'Oh! ah! Then don't say old Harry knows nothing, then. How nicely, now, you and I might get a living off this 'ere manor, if the landlords was served like the French ones was. Eh, Paul?' chuckled old Harry. 'Wouldn't we pay our taxes with pheasants and grayling, that's all, eh? Ain't old Harry right now, eh?'

The old fox was fishing for an assent, not for its own sake, for he was a fierce Tory, and would have stood up to be shot at any day, not only for his master's sake, but for the sake of a single pheasant of his master's; but he hated Tregarva for many reasons, and was daily on the watch to entrap him on some of his peculiar points, whereof he had, as we shall find, a good many.

What would have been Tregarva's answer, I cannot tell; but Lancelot, who had unintentionally overheard the greater part of the conversation, disliked being any longer a listener, and came close to them.

'Here's your gudgeons and minnows, sir, as you bespoke,' quoth Harry; 'and here's that paternoster as you gave me to rig up. Beautiful minnows, sir, white as a silver spoon.—They're the ones now, ain't they, sir, eh?'

'They'll do!'

'Well, then, don't say old Harry don't know nothing, that's all, eh?' and the old fellow toddled off, peering and twisting his head about like a starling.

'An odd old fellow that, Tregarva,' said Lancelot.

'Very, sir, considering who made him,' answered the Cornishman, touching his hat, and then thrusting his nose deeper than ever into the eel-basket.

'Beautiful stream this,' said Lancelot, who had a continual longing—right or wrong—to chat with his inferiors; and was proportionately sulky and reserved to his superiors.

'Beautiful enough, sir,' said the keeper, with an emphasis on the first word.

'Why, has it any other fault?'

'Not so wholesome as pretty, sir.'

'What harm does it do?'

'Fever, and ague, and rheumatism, sir.'

'Where?' asked Lancelot, a little amused by the man's laconic answers.

'Wherever the white fog spreads, sir.'

'Where's that?'

'Everywhere, sir.'

'And when?'

'Always, sir.'

Lancelot burst out laughing. The man looked up at him slowly and seriously.

'You wouldn't laugh, sir, if you'd seen much of the inside of these cottages round.'

'Really,' said Lancelot, 'I was only laughing at our making such very short work of such a long and serious story. Do you mean that the unhealthiness of this country is wholly caused by the river?'

'No, sir. The river-damps are God's sending; and so they are not too bad to bear. But there's more of man's sending, that is too bad to bear.'

'What do you mean?'

'Are men likely to be healthy when they are worse housed than a pig?'

'No.'

'And worse fed than a hound?'

'Good heavens! No!'

'Or packed together to sleep, like pilchards in a barrel?'

'But, my good fellow, do you mean that the labourers here are in that state?'

'It isn't far to walk, sir. Perhaps some day, when the May-fly is gone off, and the fish won't rise awhile, you could walk down and see. I beg your pardon, sir, though, for thinking of such a thing. They are not places fit for gentlemen, that's certain.' There was a staid irony in his tone, which Lancelot felt.

'But the clergyman goes?'

'Yes, sir.'

'And Miss Honoria goes?'

'Yes, God Almighty bless her!'

'And do not they see that all goes right?'

The giant twisted his huge limbs, as if trying to avoid an answer, and yet not daring to do so.

'Do clergymen go about among the poor much, sir, at college, before they are ordained?'

Lancelot smiled, and shook his head.

'I thought so, sir. Our good vicar is like the rest hereabouts. God knows, he stints neither time nor money—the souls of the poor are well looked after, and their bodies too—as far as his purse will go; but that's not far.'

'Is he ill-off, then?'

'The living's worth some forty pounds a year. The great tithes, they say, are worth better than twelve hundred; but Squire Lavington has them.'

'Oh, I see!' said Lancelot.

'I'm glad you do, sir, for I don't,' meekly answered Tregarva. 'But the vicar, sir, he is a kind man, and a good; but the poor don't understand him, nor he them. He is too learned, sir, and, saving your presence, too fond of his prayer-book.'

'One can't be too fond of a good thing.'

'Not unless you make an idol of it, sir, and fancy that men's souls were made for the prayer-book, and not the prayer-book for them.'

'But cannot he expose and redress these evils, if they exist?'

Tregarva twisted about again.

'I do not say that I think it, sir; but this I know, that every poor man in the vale thinks it—that the parsons are afraid of the landlords. They must see these things, for they are not blind; and they try to plaster them up out of their own pockets.'

'But why, in God's name, don't they strike at the root of the matter, and go straight to the landlords and tell them the truth?' asked Lancelot.

'So people say, sir. I see no reason for it except the one which I gave you. Besides, sir, you must remember, that a man can't quarrel with his own kin; and so many of them are their squire's brothers, or sons, or nephews.'

'Or good friends with him, at least.'

'Ay, sir, and, to do them justice, they had need, for the poor's sake, to keep good friends with the squire. How else are they to get a farthing for schools, or coal-subscriptions, or lying-in societies, or lending libraries, or penny clubs? If they spoke their minds to the great ones, sir, how could they keep the parish together?'

'You seem to see both sides of a question, certainly. But what a miserable state of things, that the labouring man should require all these societies, and charities, and helps from the rich!—that an industrious freeman cannot live without alms!'

'So I have thought this long time,' quietly answered Tregarva.

'But Miss Honoria,—she is not afraid to tell her father the truth?'

'Suppose, sir, when Adam and Eve were in the garden, that all the devils had come up and played their fiends' tricks before them,—do you think they'd have seen any shame in it?'

'I really cannot tell,' said Lancelot, smiling.

'Then I can, sir. They'd have seen no more harm in it than there was harm already in themselves; and that was none. A man's eyes can only see what they've learnt to see.'

Lancelot started: it was a favourite dictum of his in Carlyle's works.

'Where did you get that thought, my friend'

'By seeing, sir.'

'But what has that to do with Miss Honoria?'

'She is an angel of holiness herself, sir; and, therefore, she goes on without blushing or suspecting, where our blood would boil again. She sees people in want, and thinks it must be so, and pities them and relieves them. But she don't know want herself; and, therefore, she don't know that it makes men beasts and devils. She's as pure as God's light herself; and, therefore, she fancies every one is as spotless as she is. And there's another mistake in your charitable great people, sir. When they see poor folk sick or hungry before their eyes, they pull out their purses fast enough, God bless them; for they wouldn't like to be so themselves. But the oppression that goes on all the year round, and the want that goes on all the year round, and the filth, and the lying, and the swearing, and the profligacy, that go on all the year round, and the sickening weight of debt, and the miserable grinding anxiety from rent-day to rent-day, and Saturday night to Saturday night, that crushes a man's soul down, and drives every thought out of his head but how he is to fill his stomach and warm his back, and keep a house over his head, till he daren't for his life take his thoughts one moment off the meat that perisheth—oh, sir, they never felt this; and, therefore, they never dream that there are thousands who pass them in their daily walks who feel this, and feel nothing else!'

This outburst was uttered with an earnestness and majesty which astonished Lancelot. He forgot the subject in the speaker.

'You are a very extraordinary gamekeeper!' said he.

'When the Lord shows a man a thing, he can't well help seeing it,' answered Tregarva, in his usual staid tone.

There was a pause. The keeper looked at him with a glance, before which Lancelot's eyes fell.

'Hell is paved with hearsays, sir, and as all this talk of mine is hearsay, if you are in earnest, sir, go and see for yourself. I know you have a kind heart, and they tell me that you are a great scholar, which would to God I was! so you ought not to condescend to take my word for anything which you can look into yourself;' with which sound piece of common-sense Tregarva returned busily to his eel-lines.

'Hand me the rod and can, and help me out along the buck-stage,' said Lancelot; 'I must have some more talk with you, my fine fellow.'

'Amen,' answered Tregarva, as he assisted our lame hero along a huge beam which stretched out into the pool; and having settled him there, returned mechanically to his work, humming a Wesleyan hymn-tune.

Lancelot sat and tried to catch perch, but Tregarva's words haunted him. He lighted his cigar, and tried to think earnestly over the matter, but he had got into the wrong place for thinking. All his thoughts, all his sympathies, were drowned in the rush and whirl of the water. He forgot everything else in the mere animal enjoyment of sight and sound. Like many young men at his crisis of life, he had given himself up to the mere contemplation of Nature till he had become her slave; and now a luscious scene, a singing bird, were enough to allure his mind away from the most earnest and awful thoughts. He tried to think, but the river would not let him. It thundered and spouted out behind him from the hatches, and leapt madly past him, and caught his eyes in spite of him, and swept them away down its dancing waves, and let them go again only to sweep them down again and again, till his brain felt a delicious dizziness from the everlasting rush and the everlasting roar. And then below, how it spread, and writhed, and whirled into transparent fans, hissing and twining snakes, polished glass-wreaths, huge crystal bells, which boiled up from the bottom, and dived again beneath long threads of creamy foam, and swung round posts and roots, and rushed blackening under dark weed-fringed boughs, and gnawed at the marly banks, and shook the ever-restless bulrushes, till it was swept away and down over the white pebbles and olive weeds, in one broad rippling sheet of molten silver, towards the distant sea. Downwards it fleeted ever, and bore his thoughts floating on its oily stream; and the great trout, with their yellow sides and peacock backs, lounged among the eddies, and the silver grayling dimpled and wandered upon the shallows, and the may-flies flickered and rustled round him like water fairies, with their green gauzy wings; the coot clanked musically among the reeds; the frogs hummed their ceaseless vesper-monotone; the kingfisher darted from his hole in the bank like a blue spark of electric light; the swallows' bills snapped as they twined and hawked above the pool; the swift's wings whirred like musket-balls, as they rushed screaming past his head; and ever the river fleeted by, bearing his eyes away down the current, till its wild eddies began to glow with crimson beneath the setting sun. The complex harmony of sights and sounds slid softly over his soul, and he sank away into a still daydream, too passive for imagination, too deep for meditation, and

> 'Beauty born of murmuring sound,
> Did pass into his face.'

Blame him not. There are more things in a man's heart than ever get in through his thoughts.

On a sudden, a soft voice behind him startled him.

'Can a poor cockney artist venture himself along this timber without falling in?'

Lancelot turned.

'Come out to me, and if you stumble, the naiads will rise out of their depths, and "hold up their pearled wrists" to save their favourite.'

The artist walked timidly out along the beams, and sat down beside Lancelot, who shook him warmly by the hand.

'Welcome, Claude Mellot, and all lovely enthusiasms and symbolisms! Expound to me, now, the meaning of that water-lily leaf and its grand simple curve, as it lies sleeping there in the back eddy.'

'Oh, I am too amused to philosophise. The fair Argemone has just been treating me to her three hundred and sixty-fifth philippic against my unoffending beard.'

'Why, what fault can she find with such a graceful and natural ornament?'

'Just this, my dear fellow, that it is natural. As it is, she considers me only "intelligent-looking." If the beard were away, my face, she says, would be "so refined!" And, I suppose, if I was just a little more effeminate and pale, with a nice retreating under-jaw and a drooping lip, and a meek, peaking simper, like your starved Romish saints, I should be "so spiritual!" And if, again, to complete the climax, I did but shave my head like a Chinese, I should be a model for St. Francis himself!'

'But really, after all, why make yourself so singular by this said beard?'

'I wear it for a testimony and a sign that a man has no right to be ashamed of the mark of manhood. Oh, that one or two of your Protestant clergymen, who ought to be perfect ideal men, would have the courage to get up into the pulpit in a long beard, and testify that the very essential idea of Protestantism is the dignity and divinity of man as God made him! Our forefathers were not ashamed of their beards; but now even the soldier is only allowed to keep his moustache, while our quill-driving masses shave themselves as close as they can; and in proportion to a man's piety he wears less hair, from the young curate who shaves off his whiskers, to the Popish priest who shaves his crown!'

'What do you say, then, to cutting off nuns' hair?'

'I say, that extremes meet, and prudish Manichæism always ends in sheer indecency. Those Papists have forgotten what woman was made for, and therefore, they have forgotten that a woman's hair is her glory, for it was given to her for a covering: as says your friend, Paul the Hebrew, who, by the bye, had as fine theories of art as he had of society, if he had only lived fifteen hundred years later, and had a chance of working them out.'

'How remarkably orthodox you are!' said Lancelot, smiling.

'How do you know that I am not? You never heard me deny the old creed. But what if an artist ought to be of all creeds at once? My business is to represent the beautiful, and therefore to accept it wherever I find it. Yours is to be a philosopher, and find the true.'

'But the beautiful must be truly beautiful to be worth anything; and so you, too, must search for the true.'

'Yes; truth of form, colour, chiaroscuro. They are worthy to occupy me a life; for they are eternal—or at least that which they express: and if I am to get at the symbolised unseen, it must be through the beauty of the symbolising phenomenon. If I, who live by art, for art, in art, or you either, who seem as much a born artist as myself, am to have a religion, it must be a worship of the fountain of art—of the

> "Spirit of beauty, who doth consecrate
> With his own hues whate'er he shines upon."'

'As poor Shelley has it; and much peace of mind it gave him!' answered Lancelot. 'I have grown sick lately of such dreary tinsel abstractions. When you look through the glitter of the words, your "spirit of beauty" simply means certain shapes and colours which please you in beautiful things and in beautiful people.'

'Vile nominalist! renegade from the ideal and all its glories!' said Claude, laughing.

'I don't care sixpence now for the ideal! I want not beauty, but some beautiful thing—a woman perhaps,' and he sighed. 'But at least a person—a living, loving person—all lovely itself, and giving loveliness to all things! If I must have an ideal, let it be, for mercy's sake, a realised one.'

Claude opened his sketch-book.

'We shall get swamped in these metaphysical oceans, my dear dreamer. But lo, here come a couple, as near ideals as any in these degenerate days—the two poles of beauty: the *milieu* of which would be Venus with us Pagans, or the Virgin Mary with the Catholics. Look at them! Honoria the dark—symbolic of passionate depth; Argemone the fair, type of intellectual light! Oh, that I were a Zeuxis to unite them instead of having to paint them in two separate pictures, and split perfection in half, as everything is split in this piecemeal world!'

'You will have the honour of a sitting this afternoon, I suppose, from both beauties?'

'I hope so, for my own sake. There is no path left to immortality, or bread either, now for us poor artists but portrait-painting.'

'I envy you your path, when it leads through such Elysiums,' said Lancelot.

'Come here, gentlemen both!' cried Argemone from the bridge.

'Fairly caught!' grumbled Lancelot. 'You must go, at least; my lameness will excuse me, I hope.'

The two ladies were accompanied by Bracebridge, a gazelle which he had given Argemone, and a certain miserable cur of Honoria's adopting, who plays an important part in this story, and, therefore, deserves a little notice. Honoria had rescued him from a watery death in the village pond, by means of the colonel, who had revenged himself for a pair of wet feet by utterly corrupting the dog's morals, and teaching him every week to answer to some fresh scandalous name.

But Lancelot was not to escape. Instead of moving on, as he had hoped, the party stood looking over the bridge, and talking—he took for granted, poor thin-skinned fellow—of him. And for once his suspicions were right; for he overheard Argemone say—

'I wonder how Mr. Smith can be so rude as to sit there in my presence over his stupid perch! Smoking those horrid cigars, too! How selfish those field-sports do make men!'

'Thank you!' said the colonel, with a low bow. Lancelot rose.

'If a country girl, now, had spoken in that tone,' said he to himself, 'it would have been called at least "saucy"—but Mammon's elect ones may do anything. Well—here I come, limping to my new tyrant's feet, like Goethe's bear to Lili's.'

She drew him away, as women only know how, from the rest of the party, who were chatting and laughing with Claude. She had shown off her fancied indifference to Lancelot before them, and now began in a softer voice—

'Why will you be so shy and lonely, Mr. Smith?'

'Because I am not fit for your society.'

'Who tells you so? Why will you not become so?'

Lancelot hung down his head.

'As long as fish and game are your only society, you will become more and more *morne* and self-absorbed.'

'Really fish were the last things of which I was thinking when you came. My whole heart was filled with the beauty of nature, and nothing else.'

There was an opening for one of Argemone's preconcerted orations.

'Had you no better occupation,' she said gently, 'than nature, the first day of returning to the open air after so frightful and dangerous an accident? Were there no thanks due to One above?'

Lancelot understood her.

'How do you know that I was not even then showing my thankfulness?'

'What! with a cigar and a fishing-rod?'

'Certainly. Why not?'

Argemone really could not tell at the moment. The answer upset her scheme entirely.

'Might not that very admiration of nature have been an act of worship?' continued our hero. 'How can we better glorify the worker than by delighting in his work?'

'Ah!' sighed the lady, 'why trust to these self-willed methods, and neglect the noble and exquisite forms which the Church has prepared for us as embodiments for every feeling of our hearts?'

'*Every* feeling, Miss Lavington?'

Argemone hesitated. She had made the good old stock assertion, as in duty bound; but she could not help recollecting that there were several Popish books of devotion at that moment on her table, which seemed to her to patch a gap or two in the Prayer-book.

'My temple as yet,' said Lancelot, 'is only the heaven and the earth; my church-music I can hear all day long, whenever I have the sense to be silent, and "hear my mother sing;" my priests and preachers are every bird and bee, every flower and cloud. Am I not well enough furnished? Do you want to reduce my circular infinite chapel to an oblong hundred-foot one? My sphere harmonies to the Gregorian tones in four parts? My world-wide priesthood, with their endless variety of costume, to one not over-educated gentleman in a white sheet? And my dreams of naiads and flower-fairies, and the blue-bells ringing God's praises, as they do in "The story without an End," for the gross reality of naughty charity children, with their pockets full of apples, bawling out Hebrew psalms of which they neither feel nor understand a word?'

Argemone tried to look very much shocked at this piece of bombast. Lancelot evidently meant it as such, but he eyed her all the while as if there was solemn earnest under the surface.

'Oh, Mr. Smith!' she said, 'how can you dare talk so of a liturgy compiled by the wisest and holiest of all countries and ages! You revile that of whose beauty you are not qualified to judge!'

'There must be a beauty in it all, or such as you are would not love it.'

'Oh,' she said hopefully, 'that you would but try the Church system! How you would find it harmonise and methodise every day, every thought for you! But I cannot explain myself. Why not go to our vicar and open your doubts to him?'

'Pardon, but you must excuse me.'

'Why? He is one of the saintliest of men!'

'To tell the truth, I have been to him already.'

'You do not mean it! And what did he tell you?'

'What the rest of the world does—hearsays.'

'But did you not find him most kind?'

'I went to him to be comforted and guided. He received me as a criminal. He told me that my first duty was penitence; that as long as I lived the life I did, he could not dare to cast his pearls before swine by answering my doubts; that I was in a state incapable of appreciating spiritual truths; and, therefore, he had no right to tell me any.'

'And what did he tell you?'

'Several spiritual lies instead, I thought. He told me, hearing me quote Schiller, to beware of the Germans, for they were all Pantheists at heart. I asked him whether he included Lange and Bunsen, and it appeared that he had never read a German book in his life. He then flew furiously at Mr. Carlyle, and I found that all he knew of him was from a certain review in the *Quarterly*. He called Boehmen a theosophic Atheist. I should have burst out at that, had I not read the very words in a High Church review the day before, and hoped that he was not aware of the impudent falsehood which he was retailing. Whenever I feebly interposed an objection to anything he said (for, after all, he talked on), he told me to hear the Catholic Church. I asked him which Catholic Church? He said the English. I asked him whether it was to be the Church of the sixth century, or the thirteenth, or the seventeenth or the eighteenth? He told me the one and eternal Church which belonged as much to the nineteenth century as to the first. I begged to know whether, then, I was to hear the Church according to Simeon, or according to Newman, or according to St. Paul; for they seemed to me a little at variance? He told me, austerely enough, that the mind of the Church was embodied in her Liturgy and Articles. To which I answered, that the mind of the episcopal clergy might, perhaps, be; but, then, how happened it that they were always quarrelling and calling hard names about the sense of those very documents? And so I left him, assuring him that, living in the nineteenth century, I wanted to hear the Church of the nineteenth century, and no other; and should be most happy to listen to her, as soon as she had made up her mind what to say.'

Argemone was angry and disappointed. She felt she could not cope with Lancelot's quaint logic, which, however unsound, cut deeper into questions than she had yet looked for herself. Somehow, too, she was tongue-tied before him just when she wanted to be most eloquent in behalf of her principles; and that fretted her still more. But his manner puzzled her most of all. First he would run on with his face turned away, as if soliloquising out into the air, and then suddenly look round at her with most fascinating humility; and, then, in a moment, a dark shade would pass over his countenance, and he would look like one possessed, and his lips wreathe in a sinister artificial smile, and his wild eyes glare through and through her with such cunning understanding of himself and her, that, for the first time in her life, she quailed and felt frightened, as if in the power of a madman. She turned hastily away to shake off the spell.

He sprang after her, almost on his knees, and looked up into her beautiful face with an imploring cry.

'What, do you, too, throw me off? Will you, too, treat the poor wild uneducated sportsman as a Pariah and an outcast, because he is not ashamed to be a man?—because he cannot stuff his soul's hunger with cut-and-dried hearsays, but dares to think for himself?—because he wants to believe things, and dare not be satisfied with only believing that he ought to believe them?'

She paused, astonished.

'Ah, yes,' he went on, 'I hoped too much! What right had I to expect that you would understand me? What right, still more, to expect that you would stoop, any more than the rest of the world, to speak to me, as if I could become anything better than the wild hog I seem? Oh yes!—the chrysalis has no butterfly in it, of course! Stamp on the ugly motionless thing! And yet—you look so beautiful and good!—are all my dreams to perish, about the Alrunen and prophet-maidens, how they charmed our old fighting, hunting forefathers into purity and sweet obedience among their Saxon forests? Has woman forgotten her mission—to look at the heart and have mercy, while cold man looks at the act and condemns? Do you, too, like the rest of mankind, think no-belief better than misbelief; and smile on hypocrisy, lip-assent, practical Atheism, sooner than on the unpardonable sin of making a mistake? Will you, like the rest of this wise world, let a man's spirit rot asleep into the pit, if he will only lie quiet and not disturb your smooth respectabilities; but if he dares, in waking, to yawn in an unorthodox manner, knock him on the head at once, and "break the bruised reed," and "quench the smoking flax"? And yet you churchgoers have "renounced the world"!'

'What do you want, in Heaven's name?' asked Argemone, half terrified.

'I want *you* to tell me that. Here I am, with youth, health, strength, money, every blessing of life but one; and I am utterly miserable. I want some one to tell me what I want.'

'Is it not that you want—religion?'

'I see hundreds who have what you call religion, with whom I should scorn to change my irreligion.'

'But, Mr. Smith, are you not—are you not wicked?—They tell me so,' said Argemone, with an effort, 'And is that not the cause of your disease?'

Lancelot laughed.

'No, fairest prophetess, it is the disease itself. "Why am I what I am, when I know more and more daily what I could be?"—That is the mystery; and my sins are the fruit, and not the root of it. Who will explain that?'

Argemone began,—

'The Church—'

'Oh, Miss Lavington,' cried he, impatiently, 'will you, too, send me back to that cold abstraction? I came to you, however presumptuous, for living, human advice to a living, human heart; and will you pass off on me that Proteus-dream the Church, which in every man's mouth has a different meaning? In one book, meaning a method of education, only it has never been carried out; in another, a system of polity,—only it has never been realised;—now a set of words written in books, on whose meaning all are divided; now a body of men who are daily excommunicating each other as heretics and apostates; now a universal idea; now the narrowest and most exclusive of all parties. Really, before you ask me to hear the Church, I have a right to ask you to define what the Church is.'

'Our Articles define it,' said Argemone drily.

'The "Visible Church," at least, it defines as "a company of faithful men, in which," etc. But how does it define the "Invisible" one? And what does "faithful" mean? What if I thought Cromwell and Pierre Leroux infinitely more faithful men in their way, and better members of the "Invisible Church," than the torturer-pedant Laud, or the facing bothways Protestant-Manichee Taylor?'

It was lucky for the life of young Love that the discussion went no further: Argemone was becoming scandalised beyond all measure. But, happily, the colonel interposed,—

'Look here; tell me if you know for whom this sketch is meant?'

'Tregarva, the keeper: who can doubt?' answered they both at once.

'Has not Mellot succeeded perfectly?'

'Yes,' said Lancelot. 'But what wonder, with such a noble subject! What a grand benevolence is enthroned on that lofty forehead!'

'Oh, you would say so, indeed,' interposed Honoria, 'if you knew him! The stories that I could tell you about him! How he would go into cottages, read to sick people by the hour, dress the children, cook the food for them, as tenderly as any woman! I found out, last winter, if you will believe it, that he lived on bread and water, to give out of his own wages—which are barely twelve shillings a week—five shillings a week for more than two months to a poor labouring man, to prevent his going to the workhouse, and being parted from his wife and children.'

'Noble, indeed!' said Lancelot. 'I do not wonder now at the effect his conversation just now had on me.'

'Has he been talking to you?' said Honoria eagerly. 'He seldom speaks to any one.'

'He has to me; and so well, that were I sure that the poor were as ill off as he says, and that I had the power of altering the system a hair, I could find it in my heart to excuse all political grievance-mongers, and turn one myself.'

Claude Mellot clapped his white woman-like hands.

'Bravo! bravo! O wonderful conversion! Lancelot has at last discovered that, besides the "glorious Past," there is a Present worthy of his sublime notice! We may now hope, in time, that he will discover the existence of a Future!'

'But, Mr. Mellot,' said Honoria, 'why have you been so unfaithful to your original? why have you, like all artists, been trying to soften and refine on your model?'

'Because, my dear lady, we are bound to see everything in its ideal—not as it is, but as it ought to be, and will be, when the vices of this pitiful civilised world are exploded, and sanitary reform, and a variety of occupation, and harmonious education, let each man fulfil in body and soul the ideal which God embodied in him.'

'Fourierist!' cried Lancelot, laughing. 'But surely you never saw a face which had lost by wear less of the divine image? How thoroughly it exemplifies your great law of Protestant art, that "the Ideal is best manifested in the Peculiar." How classic, how independent of clime or race, is its bland, majestic self-possession! how thoroughly Norse its massive squareness!'

'And yet, as a Cornishman, he should be no Norseman.'

'I beg your pardon! Like all noble races, the Cornish owe their nobleness to the impurity of their blood—to its perpetual loans from foreign veins. See how the serpentine curve of his nose, his long nostril, and protruding, sharp-cut lips, mark his share of Phœnician or Jewish blood! how Norse, again, that dome-shaped forehead! how Celtic those dark curls, that restless gray eye, with its "swinden blicken," like Von Troneg Hagen's in the *Niebelungen Lied*!'

He turned: Honoria was devouring his words. He saw it, for he was in love, and young love makes man's senses as keen as woman's.

'Look! look at him now!' said Claude, in a low voice. 'How he sits, with his hands on his knees, the enormous size of his limbs quite concealed by the careless grace, with his Egyptian face, like some dumb granite Memnon!'

'Only waiting,' said Lancelot, 'for the day-star to arise on him and awake him into voice.'

He looked at Honoria as he spoke. She blushed angrily; and yet a sort of sympathy arose from that moment between Lancelot and herself.

Our hero feared he had gone too far, and tried to turn the subject off.

The smooth mill-head was alive with rising trout.

'What a huge fish leapt then!' said Lancelot carelessly; 'and close to the bridge, too!'

Honoria looked round, and uttered a piercing scream.

'Oh, my dog! my dog! Mops is in the river! That horrid gazelle has butted him in, and he'll be drowned!'

Alas! it was too true. There, a yard above the one open hatchway, through which the whole force of the stream was rushing, was the unhappy Mops, *alias* Scratch, *alias* Dirty Dick, *alias* Jack Sheppard, paddling, and sneezing, and winking, his little bald muzzle turned piteously upward to the sky.

'He will be drowned!' quoth the colonel.

There was no doubt of it; and so Mops thought, as, shivering and whining, he plied every leg, while the glassy current dragged him back and back, and Honoria sobbed like a child.

The colonel lay down on the bridge, and caught at him: his arm was a foot too short. In a moment the huge form of Tregarva plunged solemnly into the water, with a splash like seven salmon, and Mops was jerked out over the colonel's head high and dry on to the bridge.

'You'll be drowned, at least!' shouted the colonel, with an oath of Uncle Toby's own.

Tregarva saw his danger, made one desperate bound upward, and missed the bridge. The colonel caught at him, tore off a piece of his collar—the calm, solemn face of the keeper flashed past beneath him, and disappeared through the roaring gate.

They rushed to the other side of the bridge—caught one glimpse of a dark body fleeting and roaring down the foam-way. The colonel leapt the bridge-rail like a deer, rushed out along the buck-stage, tore off his coat, and sprung headlong into the boiling pool, 'rejoicing in his might,' as old Homer would say.

Lancelot, forgetting his crutches, was dashing after him, when he felt a soft hand clutching at his arm.

'Lancelot! Mr. Smith!' cried Argemone. 'You shall not go! You are too ill—weak—'

'A fellow-creature's life!'

'What is his life to yours?' she cried, in a tone of deep passion. And then, imperiously, 'Stay here, I command you!'

The magnetic touch of her hand thrilled through his whole frame. She had called him Lancelot! He shrank down, and stood spell-bound.

'Good heavens!' she cried; 'look at my sister!'

Out on the extremity of the buck-stage (how she got there neither they nor she ever knew) crouched Honoria, her face idiotic with terror, while she stared with bursting eyes into the foam. A shriek of disappointment rose from her lips, as in a moment the colonel's weather-worn head reappeared above, looking for all the world like an old gray shiny-painted seal.

'Poof! tally-ho! Poof! poof! Heave me a piece of wood, Lancelot, my boy!' And he disappeared again.

They looked round, there was not a loose bit near. Claude ran off towards the house. Lancelot, desperate, seized the bridge-rail, tore it off by sheer strength, and hurled it far into the pool. Argemone saw it, and remembered it, like a true woman. Ay, be as Manichæan-sentimental as you will, fair ladies, physical prowess, that Eden-right of manhood, is sure to tell upon your hearts!

Again the colonel's grizzled head reappeared,—and, oh joy! beneath it a draggled knot of black curls. In another instant he had hold of the rail, and quietly floating down to the shallow, dragged the lifeless giant high and dry on a patch of gravel.

Honoria never spoke. She rose, walked quietly back along the beam, passed Argemone and Lancelot without seeing them, and firmly but hurriedly led the way round the pool-side.

Before they arrived at the bank, the colonel had carried Tregarva to it. Lancelot and two or three workmen, whom his cries had attracted, lifted the body on to the meadow.

Honoria knelt quietly down on the grass, and watched, silent and motionless, the dead face, with her wide, awestruck eyes.

'God bless her for a kind soul!' whispered the wan weather-beaten field drudges, as they crowded round the body.

'Get out of the way, my men!' quoth the colonel. 'Too many cooks spoil the broth.' And he packed off one here and another there for necessaries, and commenced trying every restorative means with the ready coolness of a practised surgeon; while Lancelot, whom he ordered about like a baby, gulped down a great choking lump of envy, and then tasted the rich delight of forgetting himself in admiring obedience to a real superior.

But there Tregarva lay lifeless, with folded hands, and a quiet satisfied smile, while Honoria watched and watched with parted lips, unconscious of the presence of every one.

Five minutes!—ten!

'Carry him to the house,' said the colonel, in a despairing tone, after another attempt.

'He moves!' 'No!' 'He does!' 'He breathes!' 'Look at his eyelids!'

Slowly his eyes opened.

'Where am I? All gone? Sweet dreams—blessed dreams!'

His eye met Honoria's. One big deep sigh swelled to his lips and burst. She seemed to recollect herself, rose, passed her arm through Argemone's, and walked slowly away.

CHAPTER IV
AN 'INGLORIOUS MILTON'

Argemone, sweet prude, thought herself bound to read Honoria a lecture that night, on her reckless exhibition of feeling; but it profited little. The most consummate cunning could not have baffled Argemone's suspicions more completely than her sister's utter simplicity. She cried just as bitterly about Mops's danger as about the keeper's, and then laughed heartily at Argemone's solemnity; till at last, when pushed a little too hard, she broke out into something very like a passion, and told her sister, bitterly enough, that 'she was not accustomed to see men drowned every day, and begged to hear no more about the subject.' Whereat Argemone prudently held her tongue, knowing that under all Honoria's tenderness lay a volcano of passionate determination, which was generally kept down by her affections, but was just as likely to be maddened by them. And so this conversation only went to increase the unconscious estrangement between them, though they continued, as sisters will do, to lavish upon each other the most extravagant protestations of affection—vowing to live and die only for each other—and believing honestly, sweet souls, that they felt all they said; till real imperious Love came in, in one case of the two at least, shouldering all other affections right and left; and then the two beauties discovered, as others do, that it is not so possible or reasonable as they thought for a woman to sacrifice herself and her lover for the sake of her sister or her friend. Next morning Lancelot and the colonel started out to Tregarva's cottage, on a mission of inquiry. They found the giant propped up in bed with pillows, his magnificent features looking in their paleness more than ever like a granite Memnon. Before him lay an open *Pilgrim's Progress*, and a drawer filled with feathers and furs, which he was busily manufacturing into trout flies, reading as he worked. The room was filled with nets, guns, and keepers' tackle, while a well-filled shelf of books hung by the wall.

'Excuse my rising, gentlemen,' he said, in his slow, staid voice, 'but I am very weak, in spite of the Lord's goodness to me. You are very kind to think of coming to my poor cottage,'

'Well, my man,' said the colonel, 'and how are you after your cold bath? You are the heaviest fish I ever landed!'

'Pretty well, thank God, and you, sir. I am in your debt, sir, for the dear life. How shall I ever repay you?'

'Repay, my good fellow? You would have done as much for me.'

'May be; but you did not think of that when you jumped in; and no more must I in thanking you. God knows how a poor miner's son will ever reward you; but the mouse repaid the lion, says the story, and, at all events, I can pray for you. By the bye, gentlemen, I hope you have brought up some trolling-tackle?'

'We came up to see you, and not to fish,' said Lancelot, charmed with the stately courtesy of the man.

'Many thanks, gentlemen; but old Harry Verney was in here just now, and had seen a great jack strike, at the tail of the lower reeds. With this fresh wind he will run till noon; and you are sure of him with a dace. After that, he will not be up again on the shallows till sunset. He works the works of darkness, and comes not to the light, because his deeds are evil.'

Lancelot laughed. 'He does but follow his kind, poor fellow.'

'No doubt, sir, no doubt; all the Lord's works are good: but it is a wonder why He should have made wasps, now, and blights, and vermin, and jack, and such evil-featured things, that carry spite and cruelty in their very faces—a great wonder. Do you think, sir, all those creatures were in the Garden of Eden?'

'You are getting too deep for me,' said Lancelot. 'But why trouble your head about fishing?'

'I beg your pardon for preaching to you, sir. I'm sure I forgot myself. If you will let me, I'll get up and get you a couple of bait from the stew. You'll do us keepers a kindness, and prevent sin, sir, if you'll catch him. The squire will swear sadly—the Lord forgive him—if he hears of a pike in the trout-runs. I'll get up, if I may trouble you to go into the next room a minute.'

'Lie still, for Heaven's sake. Why bother your head about pike now?'

'It is my business, sir, and I am paid for it, and I must do it thoroughly;—and abide in the calling wherein I am called,' he added, in a sadder tone.

'You seem to be fond enough of it, and to know enough about it, at all events,' said the colonel, 'tying flies here on a sick-bed.'

'As for being fond of it, sir—those creatures of the water teach a man many lessons; and when I tie flies, I earn books.'

'How then?'

'I send my flies all over the country, sir, to Salisbury and Hungerford, and up to Winchester, even; and the money buys me many a wise book—all my delight is in reading; perhaps so much the worse for me.'

'So much the better, say,' answered Lancelot warmly. 'I'll give you an order for a couple of pounds' worth of flies at once.'

'The Lord reward you, sir,' answered the giant.

'And you shall make me the same quantity,' said the colonel. 'You can make salmon-flies?'

'I made a lot by pattern for an Irish gent, sir.'

'Well, then, we'll send you some Norway patterns, and some golden pheasant and parrot feathers. We're going to Norway this summer, you know, Lancelot—'

Tregarva looked up with a quaint, solemn hesitation.

'If you please, gentlemen, you'll forgive a man's conscience.'

'Well?'

'But I'd not like to be a party to the making of Norway flies.'

'Here's a Protectionist, with a vengeance!' laughed the colonel. 'Do you want to keep all us fishermen in England? eh? to fee English keepers?'

'No, sir. There's pretty fishing in Norway, I hear, and poor folk that want money more than we keepers. God knows we get too much—we that hang about great houses and serve great folks' pleasure—you toss the money down our throats, without our deserving it; and we spend it as we get it—a deal too fast—while hard-working labourers are starving.'

'And yet you would keep us in England?'

'Would God I could!'

'Why then, my good fellow?' asked Lancelot, who was getting intensely interested with the calm, self-possessed earnestness of the man, and longed to draw him out.

The colonel yawned.

'Well, I'll go and get myself a couple of bait. Don't you stir, my good parson-keeper. Down charge, I say! Odd if I don't find a bait-net, and a rod for myself, under the verandah.'

'You will, colonel. I remember, now, I set it there last morning; but the water washed many things out of my brains, and some things into them—and I forgot it like a goose.'

'Well, good-bye, and lie still. I know what a drowning is, and more than one. A day and a night have I been in the deep, like the man in the good book; and bed is the best of medicine for a ducking;' and the colonel shook him kindly by the hand and disappeared.

Lancelot sat down by the keeper's bed.

'You'll get those fish-hooks into your trousers, sir; and this is a poor place to sit down in.'

'I want you to say your say out, friend, fish-hooks or none.'

The keeper looked warily at the door, and when the colonel had passed the window, balancing the trolling-rod on his chin, and whistling merrily, he began,—

'"A day and a night have I been in the deep!"—and brought back no more from it! And yet the Psalms say how they that go down to the sea in ships see the works of the Lord!—If the Lord has opened their eyes to see them, that must mean—'

Lancelot waited.

'What a gallant gentleman that is, and a valiant man of war, I'll warrant,—and to have seen all the wonders he has, and yet to be wasting his span of life like that!'

Lancelot's heart smote him.

'One would think, sir,—You'll pardon me for speaking out.' And the noble face worked, as he murmured to himself, 'When ye are brought before kings and princes for my name's sake.—I dare not hold my tongue, sir. I am as one risen from the dead,'—and his face flashed up into sudden enthusiasm—'and woe to me if I speak not. Oh, why, why are you gentlemen running off to Norway, and foreign parts, whither God has not called you! Are there no graves in Egypt, that you must go out to die in the wilderness!'

Lancelot, quite unaccustomed to the language of the Dissenting poor, felt keenly the bad taste of the allusion.

'What can you mean?' he asked.

'Pardon me, sir, if I cannot speak plainly; but are there not temptations enough here in England that you must go to waste all your gifts, your scholarship, and your rank, far away there out of the sound of a church-going bell? I don't deny it's a great temptation. I have read of Norway wonders in a book of one Miss Martineau, with a strange name.'

'*Feats on the Fiord?*'

'That's it, sir. Her books are grand books to set one a-thinking; but she don't seem to see the Lord in all things, does she, sir?'

Lancelot parried the question.

'You are wandering a little from the point.'

'So I am, and thank you for the rebuke. There's where I find you scholars have the advantage of us poor fellows, who pick up knowledge as we can. Your book-learning makes you stick to the point so much better. You are taught how to think. After all—God forgive me if I'm wrong! but I sometimes think that there must be more good in that human wisdom, and philosophy falsely so called, than we Wesleyans hold. Oh, sir, what a blessing is a good education! What you gentlemen might do with it, if you did but see your own power! Are there no fish in England, sir, to be caught? precious fish, with immortal souls? And is there not One who has said, "Come with me, and I will make you fishers of men?"'

'Would you have us all turn parsons?'

'Is no one to do God's work except the parson, sir? Oh, the game that you rich folks have in your hands, if you would but play it! Such a man as Colonel Bracebridge now, with the tongue of the serpent, who can charm any living soul he likes to his will, as a stoat charms a rabbit. Or you, sir, with your tongue:—you have charmed one precious creature already. I can see it: though neither of you know it, yet I know it.'

Lancelot started, and blushed crimson.

'Oh, that I had your tongue, sir!' And the keeper blushed crimson, too, and went on hastily,—

'But why could you not charm all alike! Do not the poor want you as well as the rich?'

'What can I do for the poor, my good fellow? And what do they want? Have they not houses, work, a church, and schools,—and poor-rates to fall back on?'

The keeper smiled sadly.

'To fall back on, indeed! and down on, too. At all events, you rich might help to make Christians of them, and men of them. For I'm beginning to fancy strangely, in spite of all the preachers say, that, before ever you can make them Christians, you must make them men and women.'

'Are they not so already?'

'Oh, sir, go and see! How can a man be a man in those crowded styes, sleeping packed together like Irish pigs in a steamer, never out of the fear of want, never knowing any higher amusement than the beer-shop? Those old Greeks and Romans, as I read, were more like men than half our English labourers. Go and see! Ask that sweet heavenly angel, Miss Honoria,'—and the keeper again blushed,—'And she, too, will tell you. I think sometimes if she had been born and bred like her father's tenants' daughters, to sleep where they sleep, and hear the talk they hear, and see the things they see, what would she have been now? We mustn't think of it.' And the keeper turned his head away, and fairly burst into tears.

Lancelot was moved.

'Are the poor very immoral, then?'

'You ask the rector, sir, how many children hereabouts are born within six months of the wedding-day. None of them marry, sir, till the devil forces them. There's no sadder sight than a labourer's wedding now-a-days. You never see the parents come with them. They just get another couple, that are keeping company, like themselves, and come sneaking into church, looking all over as if they were ashamed of it—and well they may be!'

'Is it possible?'

'I say, sir, that God makes you gentlemen, gentlemen, that you may see into these things. You give away your charities kindly enough, but you don't know the folks you give to. If a few of you would but be like the blessed Lord, and stoop to go out of the road, just behind the hedge, for once, among the publicans and harlots! Were you ever at a country fair, sir? Though I suppose I am rude for fancying that you could demean yourself to such company.'

'I should not think it demeaning myself,' said Lancelot, smiling; 'but I never was at one, and I should like for once to see the real manners of the poor.'

'I'm no haunter of such places myself, God knows; but—I see you're in earnest now—will you come with me, sir,—for once? for God's sake and the poor's sake?'

'I shall be delighted.'

'Not after you've been there, I am afraid.'

'Well, it's a bargain when you are recovered. And, in the meantime, the squire's orders are, that you lie by for a few days to rest; and Miss Honoria's, too; and she has sent you down some wine.'

'She thought of me, did she?' And the still sad face blazed out radiant with pleasure, and then collapsed as suddenly into deep melancholy.

Lancelot saw it, but said nothing; and shaking him heartily by the hand, had his shake returned by an iron grasp, and slipped silently out of the cottage.

The keeper lay still, gazing on vacancy. Once he murmured to himself, —

'Through strange ways—strange ways—and though he let them wander out of the road in the wilderness;—we know how that goes on—'

And then he fell into a mixed meditation—perhaps into a prayer.

CHAPTER V
A SHAM IS WORSE THAN NOTHING

At last, after Lancelot had waited long in vain, came his cousin's answer to the letter which I gave in my second chapter.

'You are not fair to me, good cousin . . . but I have given up expecting fairness from Protestants. I do not say that the front and the back of my head have different makers, any more than that doves and vipers have . . . and yet I kill the viper when I meet him . . . and so do you. . . . And yet, are we not taught that our animal nature is throughout equally viperous? . . . The Catholic Church, at least, so teaches. . . . She believes in the corruption of human nature. She believes in the literal meaning of Scripture. She has no wish to paraphrase away St. Paul's awful words, that "in his flesh dwelleth no good thing," by the unscientific euphemisms of "fallen nature" or "corrupt humanity." The boasted discovery of phrenologists, that thought, feeling, and passion reside in this material brain and nerves of ours, has ages ago been anticipated by her simple faith in the letter of Scripture; a faith which puts to shame the irreverent vagueness and fantastic private interpretations of those who make an idol of that very letter which they dare not take literally, because it makes against their self-willed theories. . .

'And so you call me *douce* and meek? . . . You should remember what I once was, Lancelot . . . I, at least, have not forgotten . . . I have not forgotten how that very animal nature, on the possession of which you seem to pride yourself, was in me only the parent of remorse., . . I know it too well not to hate and fear it. Why do you reproach me, if I try to abjure it, and cast away the burden which I am too weak to bear? I am weak—Would you have me say that I am strong? Would you have me try to be a Prometheus, while I am longing to be once more an infant on a mother's breast? Let me alone . . . I am a weary child, who knows nothing, can do nothing, except lose its way in arguings and reasonings, and "find no end, in wandering mazes lost." Will you reproach me, because when I see a soft cradle lying open for me . . . with a Virgin Mother's face smiling down all woman's love about it . . . I long to crawl into it, and sleep awhile? I want loving, indulgent sympathy . . . I want detailed, explicit guidance . . . Have you, then, found so much of them in our former creed, that you forbid me to go to seek them elsewhere, in the Church which not only professes them as an organised system, but practises them . . . as you would find in your first half-hour's talk with one of Her priests . . . true priests . . . who know the heart of man, and pity, and console, and bear for their flock the burdens which they cannot bear themselves? You ask me who will teach a fast young man? . . . I answer, the Jesuit. Ay, start and sneer, at that delicate woman-like tenderness, that subtle instinctive sympathy, which you have never felt . . . which is as new to me, alas, as it would be to you! For if there be none now-a-days to teach such as you, who is there who will teach such as me? Do not fancy that I have not craved and searched for teachers . . . I went to one party long ago, and they commanded me, as the price of their sympathy, even of anything but their denunciations, to ignore, if not to abjure, all the very points on which I came for light—my love for the Beautiful and the Symbolic—my desire to consecrate and christianise it—my longing for a human voice to tell me with authority that I was forgiven—my desire to find some practical and palpable communion between myself and the saints of old. They told me to cast away, as an accursed chaos, a thousand years of Christian history, and believe that the devil had been for ages . . . just the ages I thought noblest, most faithful, most interpenetrated with the thought of God . . . triumphant over that church with which He had promised to be till the end of the world. No . . . by the bye, they made two exceptions—of their own choosing. One in favour of the Albigenses . . . who seemed to me, from the original documents, to have been very profligate Infidels, of whom the world was well rid . . . and the Piedmontese . . . poor, simple, ill-used folk enough, but who certainly cannot be said to have exercised much influence on the destinies of mankind . . . and all the rest was chaos and the pit. There never had been, never would be, a kingdom of God on earth, but only a few scattered individuals, each selfishly intent on the salvation of his own soul—without organisation, without unity, without common purpose, without even a masonic sign whereby to know one another when they chanced to meet . . . except Shibboleths which the hypocrite could ape, and virtues which the heathen have performed . . . Would *you* have had me accept such a "Philosophy of History"?

'And then I went to another school . . . or rather wandered up and down between those whom I have just described, and those who boast on their side prescriptive right, and apostolic succession . . . and I found that their ancient charter went back—just three hundred years . . . and there derived its transmitted virtue, it seemed to me, by something very like obtaining goods on false pretences, from the very church which it now anathematises. Disheartened, but not hopeless, I asked how it was that the priesthood, whose hands bestowed the grace of ordination, could not withdraw it . . .

whether, at least, the schismatic did not forfeit it by the very act of schism . . . and instead of any real answer to that fearful spiritual dilemma, they set me down to folios of Nag's head controversies . . . and myths of an independent British Church, now represented, strangely enough, by those Saxons who, after its wicked refusal to communicate with them, exterminated it with fire and sword, and derived its own order from St. Gregory . . . and decisions of mythical old councils (held by bishops of a different faith and practice from their own), from which I was to pick the one point which made for them, and omit the nine which made against them, while I was to believe, by a stretch of imagination . . . or common honesty . . ., which I leave you to conceive, that the Church of Syria in the fourth century was, in doctrine, practice, and constitution, like that of England in the nineteenth? . . . And what was I to gain by all this? . . . For the sake of what was I to strain logic and conscience? To believe myself a member of the same body with all the Christian nations of the earth?—to be able to hail the Frenchman, the Italian, the Spaniard, as a brother—to have hopes even of the German and the Swede . . . if not in this life, still in the life to come? No . . . to be able still to sit apart from all Christendom in the exclusive pride of insular Pharisaism; to claim for the modern littleness of England the infallibility which I denied to the primæval mother of Christendom, not to enlarge my communion to the Catholic, but excommunicate, to all practical purposes, over and above the Catholics, all other Protestants except my own sect . . . or rather, in practice, except my own party in my own sect. . . . And this was believing in one Catholic and Apostolic church! . . . this was to be my share of the communion of saints! And these were the theories which were to satisfy a soul which longed for a kingdom of God on earth, which felt that unless the highest of His promises are a mythic dream, there must be some system on the earth commissioned to fulfil those promises; some authority divinely appointed to regenerate, and rule, and guide the lives of men, and the destinies of nations; who must go mad, unless he finds that history is not a dreary aimless procession of lost spirits descending into the pit, or that the salvation of millions does not depend on an obscure and controverted hair's breadth of ecclesiastic law.

'I have tried them both, Lancelot, and found them wanting; and now but one road remains. . . . Home, to the fountain-head; to the mother of all the churches whose fancied cruelty to her children can no more destroy her motherhood, than their confest rebellion can. . . . Shall I not hear her voice, when she, and she alone cries to me, "I have authority and commission from the King of kings to regenerate the world. History is a chaos, only because mankind has been ever rebelling against me, its lawful ruler . . . and yet not a chaos . . . for I still stand, and grow rooted on the rock of ages, and under my boughs are fowl of every wing. I alone have been and am consistent, progressive, expansive, welcoming every race, and intellect and character into its proper place in my great organism . . . meeting alike the wants of the king and the beggar, the artist and the devotee . . . there is free room for all within my heaven-wide bosom. Infallibility is not the exclusive heritage of one proud and ignorant Island, but of a system which knows no distinction of language, race, or clime. The communion of saints is not a bygone tale, for my saints, redeemed from every age and every nation under heaven, still live, and love, and help and intercede. The union of heaven and earth is not a barbaric myth; for I have still my miracles, my Host, my exorcism, my absolution. The present rule of God is still, as ever, a living reality; for I rule in His name, and fulfil all His will."

'How can I turn away from such a voice? What if some of her doctrines may startle my untutored and ignorant understanding? . . . If she is the appointed teacher, she will know best what truths to teach. . . . The disciple is not above his master . . . or wise in requiring him to demonstrate the abstrusest problems . . . spiritual problems, too . . . before he allows his right to teach the elements. Humbly I must enter the temple porch; gradually and trustfully proceed with my initiation. . . . When that is past, and not before . . . shall I be a fit judge of the mysteries of the inner shrine.

'There . . . I have written a long letter . . . with my own heart's blood. . . . Think over it well, before you despise it. . . . And if you can refute it for me, and sweep the whole away like a wild dream when one awakes, none will be more thankful—paradoxical as it may seem—than your unhappy Cousin.'

And Lancelot did consider that letter, and answered it as follows:—

'It is a relief to me at least, dear Luke, that you are going to Rome in search of a great idea, and not merely from selfish superstitious terror (as I should call it) about the "salvation of your soul." And it is a new and very important thought to me, that Rome's scheme of this world, rather than of the next, forms her chief allurement. But as for that flesh and spirit question, or the apostolic succession one either; all you seem to me, as a looker on, to have logically proved, is that Protestants, orthodox and unorthodox, must be a little more scientific and careful in their use of the terms. But as for adopting your use of them, and the consequences thereof—you must pardon me, and I suspect, them too. Not that. Anything but that. Whatever is right, that is wrong. Better to be inconsistent in truth, than consistent in a mistake. And your Romish idea of man is a mistake—utterly wrong and absurd—except in the one requirement of righteousness and godliness, which Protestants and heathen philosophers have required and do require just as much as you. My dear Luke, your ideal men and women won't do—

for they are not men and women at all, but what you call "saints" . . . Your Calendar, your historic list of the Earth's worthies, won't do—not they, but others, are the people who have brought Humanity thus far. I don't deny that there are great souls among them; Beckets, and Hugh Grostêtes, and Elizabeths of Hungary. But you are the last people to praise them, for you don't understand them. Thierry honours Thomas à Becket more than all Canonisations and worshippers do, because he does see where the man's true greatness lay, and you don't. Why, you may hunt all Surius for such a biography of a mediaeval worthy as Carlyle has given of your Abbot Samson. I have read, or tried to read your Surius, and Alban Butler, and so forth—and they seemed to me bats and asses—One really pitied the poor saints and martyrs for having such blind biographers—such dunghill cocks, who overlooked the pearl of real human love and nobleness in them, in their greediness to snatch up and parade the rotten chaff of superstition, and self-torture, and spiritual dyspepsia, which had overlaid it. My dear fellow, that Calendar ruins your cause—you are "sacrés aristocrates"—kings and queens, bishops and virgins by the hundred at one end; a beggar or two at the other; and but one real human lay St. Homobonus to fill up the great gulf between—A pretty list to allure the English middle classes, or the Lancashire working-men!—Almost as charmingly suited to England as the present free, industrious, enlightened, and moral state of that Eternal City, which has been blest with the visible presence and peculiar rule, temporal as well as spiritual, too, of your Dalai Lama. His pills do not seem to have had much practical effect there. . . . My good Luke, till he can show us a little better specimen of the kingdom of Heaven organised and realised on earth, in the country which does belong to him, soil and people, body and soul, we must decline his assistance in realising that kingdom in countries which don't belong to him. If the state of Rome don't show his idea of man and society to be a rotten lie, what proof would you have? . . . perhaps the charming results of a century of Jesuitocracy, as they were represented on a French stage in the year 1793? I can't answer his arguments, you see, or yours either; I am an Englishman, and not a controversialist. The only answer I give is John Bull's old dumb instinctive "Everlasting No!" which he will stand by, if need be, with sharp shot and cold steel—"Not that; anything but that. No kingdom of Heaven at all for us, if the kingdom of Heaven is like that. No heroes at all for us, if their heroism is to consist in their being not-men. Better no society at all, but only a competitive wild-beast's den, than a sham society. Better no faith, no hope, no love, no God, than shams thereof." I take my stand on fact and nature; you may call them idols and phantoms; I say they need be so no longer to any man, since Bacon has taught us to discover the Eternal Laws under the outward phenomena. Here on blank materialism will I stand, and testify against all Religions and Gods whatsoever, if they must needs be like that Roman religion, that Roman God. I don't believe they need—not I. But if they need, they must go. We cannot have a "Deus quidam deceptor." If there be a God, these trees and stones, these beasts and birds must be His will, whatever else is not. My body, and brain, and faculties, and appetites must be His will, whatever else is not. Whatsoever I can do with them in accordance with the constitution of them and nature must be His will, whatever else is not. Those laws of Nature must reveal Him, and be revealed by Him, whatever else is not. Man's scientific conquest of nature must be one phase of His Kingdom on Earth, whatever else is not. I don't deny that there are spiritual laws which man is meant to obey—How can I, who feel in my own daily and inexplicable unhappiness the fruits of having broken them?—But I do say, that those spiritual laws must be in perfect harmony with every fresh physical law which we discover: that they cannot be intended to compete self-destructively with each other; that the spiritual cannot be intended to be perfected by ignoring or crushing the physical, unless God is a deceiver, and His universe a self-contradiction. And by this test alone will I try all theories, and dogmas, and spiritualities whatsoever— Are they in accordance with the laws of nature? And therefore when your party compare sneeringly Romish Sanctity, and English Civilisation, I say, "Take you the Sanctity, and give me the Civilisation!" The one may be a dream, for it is unnatural; the other cannot be, for it is natural; and not an evil in it at which you sneer but is discovered, day by day, to be owing to some infringement of the laws of nature. When we "draw bills on nature," as Carlyle says, "she honours them,"—our ships do sail; our mills do work; our doctors do cure; our soldiers do fight. And she does not honour yours; for your Jesuits have, by their own confession, to lie, to swindle, to get even man to accept theirs for them. So give me the political economist, the sanitary reformer, the engineer; and take your saints and virgins, relics and miracles. The spinning-jenny and the railroad, Cunard's liners and the electric telegraph, are to me, if not to you, signs that we are, on some points at least, in harmony with the universe; that there is a mighty spirit working among us, who cannot be your anarchic and destroying Devil, and therefore may be the Ordering and Creating God.'

Which of them do you think, reader, had most right on his side?

CHAPTER VI
VOGUE LA GALÈRE

Lancelot was now so far improved in health as to return to his little cottage *ornée*. He gave himself up freely to his new passion. With his comfortable fortune and good connections, the future seemed bright and possible enough as to circumstances. He knew that Argemone felt for him; how much it seemed presumptuous even to speculate, and as yet no golden-visaged meteor had arisen portentous in his amatory zodiac. No rich man had stepped in to snatch, in spite of all his own flocks and herds, at the poor man's own ewe-lamb, and set him barking at all the world, as many a poor lover has to do in defence of his morsel of enjoyment, now turned into a mere bone of contention and loadstone for all hungry kites and crows.

All that had to be done was to render himself worthy of her, and in doing so, to win her. And now he began to feel more painfully his ignorance of society, of practical life, and the outward present. He blamed himself angrily for having, as he now thought, wasted his time on ancient histories and foreign travels, while he neglected the living wonderful present, which weltered daily round him, every face embodying a living soul. For now he began to feel that those faces did hide living souls; formerly he had half believed—he had tried, but from laziness, to make himself wholly believe—that they were all empty masks, phantasies, without interest or significance for him. But, somehow, in the light of his new love for Argemone, the whole human race seemed glorified, brought nearer, endeared to him. So it must be. He had spoken of a law wider than he thought in his fancy, that the angels might learn love for all by love for an individual. Do we not all learn love so? Is it not the first touch of the mother's bosom which awakens in the infant's heart that spark of affection which is hereafter to spread itself out towards every human being, and to lose none of its devotion for its first object, as it expands itself to innumerable new ones? Is it not by love, too—by looking into loving human eyes, by feeling the care of loving hands,—that the infant first learns that there exist other beings beside itself?—that every body which it sees expresses a heart and will like its own? Be sure of it. Be sure that to have found the key to one heart is to have found the key to all; that truly to love is truly to know; and truly to love one, is the first step towards truly loving all who bear the same flesh and blood with the beloved. Like children, we must dress up even our unseen future in stage properties borrowed from the tried and palpable present, ere we can look at it without horror. We fear and hate the utterly unknown, and it only. Even pain we hate only when we cannot *know* it; when we can only feel it, without explaining it, and making it harmonise with our notions of our own deserts and destiny. And as for human beings, there surely it stands true, wherever else it may not, that all knowledge is love, and all love knowledge; that even with the meanest, we cannot gain a glimpse into their inward trials and struggles, without an increase of sympathy and affection.

Whether he reasoned thus or not, Lancelot found that his new interest in the working classes was strangely quickened by his passion. It seemed the shortest and clearest way toward a practical knowledge of the present. 'Here,' he said to himself, 'in the investigation of existing relations between poor and rich, I shall gain more real acquaintance with English society, than by dawdling centuries in exclusive drawing-rooms.'

The inquiry had not yet presented itself to him as a duty; perhaps so much the better, that it might be the more thoroughly a free-will offering of love. At least it opened a new field of amusement and knowledge; it promised him new studies of human life; and as he lay on his sofa and let his thoughts flow, Tregarva's dark revelations began to mix themselves with dreams about the regeneration of the Whitford poor, and those again with dreams about the heiress of Whitford; and many a luscious scene and noble plan rose brightly detailed in his exuberant imagination. For Lancelot, like all born artists, could only think in a concrete form. He never worked out a subject without embodying it in some set oration, dialogue, or dramatic castle in the air.

But the more he dreamt, the more he felt that a material beauty of flesh and blood required a material house, baths, and boudoirs, conservatories, and carriages; a safe material purse, and fixed material society; law and order, and the established frame-work of society, gained an importance in his eyes which they had never had before.

'Well,' he said to himself, 'I am turning quite practical and auld-warld. Those old Greeks were not so far wrong when they said that what made men citizens, patriots, heroes, was the love of wedded wife and child.'

'Wedded wife and child!'—He shrank in from the daring of the delicious thought, as if he had intruded without invitation into a hidden sanctuary, and looked round for a book to drive away the dazzling picture. But even there his thoughts were haunted by Argemone's face, and

> 'When his regard
> Was raised by intense pensiveness, two eyes,
> Two starry eyes, hung in the gloom of thought,
> And seemed, with their serene and azure smiles,
> To beckon him.'

He took up, with a new interest 'Chartism,' which alone of all Mr. Carlyle's works he had hitherto disliked, because his own luxurious day-dreams had always flowed in such sad discord with the terrible warnings of the modern seer, and his dark vistas of starvation, crime, neglect, and discontent.

'Well,' he said to himself, as he closed the book, 'I suppose it is good for us easy-going ones now and then to face the possibility of a change. Gold has grown on my back as feathers do on geese, without my own will or deed; but considering that gold, like feathers, is equally useful to those who have and those who have not, why, it is worth while for the goose to remember that he may possibly one day be plucked. And what remains? "Io," as Medea says. . . . But Argemone?' . . . And Lancelot felt, for the moment, as conservative as the tutelary genius of all special constables.

As the last thought passed through his brain, Bracebridge's little mustang slouched past the window, ridden (without a saddle) by a horseman whom there was no mistaking for no one but the immaculate colonel, the *chevalier sans peur et sans reproche*, dared to go about the country 'such a figure.' A minute afterwards he walked in, in a student's felt hat, a ragged heather-coloured coatee, and old white 'regulation drills,' shrunk half-way up his legs, a pair of embroidered Indian mocassins, and an enormous meerschaum at his button-hole.

'Where have you been this last week?'

'Over head and ears in Young England, till I fled to you for a week's common sense. A glass of cider, for mercy's sake, "to take the taste of it out of my mouth," as Bill Sykes has it.'

'Where have you been staying?'

'With young Lord Vieuxbois, among high art and painted glass, spade farms, and model smell-traps, rubricalities and sanitary reforms, and all other inventions, possible and impossible, for "stretching the old formula to meet the new fact," as your favourite prophet says.'

'Till the old formula cracks under the tension.'

'And cracks its devotees, too, I think. Here comes the cider!'

'But, my dear fellow, you must not laugh at all this. Young England or Peelite, this is all right and noble. What a yet unspoken poetry there is in that very sanitary reform! It is the great fact of the age. We shall have men arise and write epics on it, when they have learnt that "to the pure all things are pure," and that science and usefulness contain a divine element, even in their lowest appliances.'

'Write one yourself, and call it the *Chadwickiad*.'

'Why not?

'Smells and the Man I sing.

There's a beginning at once. Why don't *you* rather, with your practical power, turn sanitary reformer—the only true soldier—and conquer those real devils and "natural enemies" of Englishmen, carbonic acid and sulphuretted hydrogen?'

'*Ce n'est pas mon métier*, my dear fellow. I am miserably behind the age. People are getting so cursedly in earnest now-a-days, that I shall have to bolt to the backwoods to amuse myself in peace; or else sham dumb as the monkeys do, lest folks should find out that I'm rational, and set me to work.'

Lancelot laughed and sighed.

'But how on earth do you contrive to get on so well with men with whom you have not an idea in common!'

'*Savoir faire*, O infant Hercules! own daddy to *savoir vivre*. I am a good listener; and, therefore, the most perfect, because the most silent, of flatterers. When they talk Puginesquery, I stick my head on one side attentively, and "think the more," like the lady's parrot. I have been all the morning looking over a set of drawings for my lord's new chapel; and every soul in the party fancies me a great antiquary, just because I have been retailing to B as my own everything that A told me the moment before.'

'I envy you your tact, at all events.'

'Why the deuce should you? You may rise in time to something better than tact; to what the good book, I suppose, means by "wisdom." Young geniuses like you, who have been green enough to sell your souls to "truth," must not meddle with tact, unless you wish to fare as the donkey did when he tried to play lap-dog.'

'At all events, I would sooner remain cub till they run me down and eat me, than give up speaking my mind,' said Lancelot. 'Fool I may be, but the devil himself shan't make me knave.'

'Quite proper. On two thousand a year a man can afford to be honest. Kick out lustily right and left!—After all, the world is like a spaniel; the more you beat it, the better it likes you—if you have money. Only don't kick too hard; for, after all, it has a hundred million pair of shins to your one.'

'Don't fear that I shall run a-muck against society just now. I am too thoroughly out of my own good books. I have been for years laughing at Young England, and yet its little finger is thicker than my whole body, for it is trying to do something; and I, alas, am doing utterly nothing. I should be really glad to take a lesson of these men and their plans for social improvement.'

'You will have a fine opportunity this evening. Don't you dine at Minchampstead?'

'Yes. Do you?'

'Mr. Jingle dines everywhere, except at home. Will you take me over in your trap?'

'Done. But whom shall we meet there?'

'The Lavingtons, and Vieuxbois, and Vaurien, and a parson or two, I suppose. But between Saint Venus and Vieuxbois you may soon learn enough to make you a sadder man, if not a wiser one.'

'Why not a wiser one? Sadder than now I cannot be; or less wise, God knows.'

The colonel looked at Lancelot with one of those kindly thoughtful smiles, which came over him whenever his better child's heart could bubble up through the thick crust of worldliness.

'My young friend, you have been a little too much on the stilts heretofore. Take care that, now you are off them, you don't lie down and sleep, instead of walking honestly on your legs. Have faith in yourself; pick these men's brains, and all men's. You can do it. Say to yourself boldly, as the false prophet in India said to the missionary, "I have fire enough in my stomach to burn up" a dozen stucco and filigree reformers and "assimilate their ashes into the bargain, like one of Liebig's cabbages."'

'How can I have faith in myself, when I am playing traitor to myself every hour in the day? And yet faith in something I must have: in woman, perhaps.'

'Never!' said the colonel, energetically. 'In anything but woman? She must be led, not leader. If you love a woman, make her have faith in you. If you lean on her, you will ruin yourself, and her as well.'

Lancelot shook his head. There was a pause.

'After all, colonel, I think there must be a meaning in those old words our mothers used to teach us about "having faith in God."'

The colonel shrugged his shoulders.

'*Quien sabe*? said the Spanish girl, when they asked her who was her child's father. But here comes my kit on a clod's back, and it is time to dress for dinner.'

So to the dinner-party they went.

Lord Minchampstead was one of the few noblemen Lancelot had ever met who had aroused in him a thorough feeling of respect. He was always and in all things a strong man. Naturally keen, ready, business-like, daring, he had carved out his own way through life, and opened his oyster—the world, neither with sword nor pen, but with steam and cotton. His father was Mr. Obadiah Newbroom, of the well-known manufacturing firm of Newbroom, Stag, and Playforall. A stanch Dissenter himself, he saw with a slight pang his son Thomas turn Churchman, as soon as the young man had worked his way up to be the real head of the firm. But this was the only sorrow which Thomas Newbroom, now Lord Minchampstead, had ever given his father. 'I stood behind a loom myself, my boy, when I began life; and you must do with great means what I did with little ones. I have made a gentleman of you, you must make a nobleman of yourself.' Those were almost the last words of the stern, thrifty, old Puritan craftsman, and his son never forgot them. From a mill-owner he grew to coal-owner, shipowner, banker, railway director, money-lender to kings and princes; and last of all, as the summit of his own and his compeer's ambition, to land-owner. He had half a dozen estates in as many different counties. He had added house to house, and field to field; and at last bought Minchampstead Park and ten thousand acres, for two-thirds its real value, from that enthusiastic sportsman Lord Peu de Cervelle, whose family had come in with the Conqueror, and gone out with George IV. So, at least, they always said; but it was remarkable that their name could never be traced farther back than the dissolution of the monasteries: and Calumnious Dryasdusts would sometimes insolently father their title on James I. and one of his batches of bought peerages. But let the dead bury their dead. There was now a new lord in Minchampstead; and every country Caliban was finding, to his disgust, that he had 'got a new master,' and must perforce 'be a new man.' Oh! how the squires swore and the farmers chuckled, when the 'Parvenu' sold the Minchampstead hounds, and celebrated his 1st of September by exterminating every hare and pheasant on the estate! How the farmers swore and the labourers chuckled when he took all the cottages into his own hands and rebuilt them, set up a first-rate industrial school, gave every man a pig and a garden, and broke up all the commons 'to thin the labour-market.' Oh, how the labourers swore and the farmers chuckled, when he put up steam-engines on all his farms, refused to give away a farthing in alms, and enforced the new Poor-law to the very letter. How the country tradesmen swore, when he called them 'a pack of dilatory jobbers,' and announced his intention of employing only London workmen for his improvements. Oh! how they all swore together (behind his back, of course, for his dinners were worth eating), and the very ladies said naughty words, when the stern political economist proclaimed at his own table that 'he had bought Minchampstead for merely commercial purposes, as a profitable investment of capital, and he would see that, whatever else it did, it should *pay*.'

But the new lord heard of all the hard words with a quiet self-possessed smile. He had formed his narrow theory of the universe, and he was methodically and conscientiously carrying it out. True, too often, like poor Keats's merchant brothers,—

'Half-ignorant, he turned an easy wheel,
Which set sharp racks at work to pinch and peel.'

But of the harm which he did he was unconscious; in the good which he did he was consistent and indefatigable; infinitely superior, with all his defects, to the ignorant, extravagant do-nothing Squire Lavingtons around him. At heart, however, Mammoth-blinded, he was kindly and upright. A man of a stately presence; a broad, honest north-country face; a high square forehead, bland and unwrinkled. I sketch him here once for all, because I have no part for him after this scene in my *corps de ballet*.

Lord Minchampstead had many reasons for patronising Lancelot. In the first place, he had a true eye for a strong man wherever he met him; in the next place, Lancelot's uncle the banker, was a stanch Whig ally of his in the House. 'In the rotten-borough times, Mr. Smith,' he once said to Lancelot, 'we could have made a senator of you at once; but, for the sake of finality, we were forced to relinquish that organ of influence. The Tories had abused it, really, a little too far; and now we can only make a commissioner of you—which, after all, is a more useful post, and a more lucrative one.' But Lancelot had not as yet 'Galliolised,' as the Irish schoolmaster used to call it, and cared very little to play a political ninth fiddle.

The first thing which caught his eyes as he entered the drawing-room before dinner was Argemone listening in absorbed reverence to her favourite vicar,—a stern, prim, close-shaven, dyspeptic man, with a meek, cold smile, which might have become a cruel one. He watched and watched in vain, hoping to catch her eye; but no—there she stood, and talked and listened—

'Ah,' said Bracebridge, smiling, 'it is in vain, Smith! When did you know a woman leave the Church for one of us poor laymen?'

'Good heavens!' said Lancelot, impatiently, 'why will they make such fools of themselves with clergymen?'

'They are quite right. They always like the strong men—the fighters and the workers. In Voltaire's time they all ran after the philosophers. In the middle ages, books tell us, they worshipped the knights errant. They are always on the winning side, the cunning little beauties. In the war-time, when the soldiers had to play the world's game, the ladies all caught the red-coat fever; now, in these talking and thinking days (and be hanged to them for bores), they have the black-coat fever for the same reason. The parsons are the workers now-a-days—or rather, all the world expects them to be so. They have the game in their own hands, if they did but know how to play it.'

Lancelot stood still, sulking over many thoughts. The colonel lounged across the room towards Lord Vieuxbois, a quiet, truly high-bred young man, with a sweet open countenance, and an ample forehead, whose size would have vouched for great talents, had not the promise been contradicted by the weakness of the over-delicate mouth and chin.

'Who is that with whom you came into the room, Bracebridge?' asked Lord Vieuxbois. 'I am sure I know his face.'

'Lancelot Smith, the man who has taken the shooting-box at Lower Whitford.'

'Oh, I remember him well enough at Cambridge! He was one of a set who tried to look like blackguards, and really succeeded tolerably. They used to eschew gloves, and drink nothing but beer, and smoke disgusting short pipes; and when we established the Coverley Club in Trinity, they set up an opposition, and called themselves the Navvies. And they used to make piratical expeditions down to Lynn in eight oars, to attack bargemen, and fen girls, and shoot ducks, and sleep under turf-stacks, and come home when they had drank all the public-house taps dry. I remember the man perfectly.'

'Navvy or none,' said the colonel, 'he has just the longest head and the noblest heart of any man I ever met. If he does not distinguish himself before he dies, I know nothing of human nature.'

'Ah yes, I believe he is clever enough!—took a good degree, a better one than I did—but horribly eclectic; full of mesmerism, and German metaphysics, and all that sort of thing. I heard of him one night last spring, on which he had been seen, if you will believe it, going successively into a

Swedenborgian chapel, the Garrick's Head, and one of Elliotson's magnetic *soirées*. What can you expect after that?'

'A great deal,' said Bracebridge drily. 'With such a head as he carries on his shoulders the man might be another Mirabeau, if he held the right cards in the right rubber. And he really ought to suit you, for he raves about the middle ages, and chivalry, and has edited a book full of old ballads.'

'Oh, all the eclectics do that sort of thing; and small thanks to them. However, I will speak to him after dinner, and see what there is in him.'

And Lord Vieuxbois turned away, and, alas for Lancelot! sat next to Argemone at dinner. Lancelot, who was cross with everybody for what was nobody's fault, revenged himself all dinner-time by never speaking a word to his next neighbour, Miss Newbroom, who was longing with all her heart to talk sentiment to him about the Exhibition; and when Argemone, in the midst of a brilliant word-skirmish with Lord Vieuxbois, stole a glance at him, he chose to fancy that they were both talking of him, and looked more cross than ever.

After the ladies retired, Lancelot, in his sulky way, made up his mind that the conversation was going to be ineffably stupid; and set to to dream, sip claret, and count the minutes till he found himself in the drawing-room with Argemone. But he soon discovered, as I suppose we all have, that 'it never rains but it pours,' and that one cannot fall in with a new fact or a new acquaintance but next day twenty fresh things shall spring up as if by magic, throwing unexpected light on one's new phenomenon. Lancelot's head was full of the condition-of-the-poor question, and lo! everybody seemed destined to talk about it.

'Well, Lord Vieuxbois,' said the host, casually, 'my girls are raving about your new school. They say it is a perfect antiquarian gem.'

'Yes, tolerable, I believe. But Wales has disappointed me a little. That vile modernist naturalism is creeping back even into our painted glass. I could have wished that the artist's designs for the windows had been a little more Catholic.'

'How then?' asked the host, with a puzzled face.

'Oh, he means,' said Bracebridge, 'that the figures' wrists and ankles were not sufficiently dislocated, and the patron saint did not look quite like a starved rabbit with its neck wrung. Some of the faces, I am sorry to say, were positively like good-looking men and women.'

'Oh, I understand,' said Lord Minchampstead; 'Bracebridge's tongue is privileged, you know, Lord Vieuxbois, so you must not be angry.'

'I don't see my way into all this,' said Squire Lavington (which was very likely to be true, considering that he never looked for his way). 'I don't see how all these painted windows, and crosses, and chanting, and the deuce and the Pope only know what else, are to make boys any better.'

'We have it on the highest authority,' said Vieuxbois, 'that pictures and music are the books of the unlearned. I do not think that we have any right in the nineteenth century to contest an opinion which the fathers of the Church gave in the fourth.'

'At all events,' said Lancelot, 'it is by pictures and music, by art and song, and symbolic representations, that all nations have been educated in their adolescence! and as the youth of the individual is exactly analogous to the youth of the collective race, we should employ the same means of instruction with our children which succeeded in the early ages with the whole world.'

Lancelot might as well have held his tongue—nobody understood him but Vieuxbois, and he had been taught to scent German neology in everything, as some folks are taught to scent Jesuitry, especially when it involved an inductive law, and not a mere red-tape precedent, and, therefore, could not see that Lancelot was arguing for him. 'All very fine, Smith,' said the squire; 'it's a pity you won't leave off puzzling your head with books, and stick to fox-hunting. All you young gentlemen will do is to turn the heads of the poor with your cursed education.' The national oath followed, of course. 'Pictures and chanting! Why, when I was a boy, a good honest labouring man wanted to see nothing better than a halfpenny ballad, with a wood-cut at the top, and they worked very well then, and wanted for nothing.'

'Oh, we shall give them the halfpenny ballads in time!' said Vieuxbois, smiling.

'You will do a very good deed, then,' said mine host. 'But I am sorry to say that, as far as I can find from my agents, when the upper classes write cheap publications, the lower classes will not read them.'

'Too true,' said Vieuxbois.

'Is not the cause,' asked Lancelot, 'just that the upper classes do write them?'

'The writings of working men, certainly,' said Lord Minchampstead, 'have an enormous sale among their own class.'

'Just because they express the feelings of that class, of which I am beginning to fear that we know very little. Look again, what a noble literature of people's songs and hymns Germany has. Some of Lord Vieuxbois's friends, I know, are busy translating many of them.'

'As many of them, that is to say,' said Vieuxbois, 'as are compatible with a real Church spirit.'

'Be it so; but who wrote them? Not the German aristocracy for the people, but the German people for themselves. There is the secret of their power. Why not educate the people up to such a standard that they should be able to write their own literature?'

'What,' said Mr. Chalklands, of Chalklands, who sat opposite, 'would you have working men turn ballad writers? There would be an end of work, then, I think.'

'I have not heard,' said Lancelot, 'that the young women—*ladies*, I ought to say, if the word mean anything—who wrote the "Lowell Offering," spun less or worse cotton than their neighbours.'

'On the contrary," said Lord Minchampstead, 'we have the most noble accounts of heroic industry and self-sacrifice in girls whose education, to judge by its fruits, might shame that of most English young ladies.'

Mr. Chalklands expressed certain confused notions that, in America, factory girls carried green silk parasols, put the legs of pianos into trousers, and were too prudish to make a shirt, or to call it a shirt after it was made, he did not quite remember which.

'It is a great pity,' said Lord Minchampstead, 'that our factory girls are not in the same state of civilisation. But it is socially impossible. America is in an abnormal state. In a young country the laws of political economy do not make themselves fully felt. Here, where we have no uncleared world to drain the labour-market, we may pity and alleviate the condition of the working-classes, but we can do nothing more. All the modern schemes for the amelioration which ignore the laws of competition, must end either in pauperisation'—(with a glance at Lord Vieuxbois),—'or in the destruction of property.'

Lancelot said nothing, but thought the more. It did strike him at the moment that the few might, possibly, be made for the many, and not the many for the few; and that property was made for man, not man for property. But he contented himself with asking,—

'You think, then, my lord, that in the present state of society, no dead-lift can be given to the condition—in plain English, the wages—of working men, without the destruction of property?'

Lord Minchampstead smiled, and parried the question.

'There may be other dead-lift ameliorations, my young friend, besides a dead-lift of wages.'

So Lancelot thought, also; but Lord Minchampstead would have been a little startled could he have seen Lancelot's notion of a dead-lift. Lord Minchampstead was thinking of cheap bread and sugar. Do you think that I will tell you of what Lancelot was thinking?

But here Vieuxbois spurred in to break a last lance. He had been very much disgusted with the turn the conversation was taking, for he considered nothing more heterodox than the notion that the poor were to educate themselves. In his scheme, of course the clergy and the gentry were to educate the poor, who were to take down thankfully as much as it was thought proper to give them: and all beyond was 'self-will' and 'private judgment,' the fathers of Dissent and Chartism, Trades'-union strikes, and French Revolutions, *et si qua alia*.

'And pray, Mr. Smith, may I ask what limit you would put to education?'

'The capacities of each man,' said Lancelot. 'If man living in civilised society has one right which he can demand it is this, that the State which exists by his labour shall enable him to develop, or, at least, not hinder his developing, his whole faculties to their very utmost, however lofty that may be. While a man who might be an author remains a spade-drudge, or a journeyman while he has capacities for a master; while any man able to rise in life remains by social circumstances lower than he is willing to place himself, that man has a right to complain of the State's injustice and neglect.'

'Really, I do not see,' said Vieuxbois, 'why people should wish to rise in life. They had no such self-willed fancy in the good old times. The whole notion is a product of these modern days—'

He would have said more, but he luckily remembered at whose table he was sitting.

'I think, honestly,' said Lancelot, whose blood was up, 'that we gentlemen all run into the same fallacy. We fancy ourselves the fixed and necessary element in society, to which all others are to accommodate themselves. "Given the rights of the few rich, to find the condition of the many poor." It seems to me that other postulate is quite as fair: "Given the rights of the many poor, to find the condition of the few rich."'

Lord Minchampstead laughed.

'If you hit us so hard, Mr. Smith, I must really denounce you as a Communist. Lord Vieuxbois, shall we join the ladies?'

In the drawing-room, poor Lancelot, after rejecting overtures of fraternity from several young ladies, set himself steadily again against the wall to sulk and watch Argemone. But this time she spied in a few minutes his melancholy, moonstruck face, swam up to him, and said something kind and commonplace. She spoke in the simplicity of her heart, but he chose to think she was patronising him—she had not talked commonplaces to the vicar. He tried to say something smart and cutting,—stuttered, broke down, blushed, and shrank back again to the wall, fancying that every eye in the room was on him; and for one moment a flash of sheer hatred to Argemone swept through him.

Was Argemone patronising him? Of course she was. True, she was but three-and-twenty, and he was of the same age; but, spiritually and socially, the girl develops ten years earlier than the boy. She was flattered and worshipped by gray-headed men, and in her simplicity she thought it a noble self-sacrifice to stoop to notice the poor awkward youth. And yet if he could have seen the pure moonlight of sisterly pity which filled all her heart as she retreated, with something of a blush and something of a sigh, and her heart fluttered and fell, would he have been content? Not he. It was her love he wanted, and not her pity; it was to conquer her and possess her, and inform himself with her image, and her with his own; though as yet he did not know it; though the moment that she turned away he cursed himself for selfish vanity, and moroseness and conceit.

'Who am I to demand her all to myself? Her, the glorious, the saintly, the unfallen! Is not a look, a word, infinitely more than I deserve? And yet I pretend to admire tales of chivalry! Old knightly hearts would have fought and wandered for years to earn a tithe of the favours which have been bestowed on me unasked.'—

Peace! poor Lancelot! Thy egg is by no means addle; but the chick is breaking the shell in somewhat a cross-grained fashion.

CHAPTER VII
THE DRIVE HOME, AND WHAT CAME OF IT

Now it was not extraordinary that Squire Lavington had 'assimilated' a couple of bottles of Carbonel's best port; for however abstemious the new lord himself might be, he felt for the habits, and for the vote of an old-fashioned Whig squire. Nor was it extraordinary that he fell fast asleep the moment he got into the carriage; nor, again, that his wife and daughters were not solicitous about waking him; nor, on the other hand, that the coachman and footman, who were like all the squire's servants, of the good old sort, honest, faithful, boozing, extravagant, happy-go-lucky souls, who had 'been about the place these forty years,' were somewhat owlish and unsteady on the box. Nor was it extraordinary that there was a heavy storm of lightning, for that happened three times a-week in the chalk hills the summer through; nor, again, that under these circumstances the horses, who were of the squire's own breeding, and never thoroughly broke (nothing was done thoroughly at Whitford), went rather wildly home, and that the carriage swung alarmingly down the steep hills, and the boughs brushed the windows rather too often. But it was extraordinary that Mrs. Lavington had cast off her usual primness, and seemed to-night, for the first time in her life, in an exuberant good humour, which she evinced by snubbing her usual favourite Honoria, and lavishing caresses on Argemone, whose vagaries she usually regarded with a sort of puzzled terror, like a hen who has hatched a duckling.

'Honoria, take your feet off my dress. Argemone, my child, I hope you spent a pleasant evening?'

Argemone answered by some tossy commonplace.

A pause—and then Mrs. Lavington recommenced,—

'How very pleasing that poor young Lord Vieuxbois is, after all!'

'I thought you disliked him so much.'

'His opinions, my child; but we must hope for the best. He seems moral and well inclined, and really desirous of doing good in his way; and so successful in the House, too, I hear.'

'To me,' said Argemone, 'he seems to want life, originality, depth, everything that makes a great man. He knows nothing but what he has picked up ready-made from books. After all, his opinions are the one redeeming point in him.'

'Ah, my dear, when it pleases Heaven to open your eyes, you will see as I do!'

Poor Mrs. Lavington! Unconscious spokeswoman for the ninety-nine hundredths of the human race! What are we all doing from morning to night, but setting up our own fancies as the measure of all heaven and earth, and saying, each in his own dialect, Whig, Radical, or Tory, Papist or Protestant, 'When it pleases Heaven to open your eyes you will see as I do'?

'It is a great pity,' went on Mrs. Lavington, meditatively, 'to see a young man so benighted and thrown away. With his vast fortune, too—such a means of good! Really we ought to have seen a little more of him. I think Mr. O'Blareaway's conversation might be a blessing to him. I think of asking him over to stay a week at Whitford, to meet that sainted young man.'

Now Argemone did not think the Reverend Panurgus O'Blareaway, incumbent of Lower Whitford, at all a sainted young man, but, on the contrary, a very vulgar, slippery Irishman; and she had, somehow, tired of her late favourite, Lord Vieuxbois; so she answered tossily enough,—

'Really, mamma, a week of Lord Vieuxbois will be too much. We shall be bored to death with the Cambridge Camden Society, and ballads for the people.'

'I think, my dear,' said Mrs. Lavington (who had, half unconsciously to herself, more reasons than one for bringing the young lord to Whitford), 'I think, my dear, that his conversation, with all its faults, will be a very improving change for your father. I hope he's asleep.'

The squire's nose answered for itself.

'Really, what between Mr. Smith, and Colonel Bracebridge, and their very ineligible friend, Mr. Mellot, whom I should never have allowed to enter my house if I had suspected his religious views, the place has become a hotbed of false doctrine and heresy. I have been quite frightened when I have heard their conversation at dinner, lest the footmen should turn infidels!'

'Perhaps, mamma,' said Honoria, slyly, 'Lord Vieuxbois might convert them to something quite as bad. How shocking if old Giles, the butler, should turn Papist!'

'Honoria, you are very silly. Lord Vieuxbois, at least can be trusted. He has no liking for low companions. *He* is above joking with grooms, and taking country walks with gamekeepers.'

It was lucky that it was dark, for Honoria and Argemone both blushed crimson.

'Your poor father's mind has been quite unsettled by all their ribaldry. They have kept him so continually amused, that all my efforts to bring him to a sense of his awful state have been more unavailing than ever.'

Poor Mrs. Lavington! She had married, at eighteen, a man far her inferior in intellect; and had become—as often happens in such cases—a prude and a devotee. The squire, who really admired and respected her, confined his disgust to sly curses at the Methodists (under which name he used to include every species of religious earnestness, from Quakerism to that of Mr. Newman). Mrs. Lavington used at first to dignify these disagreeables by the name of persecution, and now she was trying to convert the old man by coldness, severity, and long curtain-lectures, utterly unintelligible to their victim, because couched in the peculiar conventional phraseology of a certain school. She forgot, poor earnest soul, that the same form of religion which had captivated a disappointed girl of twenty, might not be the most attractive one for a jovial old man of sixty.

Argemone, who a fortnight before would have chimed in with all her mother's lamentations, now felt a little nettled and jealous. She could not bear to hear Lancelot classed with the colonel.

'Indeed,' she said, 'if amusement is bad for my father, he is not likely to get much of it during Lord Vieuxbois's stay. But, of course, mamma, you will do as you please.'

'Of course I shall, my dear,' answered the good lady, in a tragedy-queen tone. 'I shall only take the liberty of adding, that it is very painful to me to find you adding to the anxiety which your unfortunate opinions give me, by throwing every possible obstacle in the way of my plans for your good.'

Argemone burst into proud tears (she often did so after a conversation with her mother). 'Plans for my good!'—And an unworthy suspicion about her mother crossed her mind, and was peremptorily expelled again. What turn the conversation would have taken next, I know not, but at that moment Honoria and her mother uttered a fearful shriek, as their side of the carriage jolted half-way up the bank, and stuck still in that pleasant position.

The squire awoke, and the ladies simultaneously clapped their hands to their ears, knowing what was coming. He thrust his head out of the window, and discharged a broadside of at least ten pounds' worth of oaths

(Bow Street valuation) at the servants, who were examining the broken wheel, with a side volley or two at Mrs. Lavington for being frightened. He often treated her and Honoria to that style of oratory. At Argemone he had never sworn but once since she left the nursery, and was so frightened at the consequences, that he took care never to do it again.

But there they were fast, with a broken wheel, plunging horses, and a drunken coachman. Luckily for them, the colonel and Lancelot were following close behind, and came to their assistance.

The colonel, as usual, solved the problem.

'Your dog-cart will carry four, Smith?'

'It will.'

'Then let the ladies get in, and Mr. Lavington drive them home.'

'What?' said the squire, 'with both my hands red-hot with the gout? You must drive three of us, colonel, and one of us must walk.'

'I will walk,' said Argemone, in her determined way.

Mrs. Lavington began something about propriety, but was stopped with another pound's worth of oaths by the squire, who, however, had tolerably recovered his good humour, and hurried Mrs. Lavington and Honoria, laughingly, into the dog-cart, saying—

'Argemone's safe enough with Smith; the servants will lead the horse behind them. It's only three miles home, and I should like to see any one speak to her twice while Smith's fists are in the way.'

Lancelot thought so too.

'You can trust yourself to me, Miss Lavington?'

'By all means. I shall enjoy the walk after—:' and she stopped. In a moment the dog-cart had rattled off, with a parting curse from the squire to the servants, who were unharnessing the horses.

Argemone took Lancelot's arm; the soft touch thrilled through and through him; and Argemone felt, she knew not why, a new sensation run through her frame. She shuddered—not with pain.

'You are cold, Miss Lavington?'

'Oh, not in the least.' Cold! when every vein was boiling so strangely! A soft luscious melancholy crept over her. She had always had a terror of darkness; but now she felt quite safe in his strength. The thought of her own unprotected girlhood drew her heart closer to him. She remembered with pleasure the stories of his personal prowess, which had once made her think him coarse and brutal. For the first time in her life she knew the delight of dependence—the holy charm of weakness. And as they paced on silently together, through the black awful night, while the servants lingered, far out of sight, about the horses, she found out how utterly she trusted to him.

'Listen!' she said. A nightingale was close to them, pouring out his whole soul in song.

'Is it not very late in the year for a nightingale?'

'He is waiting for his mate. She is rearing a late brood, I suppose.'

'What do you think it is which can stir him up to such an ecstasy of joy, and transfigure his whole heart into melody?'

'What but love, the fulness of all joy, the evoker of all song?'

'All song?—The angels sing in heaven.'

'So they say: but the angels must love if they sing.'

'They love God!'

'And no one else?'

'Oh yes: but that is universal, spiritual love; not earthly love—a narrow passion for an individual.'

'How do we know that they do not learn to love all by first loving one?'

'Oh, the angelic life is single!'

'Who told you so, Miss Lavington?'

She quoted the stock text, of course:—'"In heaven they neither marry nor are given in marriage, but are as the angels."'

'"As the tree falls, so it lies." And God forbid that those who have been true lovers on earth should contract new marriages in the next world. Love is eternal. Death may part lovers, but not love. And how do we know that these angels, as they call them, if they be really persons, may not be united in pairs by some marriage bond, infinitely more perfect than any we can dream of on earth?'

'That is a very wild view, Mr. Smith, and not sanctioned by the Church,' said Argemone, severely. (Curious and significant it is, how severe ladies are apt to be whenever they talk of the Church.)

'In plain historic fact, the early fathers and the middle-age monks did not sanction it: and are not they the very last persons to whom one would go to be taught about marriage? Strange! that people should take their notions of love from the very men who prided themselves on being bound, by their own vows, to know nothing about it!'

'They were very holy men.'

'But still men, as I take it. And do you not see that Love is, like all spiritual things, only to be understood by experience—by loving?'

'But is love spiritual?'

'Pardon me, but what a question for one who believes that "God is love!"'

'But the divines tell us that the love of human beings is earthly.'

'How did they know? They had never tried. Oh, Miss Lavington! cannot you see that in those barbarous and profligate ages of the later empire, it was impossible for men to discern the spiritual beauty of marriage, degraded as it had been by heathen brutality? Do you not see that there must have been a continual tendency in the minds of a celibate clergy to look with contempt, almost with spite, on pleasures which were forbidden to them?'

Another pause.

'It must be very delicious,' said Argemone, thoughtfully, 'for any one who believes it, to think that marriage can last through eternity. But, then, what becomes of entire love to God? How can we part our hearts between him and his creatures?'

'It is a sin, then, to love your sister? or your friend? What a low, material view of love, to fancy that you can cut it up into so many pieces, like a cake, and give to one person one tit-bit, and another to another, as the Popish books would have you believe! Love is like flame—light as many fresh flames at it as you will, it grows, instead of diminishing, by the dispersion.'

'It is a beautiful imagination.'

'But, oh, how miserable and tantalising a thought, Miss Lavington, to those who know that a priceless spirit is near them, which might be one with theirs through all eternity, like twin stars in one common atmosphere, for ever giving and receiving wisdom and might, beauty and bliss, and yet are barred from their bliss by some invisible adamantine wall, against which they must beat themselves to death, like butterflies against the window-pane, gazing, and longing, and unable to guess why they are forbidden to enjoy!'

Why did Argemone withdraw her arm from his? He knew, and he felt that she was entrusted to him. He turned away from the subject.

'I wonder whether they are safe home by this time?'

'I hope my father will not catch cold. How sad, Mr. Smith, that he will swear so. I do not like to say it; and yet you must have heard him too often yourself.'

'It is hardly a sin with him now, I think. He has become so habituated to it, that he attaches no meaning or notion whatsoever to his own oaths. I have heard him do it with a smiling face to the very beggar to whom he was giving half-a-crown. We must not judge a man of his school by the standard of our own day.'

'Let us hope so,' said Argemone, sadly.

There was another pause. At a turn of the hill road the black masses of beech-wood opened, and showed the Priory lights twinkling right below. Strange that Argemone felt sorry to find herself so near home.

'We shall go to town next week,' said she; "and then—You are going to Norway this summer, are you not?'

'No. I have learnt that my duty lies nearer home.'

'What are you going to do?'

'I wish this summer, for the first time in my life, to try and do some good—to examine a little into the real condition of English working men.'

'I am afraid, Mr. Smith, that I did not teach you that duty.'

'Oh, you have taught me priceless things! You have taught me beauty is the sacrament of heaven, and love its gate; that that which is the most luscious is also the most pure.'

'But I never spoke a word to you on such subjects.'

'There are those, Miss Lavington, to whom a human face can speak truths too deep for books.'

Argemone was silent; but she understood him. Why did she not withdraw her arm a second time?

In a moment more the colonel hailed them from the dog-cart and behind him came the britschka with a relay of servants.

They parted with a long, lingering pressure of the hand, which haunted her young palm all night in dreams. Argemone got into the carriage, Lancelot jumped into the dog cart, took the reins, and relieved his heart by galloping Sandy up the hill, and frightening the returning coachman down one bank and his led horses up the other.

'*Vogue la Galère*, Lancelot? I hope you have made good use of your time?'

But Lancelot spoke no word all the way home, and wandered till dawn in the woods around his cottage, kissing the hand which Argemone's palm had pressed.

CHAPTER VIII
WHITHER?

Some three months slipped away—right dreary months for Lancelot, for the Lavingtons went to Baden-Baden for the summer. 'The waters were necessary for their health.' . . . How wonderful it is, by the bye, that those German Brunnen are never necessary for poor people's health! . . . and they did not return till the end of August. So Lancelot buried himself up to the eyes in the Condition-of-the-Poor question—that is, in blue books, red books, sanitary reports, mine reports, factory reports; and came to the conclusion, which is now pretty generally entertained, that something was the matter—but what, no man knew, or, if they knew, thought proper to declare. Hopeless and bewildered, he left the books, and wandered day after day from farm to hamlet, and from field to tramper's tent, in hopes of finding out the secret for himself. What he saw, of course I must not say; for if I did the reviewers would declare, as usual, one and all, that I copied out of the *Morning Chronicle*; and the fact that these pages, ninety-nine hundredths of them at least, were written two years before the *Morning Chronicle* began its invaluable investigations, would be contemptuously put aside as at once impossible and arrogant. I shall therefore only say, that he saw what every one else has seen, at least heard of, and got tired of hearing—though alas! they have not got tired of seeing it; and so proceed with my story, only mentioning therein certain particulars which folks seem, to me, somewhat strangely, to have generally overlooked.

But whatever Lancelot saw, or thought he saw, I cannot say that it brought him any nearer to a solution of the question; and he at last ended by a sulky acquiescence in Sam Weller's memorable dictum: 'Who it is I can't say; but all I can say is that *somebody* ought to be wopped for this!'

But one day, turning over, as hopelessly as he was beginning to turn over everything else, a new work of Mr. Carlyle's, he fell on some such words as these:—

'The beginning and the end of what is the matter with us in these days is—that *we have forgotten God*.'

Forgotten God? That was at least a defect of which blue books had taken no note. And it was one which, on the whole—granting, for the sake of argument, any real, living, or practical existence to That Being, might be a radical one—it brought him many hours of thought, that saying; and when they were over, he rose up and went to find—Tregarva.

'Yes, he is the man. He is the only man with whom I have ever met, of whom I could be sure, that independent of his own interest, without the allurements of respectability and decency, of habit and custom, he believes in God. And he too is a poor man; he has known the struggles, temptations, sorrows of the poor. I will go to him.'

But as Lancelot rose to find him, there was put into his hand a letter, which kept him at home a while longer—none other, in fact, than the long-expected answer from Luke.

'WELL, MY DEAR COUSIN—You may possibly have some logical ground from which to deny Popery, if you deny all other religions with it; but how those who hold any received form of Christianity whatsoever can fairly side with you against Rome, I cannot see. I am sure I have been sent to Rome by them, not drawn thither by Jesuits. Not merely by their defects and inconsistencies; not merely because they go on taunting us, and shrieking at us with the cry that we ought to go to Rome, till we at last, wearied out, take them at their word, and do at their bidding the thing we used to shrink from with terror—not this merely but the very doctrines we hold in common with them, have sent me to Rome. For would these men have known of them if Rome had not been? The Trinity—the Atonement—the Inspiration of Scripture.—A future state—that point on which the present generation, without a smattering of psychological science, without even the old belief in apparitions, dogmatises so narrowly and arrogantly—what would they have known of them but for Rome? And she says there are three realms in the future state . . . heaven, hell, and purgatory . . . What right have they to throw away the latter, and arbitrarily retain the two former? I am told that Scripture gives no warrant for a third state. She says that it does—that it teaches that implicitly, as it teaches other, the very highest doctrines; some hold, the Trinity itself. . . . It may be proved from Scripture; for it may be proved from the love and justice of God revealed in Scripture. The Protestants divide—in theory, that is—mankind into two classes, the righteous, who are destined to infinite bliss; the wicked, who are doomed to infinite torment; in which latter class, to make their arbitrary division exhaustive, they put of course nine hundred and ninety-nine out of the thousand, and doom to everlasting companionship with Borgias and Cagliostros, the gentle, frivolous girl, or the peevish boy, who would have shrunk, in life, with horror from the contact. . . . Well, at least, their hell is hellish enough . . . if it were but just. . . . But I, Lancelot, I cannot believe it! I will not believe it! I had a brother once—affectionate, simple, generous, full of noble aspirations—but without, alas! a thought of God; yielding in a hundred little points, and some great ones, to the infernal temptations of a public school. . . . He died at seventeen. Where is he now? Lancelot! where is he now? Never for a day has that thought left my mind for years. Not in heaven—for he has no right there; Protestants would say that as well as I. . . . Where, then?—Lancelot! not in that other place. I cannot, I will not believe it. For the sake of God's honour, as well as of my own sanity, I will not believe it! There must be some third place—some intermediate chance, some door of hope—some purifying and redeeming process beyond the grave. . . . Why not a purifying fire? Ages of that are surely punishment enough—and if there be a fire of hell, why not a fire of purgatory? . . . After all, the idea of purgatory as a fire is only an opinion, not a dogma of the Church. . . . But if the gross flesh which has sinned is to be punished by the matter which it has abused, why may it not be purified by it?'

'You may laugh, if you will, at both, and say again, as I have heard you say ere now, that the popular Christian paradise and hell are but a Pagan Olympus and Tartarus, as grossly material as Mahomet's, without the honest thorough-going sexuality, which you thought made his notion logical and consistent. . . . Well, you may say that, but Protestants cannot; for their idea of heaven and ours is the same—with this exception, that theirs will contain but a thin band of saved ones, while ours will fill and grow to all eternity. . . . I tell you, Lancelot, it is just the very doctrines for which England most curses Rome, and this very purgatory at the head of them, which constitute her strength and her allurement; which appeal to the reason, the conscience, the heart of men, like me, who have revolted from the novel superstition which looks pitilessly on at the fond memories of the brother, the prayers of the orphan, the doubled desolation of the widow, with its cold terrible assurance, "There is no hope for thy loved and lost ones—no hope, but hell for evermore!"

'I do not expect to convert you. You have your metempsychosis, and your theories of progressive incarnation, and your monads, and your spirits of the stars and flowers. I have not forgotten a certain talk of ours over Falk Von Müller's *Recollections of Goethe*, and how you materialists are often the most fantastic of theorists. . . . I do not expect, I say, to convert you. I only want to show you there is no use trying to show the self-satisfied Pharisees of the popular sect—why, in spite of all their curses, men still go back to Rome.'

Lancelot read this, and re-read it; and smiled, but sadly—and the more he read, the stronger its arguments seemed to him, and he rejoiced thereat.

For there is a bad pleasure—happy he who has not felt it—in a pitiless reductio ad absurdum, which asks tauntingly, 'Why do you not follow out your own conclusions?'—instead of thanking God that people do not follow them out, and that their hearts are sounder than their heads. Was it with this feeling that the fancy took possession of him, to show the letter to Tregarva? I hope not—perhaps he did not altogether wish to lead him into temptation, any more than I wish to lead my readers, but only to make him, just as I wish to make them, face manfully a real awful question now racking the hearts of hundreds, and see how they will be able to answer the sophist fiend—for honestly, such he is—when their time comes, as come it will. At least he wanted to test at once Tregarva's knowledge and his logic. As for his 'faith,' alas! he had not so much reverence for it as to care what effect Luke's arguments might have there. 'The whole man,' quoth Lancelot to himself, 'is a novel phenomenon; and all phenomena, however magnificent, are surely fair subjects for experiment. Magendie may have gone too far, certainly, in dissecting a live dog—but what harm in my pulling the mane of a dead lion?'

So he showed the letter to Tregarva as they were fishing together one day—for Lancelot had been installed duly in the Whitford trout preserves'—Tregarva read it slowly; asked, shrewdly enough, the meaning of a word or two as he went on; at last folded it up deliberately, and returned it to its owner with a deep sigh. Lancelot said nothing for a few minutes; but the giant seemed so little inclined to open the conversation, that he was forced at last to ask him what he thought of it.

'It isn't a matter for thinking, sir, to my mind—There's a nice fish on the feed there, just over-right that alder.'

'Hang the fish! Why not a matter for thinking?'

'To my mind, sir, a man may think a deal too much about many matters that come in his way.'

'What should he do with them, then?'

'Mind his own business.'

'Pleasant for those whom they concern!—That's rather a cold-blooded speech for you, Tregarva!'

The Cornishman looked up at him earnestly. His eyes were glittering—was it with tears?

'Don't fancy I don't feel for the poor young gentleman—God help him!—I've been through it all—or not through it, that's to say. I had a brother once, as fine a young fellow as ever handled pick, as kind-hearted as a woman, and as honest as the sun in Heaven.—But he would drink, sir;—that one temptation, he never could stand it. And one day at the shaft's mouth, reaching after the kibble-chain—maybe he was in liquor, maybe not—the Lord knows; but—'

'I didn't know him again, sir, when we picked him up, any more than—' and the strong man shuddered from head to foot, and beat impatiently on the ground with his heavy heel, as if to crush down the rising horror.

'Where is he, sir?'

A long pause.

'Do you think I didn't ask that, sir, for years and years after, of God, and my own soul, and heaven and earth, and the things under the earth, too? For many a night did I go down that mine out of my turn, and sat for hours in that level, watching and watching, if perhaps the spirit of him might haunt about, and tell his poor brother one word of news—one way or the other—anything would have been a comfort—but the doubt I couldn't bear. And yet at last I learnt to bear it—and what's more, I learnt not to care for it. It's a bold word—there's one who knows whether or not it is a true one.'

'Good Heavens!—and what then did you say to yourself?'

'I said this, sir—or rather, one came as I was on my knees, and said it to me—What's done you can't mend. What's left, you can. Whatever has happened is God's concern now, and none but His. Do you see that as far as you can no such thing ever happen again, on the face of His earth. And from that day, sir, I gave myself up to that one thing, and will until I die, to save the poor young fellows like myself, who are left now-a-days to the Devil, body and soul, just when they are in the prime of their power to work for God.'

'Ah!' said Lancelot—'if poor Luke's spirit were but as strong as yours!'

'I strong?' answered he, with a sad smile; 'and so you think, sir. But it's written, and it's true—"The heart knoweth its own bitterness."'

'Then you absolutely refuse to try to fancy your—his present state?'

'Yes, sir, because if I did fancy it, that would be a certain sign I didn't know it. If we can't conceive what God has prepared for those that we know loved Him, how much less can we for them of whom we don't know whether they loved Him or not?'

'Well,' thought Lancelot to himself, 'I did not do so very wrong in trusting your intellect to cut through a sophism.'

'But what do you believe, Tregarva?'

'I believe this, sir—and your cousin will believe the same, if he will only give up, as I am sore afraid he will need to some day, sticking to arguments and doctrines about the Lord, and love and trust the Lord himself. I believe, sir, that the judge of all the earth will do right—and what's right can't be wrong, nor cruel either, else it would not be like Him who loved us to the death, that's all I know; and that's enough for me. To whom little is given, of him is little required. He that didn't know his Master's will, will be beaten with few stripes, and he that did know it, as I do, will be beaten with many, if he neglects it—and that latter, not the former, is my concern.'

'Well,' thought Lancelot to himself, 'this great heart has gone down to the root of the matter—the right and wrong of it. He, at least, has not forgotten God. Well, I would give up all the Teleologies and cosmogonies that I ever dreamt or read, just to believe what he believes—Heigho and well-a-day!—Paul! hist? I'll swear that was an otter!'

'I hope not, sir, I'm sure. I haven't seen the spraint of one here this two years.'

'There again—don't you see something move under that marl bank?'

Tregarva watched a moment, and then ran up to the spot, and throwing himself on his face on the edge, leant over, grappled something—and was instantly, to Lancelot's astonishment, grappled in his turn by a rough, lank, white dog, whose teeth, however, could not get through the velveteen sleeve.

'I'll give in, keeper! I'll give in. Doan't ye harm the dog! he's deaf as a post, you knows.'

'I won't harm him if you take him off, and come up quietly.'

This mysterious conversation was carried on with a human head, which peeped above the water, its arms supporting from beneath the growling cur—such a visage as only worn-out poachers, or trampling drovers, or London chiffonniers carry; pear-shaped and retreating to a narrow peak above, while below, the bleared cheeks, and drooping lips, and peering purblind eyes, perplexed, hopeless, defiant, and yet sneaking, bespeak *their* share in the 'inheritance of the kingdom of heaven.'—Savages without the resources of a savage—slaves without the protection of a master—to whom the cart-whip and the rice-swamp would be a change for the better—for there, at least, is food and shelter.

Slowly and distrustfully a dripping scarecrow of rags and bones rose from his hiding-place in the water, and then stopped suddenly, and seemed inclined to dash through the river; but Tregarva held him fast.

'There's two on ye! That's a shame! I'll surrender to no man but you, Paul. Hold off, or I'll set the dog on ye!'

'It's a gentleman fishing. He won't tell—will you, sir?' And he turned to Lancelot. 'Have pity on the poor creature, sir, for God's sake—it isn't often he gets it.'

'I won't tell, my man. I've not seen you doing any harm. Come out like a man, and let's have a look at you.'

The creature crawled up the bank, and stood, abject and shivering, with the dog growling from between his legs.

'I was only looking for a kingfisher's nest: indeed now, I was, Paul Tregarva.'

'Don't lie, you were setting night-lines. I saw a minnow lie on the bank as I came up. Don't lie; I hate liars.'

'Well indeed, then—a man must live somehow.'

'You don't seem to live by this trade, my friend,' quoth Lancelot; 'I cannot say it seems a prosperous business, by the look of your coat and trousers.'

'That Tim Goddard stole all my clothes, and no good may they do him; last time as I went to gaol I gave them him to kep, and he went off for a navvy meantime; so there I am.'

'If you will play with the dogs,' quoth Tregarva, 'you know what you will be bit by. Haven't I warned you? Of course you won't prosper: as you make your bed, so you must lie in it. The Lord can't be expected to let those prosper that forget Him. What mercy would it be to you if He did let you prosper by setting snares all church-time, as you were last Sunday, instead of going to church?'

'I say, Paul Tregarva, I've told you my mind about that afore. If I don't do what I knows to be right and good already, there ain't no use in me a damning myself all the deeper by going to church to hear more.'

'God help you!' quoth poor Paul.

'Now, I say,' quoth Crawy, with the air of a man who took the whole thing as a matter of course, no more to be repined at than the rain and wind—'what be you a going to do with me this time? I do hope you won't have me up to bench. 'Tain't a month now as I'm out o' prizzum along o' they fir-toppings, and I should, you see—' with a look up and down and round at the gay hay-meadows, and the fleet water, and the soft gleaming clouds, which to Lancelot seemed most pathetic,—'I should like to ha' a spell o' fresh air, like, afore I goes in again.'

Tregarva stood over him and looked down at him, like some huge stately bloodhound on a trembling mangy cur. 'Good heavens!' thought Lancelot, as his eye wandered from the sad steadfast dignity of the one, to the dogged helpless misery of the other—'can those two be really fellow-citizens? fellow-Christians?—even animals of the same species? Hard to believe!'

True, Lancelot; but to quote you against yourself, Bacon, or rather the instinct which taught Bacon, teaches you to discern the invisible common law under the deceitful phenomena of sense.

'I must have those night-lines, Crawy,' quoth Tregarva, at length.

'Then I must starve. You might ever so well take away the dog. They're the life of me.'

'They're the death of you. Why don't you go and work, instead of idling about, stealing trout?'

'Be you a laughing at a poor fellow in his trouble? Who'd gie me a day's work, I'd like to know? It's twenty year too late for that!'

Lancelot stood listening. Yes, that wretch, too, was a man and a brother—at least so books used to say. Time was, when he had looked on a poacher as a Pariah 'hostem humani generis'—and only deplored that the law forbade him to shoot them down, like cats and otters; but he had begun to change his mind.

He had learnt, and learnt rightly, the self-indulgence, the danger, the cruelty, of indiscriminate alms. It looked well enough in theory, on paper. 'But—but—but,' thought Lancelot, 'in practice, one can't help feeling a little of that un-economic feeling called pity. No doubt the fellow has committed an unpardonable sin in daring to come into the world when there was no call for him; one used to think, certainly, that children's opinions were not consulted on such points before they were born, and that therefore it might be hard to visit the sins of the fathers on the children, even though the labour-market were a little overstocked—"mais nous avons changé tout cela," like M. Jourdain's doctors. No doubt, too, the fellow might have got work if he had chosen—in Kamschatka or the Cannibal Islands; for the political economists have proved, beyond a doubt, that there is work somewhere or other for every one who chooses to work. But as, unfortunately, society has neglected to inform him of the state of the Cannibal Island labour-market, or to pay his passage thither when informed thereof, he has had to choose in the somewhat limited labour-field of the Whitford Priors' union, whose workhouse is already every winter filled with abler-bodied men than he, between starvation—and this—. Well, as for employing him, one would have thought that there was a little work waiting to be done in those five miles of heather and snipe-bog, which I used to tramp over last winter—but those, it seems, are still on the "margin of cultivation," and not a remunerative investment—that is, to capitalists. I wonder if any one had made Crawy a present of ten acres of them when he came of age, and commanded him to till that or be hanged, whether he would not have found it a profitable investment? But bygones are bygones, and there he is, and the moors, thanks to the rights of property—in this case the rights of the dog in the manger—belong to poor old Lavington—that is, the game and timber on them; and neither Crawy nor any one else can touch them. What can I do for him? Convert him? to what? For the next life, even Tregarva's talisman seems to fail. And for this life—perhaps if he had had a few more practical proofs of a divine justice and government—that "kingdom of heaven" of which Luke talks, in the sensible bodily matters which he does appreciate, he might not be so unwilling to trust to it for the invisible spiritual matters which he does not appreciate. At all events, one has but one chance of winning him, and that is, through those five senses which he has left. What if he does spend the money in gross animal enjoyment? What will the amount of it be, compared with the animal enjoyments which my station allows me daily without reproach! A little more bacon—a little more beer—a little more tobacco; at all events they will be more important to him than a pair of new boots or an extra box of cigars to me.'—And Lancelot put his hand in his pocket, and pulled out a sovereign. No doubt he was a great goose; but if you can answer his arguments, reader, I cannot.

'Look here—what are your night-lines worth?'

'A matter of seven shilling; ain't they now, Paul Tregarva?'

'I should suppose they are.'

'Then do you give me the lines, one and all, and there's a sovereign for you.—No, I can't trust you with it all at once. I'll give it to Tregarva, and he shall allow you four shillings a week as long as it lasts, if you'll promise to keep off Squire Lavington's river.'

It was pathetic, and yet disgusting, to see the abject joy of the poor creature. 'Well,' thought Lancelot, 'if he deserves to be wretched, so do I—why, therefore, if we are one as bad as the other, should I not make his wretchedness a little less for the time being?'

'I waint come a-near the water. You trust me—I minds them as is kind to me'—and a thought seemed suddenly to lighten up his dull intelligence.

'I say, Paul, hark you here. I see that Bantam into D * * * t'other day.'

'What! is he down already?'

'With a dog-cart; he and another of his pals; and I see 'em take out a silk flue, I did. So, says I, you maunt be trying that ere along o' the Whitford trout; they kepers is out o' nights so sure as the moon.'

'You didn't know that. Lying again!'

'No, but I sayed it in course. I didn't want they a-robbing here; so I think they worked mainly up Squire Vaurien's water.'

'I wish I'd caught them here,' quoth Tregarva, grimly enough; 'though I don't think they came, or I should have seen the track on the banks.'

'But he sayed like, as how he should be down here again about pheasant shooting.'

'Trust him for it. Let us know, now, if you see him.'

'And that I will, too. I wouldn't save a feather for that 'ere old rascal, Harry. If the devil don't have he, I don't see no use in keeping no devil. But I minds them as has mercy on me, though my name is Crawy. Ay,' he added, bitterly, "tain't so many kind turns as I gets in this life, that I can afford to forget e'er a one.' And he sneaked off, with the deaf dog at his heels.

'How did that fellow get his name, Tregarva?'

'Oh, most of them have nicknames round here. Some of them hardly know their own real names, sir.' ('A sure sign of low civilisation,' thought Lancelot.) 'But he got his a foolish way; and yet it was the ruin of him. When he was a boy of fifteen, he got miching away in church-time, as boys will, and took off his clothes to get in somewhere here in this very river, groping in the banks after craw-fish; and as the devil—for I can think no less—would have it, a big one catches hold of him by the fingers with one claw, and a root with the other, and holds him there till Squire Lavington comes out to take his walk after church, and there he caught the boy, and gave him a thrashing there and then, naked as he stood. And the story got wind, and all the chaps round called him Crawy ever afterwards, and the poor fellow got quite reckless from that day, and never looked any one in the face again; and being ashamed of himself, you see, sir, was never ashamed of anything else—and there he is. That dog's his only friend, and gets a livelihood for them both. It's growing old now; and when it dies, he'll starve.'

'Well—the world has no right to blame him for not doing his duty, till it has done its own by him a little better.'

'But the world will, sir, because it hates its duty, and cries all day long, like Cain, "Am I my brother's keeper?"'

'Do you think it knows its duty? I have found it easy enough to see that something is diseased, Tregarva; but to find the medicine first, and to administer it afterwards, is a very different matter.'

'Well—I suppose the world will never be mended till the day of judgment.'

'In plain English, not mended till it is destroyed. Hopeful for the poor world! I should fancy, if I believed that, that the devil in the old history—which you believe—had had the best of it with a vengeance, when he brought sin into the world, and ruined it. I dare not believe that. How dare you, who say that God sent His Son into the world to defeat the devil?'

Tregarva was silent a while.

'Learning and the Gospel together ought to do something, sir, towards mending it. One would think so. But the prophecies are against that.'

'As folks happen to read them just now. A hundred years hence they may be finding the very opposite meaning in them. Come, Tregarva,—Suppose I teach you a little of the learning, and you teach me a little of the Gospel—do you think we two could mend the world between us, or even mend Whitford Priors?'

'God knows, sir,' said Tregarva.

'Tregarva,' said Lancelot, as they were landing the next trout, 'where will that Crawy go, when he dies?'

'God knows, sir,' said Tregarva.

Lancelot went thoughtful home, and sat down—not to answer Luke's letter—for he knew no answer but Tregarva's, and that, alas! he could not give, for he did not believe it, but only longed to believe it. So he turned off the subject by a question—

'You speak of yourself as being already a member of the Romish communion. How is this? Have you given up your curacy? Have you told your father? I fancy that if you had done so I must have heard of it ere now. I entreat you to tell me the state of the case, for, heathen as I am, I am still an Englishman; and there are certain old superstitions still lingering among us—whencesoever we may have got them first—about truth and common honesty—you understand me.—

'Do not be angry. But there is a prejudice against the truthfulness of Romish priests and Romish converts.—It's no affair of mine. I see quite enough Protestant rogues and liars, to prevent my having any pleasure in proving Romanists, or any other persons, rogues and liars also. But I am—if not fond of you—at least sufficiently fond to be anxious for your good name. You used to be an open-hearted fellow enough. Do prove to the world that cœlum, non animum mutant, qui trans mare currunt.'

CHAPTER IX
HARRY VERNEY HEARS HIS LAST SHOT FIRED

The day after the Lavingtons' return, when Lancelot walked up to the Priory with a fluttering heart to inquire after all parties, and see one, he found the squire in a great state of excitement.

A large gang of poachers, who had come down from London by rail, had been devastating all the covers round, to stock the London markets by the first of October, and intended, as Tregarva had discovered, to pay Mr. Lavington's preserves a visit that night. They didn't care for country justices, not they. Weren't all their fines paid by highly respectable game-dealers at the West end? They owned three dog-carts among them; a parcel by railway would bring them down bail to any amount; they tossed their money away at the public-houses, like gentlemen; thanks to the Game Laws, their profits ran high, and when they had swept the country pretty clean of game, why, they would just finish off the season by a stray highway robbery or two, and vanish into Babylon and their native night.

Such was Harry Verney's information as he strutted about the courtyard waiting for the squire's orders.

'But they've put their nose into a furze-bush, Muster Smith, they have. We've got our posse-commontaturs, fourteen men, sir, as'll play the whole vale to cricket, and whap them; and every one'll fight, for they're half poachers themselves, you see' (and Harry winked and chuckled); 'and they can't abide no interlopers to come down and take the sport out of their mouths.'

'But are you sure they'll come to-night?'

'That 'ere Paul says so. Wonder how he found out—some of his underhand, colloguing, Methodist ways, I'll warrant. I seed him preaching to that 'ere Crawy, three or four times when he ought to have hauled him up. He consorts with them poachers, sir, uncommon. I hope he ben't one himself, that's all.'

'Nonsense, Harry!'

'Oh? Eh? Don't say old Harry don't know nothing, that's all. I've fixed his flint, anyhow.'

'Ah! Smith!' shouted the squire out of his study window, with a cheerful and appropriate oath. 'The very man I wanted to see! You must lead these keepers for me to-night. They always fight better with a gentleman among them. Breeding tells, you know—breeding tells.'

Lancelot felt a strong disgust at the occupation, but he was under too many obligations to the squire to refuse.

'Ay, I knew you were game,' said the old man. 'And you'll find it capital fun. I used to think it so, I know, when I was young. Many a shindy have I had here in my uncle's time, under the very windows, before the chase was disparked, when the fellows used to come down after the deer.'

Just then Lancelot turned and saw Argemone standing close to him. He almost sprang towards her—and retreated, for he saw that she had overheard the conversation between him and her father.

'What! Mr. Smith!' said she in a tone in which tenderness and contempt, pity and affected carelessness, were strangely mingled. 'So! you are going to turn gamekeeper to-night?'

Lancelot was blundering out something, when the squire interposed.

'Let her alone, Smith. Women will be tender-hearted, you know. Quite right—but they don't understand these things. They fight with their tongues, and we with our fists; and then they fancy their weapons don't hurt—Ha! ha! ha!'

'Mr. Smith,' said Argemone, in a low, determined voice, 'if you have promised my father to go on this horrid business—go. But promise me, too, that you will only look on, or I will never—'

Argemone had not time to finish her sentence before Lancelot had promised seven times over, and meant to keep his promise, as we all do.

About ten o'clock that evening Lancelot and Tregarva were walking stealthily up a ride in one of the home covers, at the head of some fifteen fine young fellows, keepers, grooms, and *not extempore* 'watchers,' whom old Harry was marshalling and tutoring, with exhortations as many and as animated as if their ambition was *'Mourir pour la patrie.'*

'How does this sort of work suit you, Tregarva, for I don't like it at all! The fighting's all very well, but it's a poor cause.'

'Oh, sir, I have no mercy on these Londoners. If it was these poor half-starved labourers, that snare the same hares that have been eating up their garden-stuff all the week, I can't touch them, sir, and that's truth; but these ruffians—And yet, sir, wouldn't it be better for the parsons to preach to them, than for the keepers to break their heads?'

'Oh?' said Lancelot, 'the parsons say all to them that they can.'

Tregarva shook his head.

'I doubt that, sir. But, no doubt, there's a great change for the better in the parsons. I remember the time, sir, that there wasn't an earnest clergyman in the vale; and now every other man you meet is trying to do his best. But those London parsons, sir, what's the matter with them? For all their societies and their schools, the devil seems to keep ahead of them sadly. I doubt they haven't found the right fly yet for publicans and sinners to rise at.'

A distant shot in the cover.

'There they are, sir. I thought that Crawy wouldn't lead me false when I let him off.'

'Well, fight away, then, and win. I have promised Miss Lavington not to lift a hand in the business.'

'Then you're a lucky man, sir. But the squire's game is his own, and we must do our duty by our master.'

There was a rustle in the bushes, and a tramp of feet on the turf.

'There they are, sir, sure enough. The Lord keep us from murder this night!' And Tregarva pulled off his neckcloth, and shook his huge limbs, as if to feel that they were all in their places, in a way that augured ill for the man who came across him.

They turned the corner of a ride, and, in an instant, found themselves face to face with five or six armed men, with blackened faces, who, without speaking a word, dashed at them, and the fight began; reinforcements came up on each side, and the engagement became general.

> 'The forest-laws were sharp and stern,
>   The forest blood was keen,
> They lashed together for life and death
>   Beneath the hollies green.
>
> 'The metal good and the walnut-wood
>   Did soon in splinters flee;
> They tossed the orts to south and north,
>   And grappled knee to knee.

> 'They wrestled up, they wrestled down,
> They wrestled still and sore;
> The herbage sweet beneath their feet
> Was stamped to mud and gore.'

And all the while the broad still moon stared down on them grim and cold, as if with a saturnine sneer at the whole humbug; and the silly birds about whom all this butchery went on, slept quietly over their heads, every one with his head under his wing. Oh! if pheasants had but understanding, how they would split their sides with chuckling and crowing at the follies which civilised Christian men perpetrate for their precious sake!

Had I the pen of Homer (though they say he never used one), or even that of the worthy who wasted precious years in writing a *Homer Burlesqued*, what heroic exploits might not I immortalise! In every stupid serf and cunning ruffian there, there was a heart as brave as Ajax's own; but then they fought with sticks instead of lances, and hammered away on fustian jackets instead of brazen shields; and, therefore, poor fellows, they were beneath 'the dignity of poetry,' whatever that may mean. If one of your squeamish 'dignity-of-poetry' critics had just had his head among the gun-stocks for five minutes that night, he would have found it grim tragic earnest enough; not without a touch of fun though, here and there.

Lancelot leant against a tree and watched the riot with folded arms, mindful of his promise to Argemone, and envied Tregarva as he hurled his assailants right and left with immense strength, and led the van of battle royally. Little would Argemone have valued the real proof of love which he was giving her as he looked on sulkily, while his fingers tingled with longing to be up and doing. Strange—that mere lust of fighting, common to man and animals, whose traces even the lamb and the civilised child evince in their mock-fights, the earliest and most natural form of play. Is it, after all, the one human propensity which is utterly evil, incapable of being turned to any righteous use? Gross and animal, no doubt it is, but not the less really pleasant, as every Irishman and many an Englishman knows well enough. A curious instance of this, by the bye, occurred in Paris during the February Revolution. A fat English coachman went out, from mere curiosity, to see the fighting. As he stood and watched, a new passion crept over him; he grew madder and madder as the bullets whistled past him; at last, when men began to drop by his side, he could stand it no longer, seized a musket, and rushed in, careless which side he took,—

'To drink delight of battle with his peers.'

He was not heard of for a day or two, and then they found him stiff and cold, lying on his face across a barricade, with a bullet through his heart.

Sedentary persons may call him a sinful fool. Be it so. *Homo sum: humani nihil à me alienum puto.*

Lancelot, I verily believe, would have kept his promise, though he saw that the keepers gave ground, finding Cockney skill too much for their clumsy strength; but at last Harry Verney, who had been fighting as venomously as a wild cat, and had been once before saved from a broken skull by Tregarva, rolled over at his very feet with a couple of poachers on him.

'You won't see an old man murdered, Mr. Smith?' cried he, imploringly.

Lancelot tore the ruffians off the old man right and left. One of them struck him; he returned the blow; and, in an instant, promises and Argemone, philosophy and anti-game-law prejudices, were swept out of his head, and 'he went,' as the old romances say, 'hurling into the midst of the press,' as mere a wild animal for the moment as angry bull or boar. An instant afterwards, though, he burst out laughing, in spite of himself, as 'The Battersea Bantam,' who had been ineffectually dancing round Tregarva like a gamecock spurring at a bull, turned off with a voice of ineffable disgust,—

'That big cove's a yokel; ta'nt creditable to waste science on him. You're my man, if you please, sir,'—and the little wiry lump of courage and conceit, rascality and good humour, flew at Lancelot, who was twice his size, 'with a heroism worthy of a better cause,' as respectable papers, when they are not too frightened, say of the French.

'Do you want any more?' asked Lancelot.

'Quite a pleasure, sir, to meet a scientific gen'lman. Beg your pardon, sir; stay a moment while I wipes my face. Now, sir, time, if you please.'

Alas for the little man! in another moment he tumbled over and lay senseless—Lancelot thought he had killed him. The gang saw their champion fall, gave ground, and limped off, leaving three of their party groaning on the ground, beside as many Whitford men.

As it was in the beginning, so is it to be to the end, my foolish brothers! From the poacher to the prime minister—wearying yourselves for very vanity! The soldier is not the only man in England who is fool enough to be shot at for a shilling a day.

But while all the rest were busy picking up the wounded men and securing the prisoners, Harry Verney alone held on, and as the poachers retreated slowly up the ride, he followed them, peering into the gloom, as if in hopes of recognising some old enemy.

'Stand back, Harry Verney; we know you, and we'd be loth to harm an old man,' cried a voice out of the darkness.

'Eh? Do you think old Harry'd turn back when he was once on the track of ye? You soft-fisted, gin-drinking, counter-skipping Cockney rascals, that fancy you're to carry the county before you, because you get your fines paid by London-tradesmen! Eh? What do you take old Harry for?'

'Go back, you old fool!' and a volley of oaths followed. 'If you follow us, we'll fire at you, as sure as the moon's in heaven!'

'Fire away, then! I'll follow you to—!' and the old man paced stealthily but firmly up to them.

Tregarva saw his danger and sprang forward, but it was too late.

'What, you will have it, then?'

A sharp crack followed,—a bright flash in the darkness—every white birch-stem and jagged oak-leaf shone out for a moment as bright as day—and in front of the glare Lancelot saw the old man throw his arms wildly upward, fall forward, and disappear on the dark ground.

'You've done it! off with you!' And the rascals rushed off up the ride.

In a moment Tregarva was by the old man's side, and lifted him tenderly up.

'They've done for me, Paul. Old Harry's got his gruel. He's heard his last shot fired. I knowed it 'ud come to this, and I said it. Eh? Didn't I, now, Paul?' And as the old man spoke, the workings of his lungs pumped great jets of blood out over the still heather-flowers as they slept in the moonshine, and dabbled them with smoking gore.

'Here, men,' shouted the colonel, 'up with him at once, and home! Here, put a brace of your guns together, muzzle and lock. Help him to sit on them, Lancelot. There, Harry, put your arms round their necks. Tregarva, hold him up behind. Now then, men, left legs foremost—keep step—march!' And they moved off towards the Priory.

'You seem to know everything, colonel,' said Lancelot.

The colonel did not answer for a moment.

'Lancelot, I learnt this dodge from the only friend I ever had in the world, or ever shall have; and a week after I marched him home to his deathbed in this very way.'

'Paul—Paul Tregarva,' whispered old Harry, 'put your head down here: wipe my mouth, there's a man; it's wet, uncommon wet.' It was his own life-blood. 'I've been a beast to you, Paul. I've hated you, and envied you, and tried to ruin you. And now you've saved my life once this night; and here you be a-nursing of me as my own son might do, if he was here, poor fellow! I've ruined you, Paul; the Lord forgive me!'

'Pray! pray!' said Paul, 'and He will forgive you. He is all mercy. He pardoned the thief on the cross—'

'No, Paul, no thief,—not so bad as that, I hope, anyhow; never touched a feather of the squire's. But you dropped a song, Paul, a bit of writing.'

Paul turned pale.

'And—the Lord forgive me!—I put it in the squire's fly-book.'

'The Lord forgive you! Amen!' said Paul, solemnly.

Wearily and slowly they stepped on towards the old man's cottage. A messenger had gone on before, and in a few minutes the squire, Mrs. Lavington, and the girls, were round the bed of their old retainer.

They sent off right and left for the doctor and the vicar; the squire was in a frenzy of rage and grief.

'Don't take on, master, don't take on,' said old Harry, as he lay; while the colonel and Honoria in vain endeavoured to stanch the wound. 'I knowed it would be so, sooner or later; 'tis all in the way of business. They haven't carried off a bird, squire, not a bird; we was too many for 'em—eh, Paul, eh?'

'Where is that cursed doctor?' said the squire. 'Save him, colonel, save him; and I'll give you—'

Alas! the charge of shot at a few feet distance had entered like a bullet, tearing a great ragged hole.—There was no hope, and the colonel knew it; but he said nothing.

'The second keeper,' sighed Argemone, 'who has been killed here! Oh, Mr. Smith, must this be? Is God's blessing on all this?'

Lancelot said nothing. The old man lighted up at Argemone's voice.

'There's the beauty, there's the pride of Whitford. And sweet Miss Honor, too,—so kind to nurse a poor old man! But she never would let him teach her to catch perch, would she? She was always too tender-hearted. Ah, squire, when we're dead and gone,—dead and gone,—squire, they'll be the pride of Whitford still! And they'll keep up the old place—won't you, my darlings? And the old name, too! For, you know, there must always be a Lavington in Whitford Priors, till the Nun's pool runs up to Ashy Down.'

'And a curse upon the Lavingtons,' sighed Argemone to herself in an undertone.

Lancelot heard what she said.

The vicar entered, but he was too late. The old man's strength was failing, and his mind began to wander.

'Windy,' he murmured to himself, 'windy, dark and windy—birds won't lie—not old Harry's fault. How black it grows! We must be gone by nightfall, squire. Where's that young dog gone? Arter the larks, the brute.'

Old Squire Lavington sobbed like a child.

'You will soon be home, my man,' said the vicar. 'Remember that you have a Saviour in heaven. Cast yourself on His mercy.'

Harry shook his head.

'Very good words, very kind,—very heavy gamebag, though. Never get home, never any more at all. Where's my boy Tom to carry it? Send for my boy Tom. He was always a good boy till he got along with them poachers.'

'Listen,' he said, 'listen! There's bells a-ringing—ringing in my head. Come you here, Paul Tregarva.'

He pulled Tregarva's face down to his own, and whispered,—

'Them's the bells a-ringing for Miss Honor's wedding.'

Paul started and drew back. Harry chuckled and grinned for a moment in his old foxy, peering way, and then wandered off again.

'What's that thumping and roaring?' Alas! it was the failing pulsation of his own heart. 'It's the weir, the weir—a-washing me away—thundering over me.—Squire, I'm drowning,—drowning and choking! Oh, Lord, how deep! Now it's running quieter—now I can breathe again—swift and oily—running on, running on, down to the sea. See how the grayling sparkle! There's a pike! 'Tain't my fault, squire, so help me—Don't swear, now, squire; old men and dying maun't swear, squire. How steady the river runs down? Lower and slower—lower and slower: now it's quite still—still—still—'

His voice sank away—he was dead!

No! once more the light flashed up in the socket. He sprang upright in the bed, and held out his withered paw with a kind of wild majesty, as he shouted,—

'There ain't such a head of hares on any manor in the county. And them's the last words of Harry Verney!'

He fell back—shuddered—a rattle in his throat—another—and all was over.

CHAPTER X
'MURDER WILL OUT,' AND LOVE TOO

Argemone need never have known of Lancelot's share in the poaching affray; but he dared not conceal anything from her. And so he boldly went up the next day to the Priory, not to beg pardon, but to justify himself, and succeeded. And, before long, he found himself fairly installed as her pupil, nominally in spiritual matters, but really in subjects of which she little dreamed.

Every day he came to read and talk with her, and whatever objections Mrs. Lavington expressed were silenced by Argemone. She would have it so, and her mother neither dared nor knew how to control her. The daughter had utterly out-read and out-thought her less educated parent, who was clinging in honest bigotry to the old forms, while Argemone was wandering forth over the chaos of the strange new age,—a poor homeless Noah's dove, seeking rest for the sole of her foot and finding none. And now all motherly influence and sympathy had vanished, and Mrs. Lavington, in fear and wonder, let her daughter go her own way. She could not have done better, perhaps; for Providence had found for Argemone a better guide than her mother could have done, and her new pupil was rapidly becoming her teacher. She was matched, for the first time, with a man who was her own equal in intellect and knowledge; and she felt how real was that sexual difference which she had been accustomed to consider as an insolent calumny against woman. Proudly and indignantly she struggled against the conviction, but in vain. Again and again she argued with him, and was vanquished,—or, at least, what is far better, made to see how many different sides there are to every question. All appeals to authority he answered with a contemptuous smile. 'The best authorities?' he used to say. 'On what question do not the best authorities flatly contradict each other? And why? Because every man believes just what it suits him to believe. Don't fancy that men reason themselves into convictions; the prejudices and feelings of their hearts give them some idea or theory, and then they find facts at their leisure to prove their theory true. Every man sees facts through narrow spectacles, red, or green, or blue, as his nation or his temperament colours them: and he is quite right, only he must allow us the liberty of having our spectacles too. Authority is only good for proving facts. We must draw our own conclusions.' And Argemone began to suspect that he was right,—at least to see that her opinions were mere hearsays, picked up at her own will and fancy; while his were living, daily-growing ideas. Her mind was beside his as the vase of cut flowers by the side of the rugged tree, whose roots are feeding deep in the mother earth. In him she first learnt how one great truth received into the depths of the soul germinates there, and bears fruit a thousandfold; explaining, and connecting, and glorifying innumerable things, apparently the most unlike and insignificant; and daily she became a more reverent listener, and gave herself up, half against her will and conscience, to the guidance of a man whom she knew to be her inferior in morals and in orthodoxy. She had worshipped intellect, and now it had become her tyrant; and she was ready to give up every belief which she once had prized, to flutter like a moth round its fascinating brilliance.

Who can blame her, poor girl? For Lancelot's humility was even more irresistible than his eloquence. He assumed no superiority. He demanded her assent to truths, not because they were his opinions, but simply for the truth's sake; and on all points which touched the heart he looked up to her as infallible and inspired. In questions of morality, of taste, of feeling, he listened not as a lover to his mistress, but rather as a baby to its mother; and thus, half unconsciously to himself, he taught her where her true kingdom lay,—that the heart, and not the brain, enshrines the priceless pearl of womanhood, the oracular jewel, the 'Urim and Thummim,' before which gross man can only inquire and adore.

And, in the meantime, a change was passing upon Lancelot. His morbid vanity—that brawl-begotten child of struggling self-conceit and self-disgust—was vanishing away; and as Mr. Tennyson says in one of those priceless idyls of his, before which the shade of Theocritus must hide his diminished head,—

> 'He was altered, and began
>   To move about the house with joy,
>   And with the certain step of man.'

He had, at last, found one person who could appreciate him. And in deliberate confidence he set to work to conquer her, and make her his own. It was a traitorous return, but a very natural one. And she, sweet creature! walked straight into the pleasant snare, utterly blind, because she fancied that she saw clearly. In the pride of her mysticism, she had fancied herself above so commonplace a passion as love. It was a curious feature of lower humanity, which she might investigate and analyse harmlessly as a cold scientific spectator; and, in her mingled pride and purity, she used to indulge Lancelot in metaphysical disquisitions about love and beauty, like that first one in their walk home from Minchampstead, from which a less celestially innocent soul would have shrunk. She thought, forsooth, as the old proverb says, that she could deal in honey, without putting her hand to her mouth. But Lancelot knew better, and marked her for his own. And daily his self-confidence and sense of rightful power developed, and with them, paradoxical as it may seem, the bitterest self-abasement. The contact of her stainless innocence, the growing certainty that the destiny of that innocence was irrevocably bound up with his own, made him shrink from her whenever he remembered his own guilty career. To remember that there were passages in it which she must never know—that she would cast him from her with abhorrence if she once really understood their vileness? To think that, amid all the closest bonds of love, there must for ever be an awful, silent gulf in the past, of which they must never speak!—That she would bring to him what he could never, never bring to her!—The thought was unbearable. And as hideous recollections used to rise before him, devilish caricatures of his former self, mopping and mowing at him in his dreams, he would start from his lonely bed, and pace the room for hours, or saddle his horse, and ride all night long aimlessly through the awful woods, vainly trying to escape himself. How gladly, at those moments, he would have welcomed centuries of a material hell, to escape from the more awful spiritual hell within him,—to buy back that pearl of innocence which he had cast recklessly to be trampled under the feet of his own swinish passions! But, no; that which was done could never be undone,—never, to all eternity. And more than once, as he wandered restlessly from one room to another, the barrels of his pistols seemed to glitter with a cold, devilish smile, and call to him,—

'Come to us! and with one touch of your finger, send that bursting spirit which throbs against your brow to flit forth free, and nevermore to defile her purity by your presence!'

But no, again: a voice within seemed to command him to go on, and claim her, and win her, spite of his own vileness. And in after years, slowly, and in fear and trembling, he knew it for the voice of God, who had been leading him to become worthy of her through that bitter shame of his own unworthiness.

As One higher than them would have it, she took a fancy to read Homer in the original, and Lancelot could do no less than offer his services as translator. She would prepare for him portions of the Odyssey, and every day that he came up to the Priory he used to comment on it to her; and so for many a week, in the dark wainscoted library, and in the clipt yew-alleys of the old gardens, and under the brown autumn trees, they quarried together in that unexhausted mine, among the records of the rich Titan-youth of man. And step by step Lancelot opened to her the everlasting significance of the poem; the unconscious purity which lingers in it, like the last rays of the Paradise dawn; its sense of the dignity of man as man; the religious reverence with which it speaks of all human ties, human strength and beauty—ay, even of merely animal human appetites, as God-given and Godlike symbols. She could not but listen and admire, when he introduced her to the sheer paganism of Schiller's Gods of Greece; for on this subject he was more eloquent than on any. He had gradually, in fact, as we have seen, dropped all faith in anything but Nature; the slightest fact about a bone or a weed was more important to him than all the books of divinity which Argemone lent him—to be laid by unread.

'What *do* you believe in?' she asked him one day, sadly.

'In *this*!' he said, stamping his foot on the ground. 'In the earth I stand on, and the things I see walking and growing on it. There may be something beside it—what you call a spiritual world. But if He who made me intended me to think of spirit first, He would have let me see it first. But as He has given me material senses, and put me in a material world, I take it as a fair hint that I am meant to use those senses first, whatever may come after. I may be intended to understand the unseen world, but if so, it must be, as I suspect, by understanding the visible one: and there are enough wonders there to occupy me for some time to come.'

'But the Bible?' (Argemone had given up long ago wasting words about the 'Church.')

'My only Bible as yet is Bacon. I know that he is right, whoever is wrong. If that Hebrew Bible is to be believed by me, it must agree with what I know already from science.'

What was to be done with so intractable a heretic? Call him an infidel and a Materialist, of course, and cast him off with horror. But Argemone was beginning to find out that, when people are really in earnest, it may be better sometimes to leave God's methods of educating them alone, instead of calling the poor honest seekers hard names, which the speakers themselves don't understand.

But words would fail sometimes, and in default of them Lancelot had recourse to drawings, and manifested in them a talent for thinking in visible forms which put the climax to all Argemone's wonder. A single profile, even a mere mathematical figure, would, in his hands, become the illustration of a spiritual truth. And, in time, every fresh lesson on the Odyssey was accompanied by its illustration,—some bold and simple outline drawing. In Argemone's eyes, the sketches were immaculate and inspired; for their chief, almost their only fault, was just those mere anatomical slips which a woman would hardly perceive, provided the forms were generally graceful and bold.

One day his fancy attempted a bolder flight. He brought a large pen-and-ink drawing, and laying it silently on the table before her, fixed his eyes intensely on her face. The sketch was labelled, the 'Triumph of Woman.' In the foreground, to the right and left, were scattered groups of men, in the dresses and insignia of every period and occupation. The distance showed, in a few bold outlines, a dreary desert, broken by alpine ridges, and furrowed here and there by a wandering watercourse. Long shadows pointed to the half-risen sun, whose disc was climbing above the waste horizon. And in front of the sun, down the path of the morning beams, came Woman, clothed only in the armour of her own loveliness. Her bearing was stately, and yet modest; in her face pensive tenderness seemed wedded with earnest joy. In her right hand lay a cross, the emblem of self-sacrifice. Her path across the desert was marked by the flowers which sprang up beneath her steps; the wild gazelle stept forward trustingly to lick her hand; a single wandering butterfly fluttered round her head. As the group, one by one, caught sight of her, a human tenderness and intelligence seemed to light up every face. The scholar dropt his book, the miser his gold, the savage his weapons; even in the visage of the half-slumbering sot some nobler recollection seemed wistfully to struggle into life. The artist caught up his pencil, the poet his lyre, with eyes that beamed forth sudden inspiration. The sage, whose broad brow rose above the group like some torrent furrowed Alp, scathed with all the temptations and all the sorrows of his race, watched with a thoughtful smile that preacher more mighty than himself. A youth, decked out in the most fantastic fopperies of the middle age, stood with clasped hands and brimming eyes, as remorse and pleasure struggled in his face; and as he looked, the fierce sensual features seemed to melt, and his flesh came again to him like the flesh of a little child. The slave forgot his fetters; little children clapped their hands; and the toil-worn, stunted, savage woman sprung forward to kneel at her feet, and see herself transfigured in that new and divine ideal of her sex.

Descriptions of drawings are clumsy things at best; the reader must fill up the sketch for himself by the eye of faith.

Entranced in wonder and pleasure, Argemone let her eyes wander over the drawing. And her feelings for Lancelot amounted almost to worship, as she apprehended the harmonious unity of the manifold conception,—the rugged boldness of the groups in front, the soft grandeur of the figure which was the lodestar of all their emotions—the virginal purity of the whole. And when she fancied that she traced in those bland aquiline lineaments, and in the crisp ringlets which floated like a cloud down to the knees of the figure, some traces of her own likeness, a dream of a new destiny flitted before her,—she blushed to her very neck; and as she bent her face over the drawing and gazed, her whole soul seemed to rise into her eyes, and a single tear dropped upon the paper. She laid her hand over it, and then turned hastily away.

'You do not like it! I have been too bold,'—said Lancelot, fearfully.

'Oh, no! no! It is so beautiful—so full of deep wisdom! But—but—You may leave it.'

Lancelot slipped silently out of the room, he hardly knew why; and when he was gone, Argemone caught up the drawing, pressed it to her bosom, covered it with kisses, and hid it, as too precious for any eyes but her own, in the farthest corner of her secrétaire.

And yet she fancied that she was not in love!

The vicar saw the growth of this intimacy with a fast-lengthening face; for it was very evident that Argemone could not serve two masters so utterly contradictory as himself and Lancelot, and that either the lover or the father-confessor must speedily resign office. The vicar had had great disadvantages, by the bye, in fulfilling the latter function; for his visits at the Priory had been all but forbidden; and Argemone's 'spiritual state' had been directed by means of a secret correspondence,—a method which some clergymen, and some young ladies too, have discovered, in the last few years, to be quite consistent with moral delicacy and filial obedience. John Bull, like a stupid fellow as he is, has still his doubts upon the point; but he should remember that though St. Paul tells women when they want advice to ask their husbands at home, yet if the poor woman has no husband, or, as often happens, her husband's advice is unpleasant, to whom is she to go but to the next best substitute, her spiritual cicisbeo, or favourite clergyman? In sad earnest, neither husband nor parent deserves pity in the immense majority of such cases. Woman will have guidance. It is her delight and glory to be led; and if her husband or her parents will not meet the cravings of her intellect, she must go elsewhere to find a teacher, and run into the wildest extravagances of private judgment, in the very hope of getting rid of it, just as poor Argemone had been led to do.

And, indeed, she had, of late, wandered into very strange paths: would to God they were as uncommon as strange! Both she and the vicar had a great wish that she should lead a 'devoted life;' but then they both disdained to use common means for their object. The good old English plan of district visiting, by which ladies can have mercy on the bodies and souls of those below them, without casting off the holy discipline which a home, even the most ungenial, alone supplies, savoured too much of mere 'Protestantism.' It might be God's plan for christianising England just now, but that was no reason, alas! for its being their plan: they wanted something more 'Catholic,' more in accordance with Church principles (for, indeed, is it not the business of the Church to correct the errors of Providence!); and what they sought they found at once in a certain favourite establishment of the vicar's, a Church-of-England *béguinage*, or quasi-Protestant nunnery, which he fostered in a neighbouring city, and went thither on all high tides to confess the young ladies, who were in all things nuns, but bound by no vows, except, of course, such as they might choose to make for themselves in private.

Here they laboured among the lowest haunts of misery and sin, piously and self-denyingly enough, sweet souls! in hope of 'the peculiar crown,' and a higher place in heaven than the relations whom they had left behind them 'in the world,' and unshackled by the interference of parents, and other such merely fleshly relationships, which, as they cannot have been instituted by God merely to be trampled under foot on the path to holiness, and cannot well have instituted themselves (unless, after all, the Materialists are right, and this world does grind of itself, except when its Maker happens to interfere once every thousand years), must needs have been instituted by the devil. And so more than one girl in that nunnery, and out of it, too, believed in her inmost heart, though her 'Catholic principles,' by a happy inconsistency, forbade her to say so.

In a moment of excitement, fascinated by the romance of the notion, Argemone had proposed to her mother to allow her to enter this *béguinage*, and called in the vicar as advocate; which produced a correspondence between him and Mrs. Lavington, stormy on her side, provokingly calm on his: and when the poor lady, tired of raging, had descended to an affecting appeal to his human sympathies, entreating him to spare a mother's feelings, he had answered with the same impassive fanaticism, that 'he was surprised at her putting a mother's selfish feelings in competition with the sanctity of her child,' and that 'had his own daughter shown such a desire for a higher vocation, he should have esteemed it the very highest honour;' to which Mrs. Lavington answered, naively enough, that 'it depended very much on what his daughter was like.'—So he was all but forbidden the house. Nevertheless he contrived, by means of this same secret correspondence, to keep alive in Argemone's mind the longing to turn nun, and fancied honestly that he was doing God service, while he was pampering the poor girl's lust for singularity and self-glorification.

But, lately, Argemone's letters had become less frequent and less confiding; and the vicar, who well knew the reason, had resolved to bring the matter to a crisis.

So he wrote earnestly and peremptorily to his pupil, urging her, with all his subtle and refined eloquence, to make a final appeal to her mother, and if that failed, to act 'as her conscience should direct her;' and enclosed an answer from the superior of the convent, to a letter which Argemone had in a mad moment asked him to write. The superior's letter spoke of Argemone's joining her as a settled matter, and of her room as ready for her, while it lauded to the skies the peaceful activity and usefulness of the establishment. This letter troubled Argemone exceedingly. She had never before been compelled to face her own feelings, either about the nunnery or about Lancelot. She had taken up the fancy of becoming a Sister of Charity, not as Honoria might have done, from genuine love of the poor, but from 'a sense of duty.' Almsgiving and visiting the sick were one of the methods of earning heaven prescribed by her new creed. She was ashamed of her own laziness by the side of Honoria's simple benevolence; and, sad though it may be to have to say it, she longed to outdo her by some signal act of self-sacrifice. She had looked to this nunnery, too, as an escape, once and for all, from her own luxury, just as people who have not strength to be temperate take refuge in teetotalism; and the thought of menial services towards the poor, however distasteful to her, came in quite prettily to fill up the little ideal of a life of romantic asceticisms and mystic contemplation, which gave the true charm in her eyes to her wild project. But now—just as a field had opened to her cravings after poetry and art, wider and richer than she had ever imagined—just as those simple childlike views of man and nature, which she had learnt to despise, were assuming an awful holiness in her eyes—just as she had found a human soul to whose regeneration she could devote all her energies,—to be required to give all up, perhaps for ever (and she felt that if at all, it ought to be for ever);—it was too much for her little heart to bear; and she cried bitterly; and tried to pray, and could not; and longed for a strong and tender bosom on which to lay her head, and pour out all her doubts and struggles; and there was none. Her mother did not understand—hardly loved her. Honoria loved her; but understood her even less than her mother. Pride—the pride of intellect, the pride of self-will—had long since sealed her lips to her own family. . . .

And then, out of the darkness of her heart, Lancelot's image rose before her stronger than all, tenderer than all; and as she remembered his magical faculty of anticipating all her thoughts, embodying for her all her vague surmises, he seemed to beckon her towards him.—She shuddered and turned away. And now she first became conscious how he had haunted her thoughts in the last few months, not as a soul to be saved, but as a living man—his face, his figure, his voice, his every gesture and expression, rising clear before her, in spite of herself, by day and night.

And then she thought of his last drawing, and the looks which had accompanied it,—unmistakable looks of passionate and adoring love. There was no denying it—she had always known that he loved her, but she had never dared to confess it to herself. But now the earthquake was come, and all the secrets of her heart burst upward to the light, and she faced the thought in shame and terror. 'How unjust I have been to him! how cruel! thus to entice him on in hopeless love!'

She lifted up her eyes, and saw in the mirror opposite the reflection of her own exquisite beauty.

'I could have known what I was doing! I knew all the while! And yet it is so delicious to feel that any one loves me! Is it selfishness? It is selfishness, to pamper my vanity on an affection which I do not, will not return. I will not be thus in debt to him, even for his love. I do not love him—I do not; and even if I did, to give myself up to a man of whom I know so little, who is not even a Christian, much less a Churchman! Ay! and to give up my will to any man! to become the subject, the slave, of another human being! I, who have worshipped the belief in woman's independence, the hope of woman's enfranchisement, who have felt how glorious it is to live like the angels, single and self-sustained! What if I cut the Gordian knot, and here make, once for all, a vow of perpetual celibacy?'

She flung herself on her knees—she could not collect her thoughts.

'No,' she said, 'I am not prepared for this. It is too solemn to be undertaken in this miserable whirlwind of passion. I will fast, and meditate, and go up formally to the little chapel, and there devote myself to God; and, in the meantime, to write at once to the superior of the Béguines; to go to my mother, and tell her once for all—What? Must I lose him?—must I give him up? Not his love—I cannot give up that—would that I could! but no! he will love me for ever. I know it as well as if an angel told me. But to give up him! Never to see him! never to hear his voice! never to walk with him among the beech woods any more! Oh, Argemone! Argemone! miserable girl! and is it come to this?' And she threw herself on the sofa, and hid her face in her hands.

Yes, Argemone, it is come to this; and the best thing you can do, is just what you are doing—to lie there and cry yourself to sleep, while the angels are laughing kindly (if a solemn public, who settles everything for them, will permit them to laugh) at the rickety old windmill of sham-Popery which you have taken for a real giant.

At that same day and hour, as it chanced, Lancelot, little dreaming what the said windmill was grinding for him, was scribbling a hasty and angry answer to a letter of Luke's, which, perhaps, came that very morning in order to put him into a proper temper for the demolishing of windmills. It ran thus,—

'Ay, my good Cousin,—So I expected—

'Suave mari magno turbantibus æquora ventis
E terra magnum alterius spectare laborem . . .

Pleasant and easy for you Protestants (for I will call you what you are, in spite of your own denials, a truly consistent and logical Protestant—and therefore a Materialist)—easy for you, I say, to sit on the shore, in cold, cruel self-satisfaction, and tell the poor wretch buffeting with the waves what he ought to do while he is choking and drowning. . . . Thank Heaven, the storm has stranded me upon the everlasting Rock of Peter;—but it has been a sore trouble to reach it. Protestants, who look at creeds as things to be changed like coats, whenever they seem not to fit them, little know what we Catholic-hearted ones suffer. . . . If they did, they would be more merciful and more chary in the requirements of us, just as we are in the very throe of a new-born existence. The excellent man, to whose care I have committed myself, has a wise and a tender heart . . . he saw no harm in my concealing from my father the spiritual reason of my giving up my curacy (for I have given it up), and only giving the outward, but equally true reason, that I found it on the whole an ineligible and distressing post. . . . I know you will apply to such an act that disgusting monosyllable of which Protestants are so fond. He felt with me and for me—for my horror of giving pain to my father, and for my wearied and excited state of mind; and strangely enough—to show how differently, according to the difference of the organs, the same object may appear to two people—he quoted in my favour that very verse which you wrest against me. He wished me to show my father that I had only changed my heaven, and not my character, by becoming an Ultramontane-Catholic . . . that, as far as his esteem and affection were founded on anything in me, the ground of it did not vanish with my conversion. If I had told him at once of my altered opinions, he would have henceforth viewed every word and action with a perjudiced eye. . . . Protestants are so bigoted . . . but if, after seeing me for a month or two the same Luke that he had ever known me, he were gradually informed that I had all the while held that creed which he had considered incompatible with such a life as I hope mine would be—you must see the effect which it ought to have. . . . I don't doubt that you will complain of all this. . . . All I can say is, that I cannot sympathise with that superstitious reverence for mere verbal truth, which is so common among Protestants. . . . It seems to me they throw away the spirit of truth, in their idolatry of its letter. For instance,—what is the use of informing a man of a true fact but to induce a true opinion in him? But if, by clinging to the exact letter of the fact, you create a false opinion in his mind, as I should do in my father's case, if by telling him at once of my change, I gave him an unjust horror of Catholicism,—you do not tell him the truth. . . . You may speak what is true to you,—but it becomes an error when received into his mind. . . . If his mind is a refracting and polarising medium—if the crystalline lens of his soul's eye has been changed into tourmaline or Labrador spar—the only way to give him a true image of the fact, is to present it to him already properly altered in form, and adapted to suit the obliquity of his vision; in order that the very refractive power of his faculties may, instead of distorting it, correct it, and make it straight for him; and so a verbal wrong in fact may possess him with a right opinion. . . .

'You see the whole question turns on your Protestant deification of the intellect. . . . If you really believed, as you all say you do, that the nature of man, and therefore his intellect among the rest, was utterly corrupt, you would not be so superstitiously careful to tell the truth . . . as you call it; because you would know that man's heart, if not his head, would needs turn the truth into a lie by its own corruption. . . . The proper use of reasoning is to produce opinion,—and if the subject in which you wish to produce the opinion is diseased, you must adapt the medicine accordingly.'

To all which Lancelot, with several strong curses, scrawled the following answer:—

'And this is my Cousin Luke!—Well, I shall believe henceforward that there is, after all, a thousand times greater moral gulf fixed between Popery and Tractarianism, than between Tractarianism and the extremest Protestantism. My dear fellow,—I won't bother you, by cutting up your charming ambiguous middle terms, which make reason and reasoning identical, or your theory that the office of reasoning is to induce opinions—(the devil take opinions, right or wrong—I want facts, faith in real facts!)—or about deifying the intellect—as if all sound intellect was not in itself divine light—a revelation to man of absolute laws independent of him, as the very heathens hold. But this I will do—thank you most sincerely for the compliment you pay us Cismontane heretics. We do retain some dim belief in a God—even I am beginning to believe in believing in Him. And therefore, as I begin to suppose, it is, that we reverence facts, as the work of God, His acted words and will, which we dare not falsify; which we believe will tell their own story better than we can tell it for them. If our eyes are dimmed, we think it safer to clear them, which do belong to us, than to bedevil, by the light of those very *already dimmed* eyes, the objects round, which do not belong to us. Whether we are consistent or not about the corruptness of man, we are about the incorruptness of God; and therefore about that of the facts by which God teaches men: and believe, and will continue to believe, that the blackest of all sins, the deepest of all Atheisms, that which, above all things, proves no faith in God's government of the universe, no sense of His presence, no understanding of His character, is—a lie.

'One word more—Unless you tell your father within twenty-four hours after receiving this letter, I will. And I, being a Protestant (if cursing Popery means Protestantism), mean what I say.'

As Lancelot walked up to the Priory that morning, the Reverend Panurgus O'Blareaway dashed out of a cottage by the roadside, and seized him unceremoniously by the shoulders. He was a specimen of humanity which Lancelot could not help at once liking and despising; a quaint mixture of conceit and earnestness, uniting the shrewdness of a stockjobber with the frolic of a schoolboy broke loose. He was rector of a place in the west of Ireland, containing some ten Protestants and some thousand Papists. Being, unfortunately for himself, a red-hot Orangeman, he had thought fit to quarrel with the priest, in consequence of which he found himself deprived both of tithes and congregation; and after receiving three or four Rockite letters, and a charge of slugs through his hat (of which he always talked as if being shot at was the most pleasant and amusing feature of Irish life), he repaired to England, and there, after trying to set up as popular preacher in London, declaiming at Exeter Hall, and writing for all the third-rate magazines, found himself incumbent of Lower Whitford. He worked there, as he said himself, 'like a horse;' spent his mornings in the schools, his afternoons in the cottages; preached four or five extempore sermons every week to overflowing congregations; took the lead, by virtue of the 'gift of the gab,' at all 'religious' meetings for ten miles round; and really did a great deal of good in his way. He had an unblushing candour about his own worldly ambition, with a tremendous brogue; and prided himself on exaggerating deliberately both of these excellences.

'The top of the morning to ye, Mr. Smith. Ye haven't such a thing as a cegar about ye? I've been preaching to school-children till me throat's as dry as the slave of a lime-burner's coat.'

'I am very sorry; but, really, I have left my case at home.'

'Oh! ah! faix and I forgot. Ye mustn't be smokin' the nasty things going up to the castle. Och, Mr. Smith, but you're the lucky man!'

'I am much obliged to you for the compliment,' said Lancelot, gruffly; 'but really I don't see how I deserve it.'

'Desarve it! Sure luck's all, and that's your luck, and not your deserts at all. To have the handsomest girl in the county dying for love of ye'—(Panurgus had a happy knack of blurting out truths—when they were pleasant ones). 'And she just the beautifulest creature that ever spilte shoe-leather, barring Lady Philandria Mountflunkey, of Castle Mountflunkey, Quane's County, that shall be nameless.'

'Upon my word, O'Blareaway, you seem to be better acquainted with my matters than I am. Don't you think, on the whole, it might be better to mind your own business?'

'Me own business! Poker o' Moses! and ain't it me own business? Haven't ye spilte my tenderest hopes? And good luck to ye in that same, for ye're as pretty a rider as ever kicked coping-stones out of a wall; and poor Paddy loves a sportsman by nature. Och! but ye've got a hand of trumps this time. Didn't I mate the vicar the other day, and spake my mind to him?'

'What do you mean?' asked Lancelot, with a strong expletive.

'Faix, I told him he might as well *Faugh a ballagh*—make a rid road, and get out of that, with his bowings and his crossings, and his Popery made asy for small minds, for there was a gun a-field that would wipe his eye,—maning yourself, ye Prathestant.'

'All I can say is, that you had really better mind your own business, and I'll mind my own.'

'Och,' said the good-natured Irishman, 'and it's you must mind my business, and I'll mind yours; and that's all fair and aqual. Ye've cut me out intirely at the Priory, ye Tory, and so ye're bound to give me a lift somehow. Couldn't ye look me out a fine fat widow, with an illigant little fortune? For what's England made for except to find poor Paddy a wife and money? Ah, ye may laugh, but I'd buy me a chapel at the West-end: me talents are thrown away here intirely, wasting me swateness on the desert air, as Tom Moore says' (Panurgus used to attribute all quotations whatsoever to Irish geniuses); 'and I flatter meself I'm the boy to shute the Gospel to the aristocracy.'

Lancelot burst into a roar of laughter, and escaped over the next gate: but the Irishman's coarse hints stuck by him as they were intended to do. 'Dying for the love of me!' He knew it was an impudent exaggeration, but, somehow, it gave him confidence; 'there is no smoke,' he thought, 'without fire.' And his heart beat high with new hopes, for which he laughed at himself all the while. It was just the cordial which he needed. That conversation determined the history of his life.

He met Argemone that morning in the library, as usual; but he soon found that she was not thinking of Homer. She was moody and abstracted; and he could not help at last saying,—

'I am afraid I and my classics are *de trop* this morning, Miss Lavington.'

'Oh, no, no. Never that.' She turned away her head. He fancied that it was to hide a tear.

Suddenly she rose, and turned to him with a clear, calm, gentle gaze.

'Listen to me, Mr. Smith. We must part to-day, and for ever. This intimacy has gone on—too long, I am afraid, for your happiness. And now, like all pleasant things in this miserable world, it must cease. I cannot tell you why; but you will trust me. I thank you for it—I thank God for it. I have learnt things from it which I shall never forget. I have learnt, at least from it, to esteem and honour you. You have vast powers. Nothing, nothing, I believe, is too high for you to attempt and succeed. But we must part; and now, God be with you. Oh, that you would but believe that these glorious talents are His loan! That you would but be a true and loyal knight to him who said—"Learn of me, for I am meek and lowly of heart, and ye shall find rest unto your souls!"—Ay,' she went on, more and more passionately, for she felt that not she, but One mightier than herself was speaking through her, 'then you might be great indeed. Then I might watch your name from afar, rising higher and higher daily in the ranks of God's own heroes. I see it—and you have taught me to see it—that you are meant for a faith nobler and deeper than all doctrines and systems can give. You must become the philosopher, who can discover new truths—the artist who can embody them in new forms, while poor I—And that is another reason why we should part.—Hush! hear me out. I must not be a clog, to drag you down in your course. Take this, and farewell; and remember that you once had a friend called Argemone.'

She put into his hands a little Bible. He took it, and laid it down on the table.

For a minute he stood silent and rooted to the spot. Disappointment, shame, rage, hatred, all boiled up madly within him. The bitterest insults rose to his lips—'Flirt, cold-hearted pedant, fanatic!' but they sank again unspoken, as he looked into the celestial azure of those eyes, calm and pure as a soft evening sky. A mighty struggle between good and evil shook his heart to the roots; and, for the first time in his life, his soul breathed out one real prayer, that God would help him now or never to play the man. And in a moment the darkness passed; a new spirit called out all the latent strength within him; and gently and proudly he answered her,—

'Yes, I will go. I have had mad dreams, conceited and insolent, and have met with my deserts. Brute and fool as I am, I have aspired even to you! And I have gained, in the sunshine of your condescension, strength and purity.—Is not that enough for me? And now I will show you that I love you—by obeying you. You tell me to depart—I go for ever.'

He turned away. Why did she almost spring after him?

'Lancelot! one word! Do not misunderstand me, as I know you will. You will think me so cold, heartless, fickle.—Oh, you do not know—you never can know—how much I, too, have felt!'

He stopped, spell-bound. In an instant his conversation with the Irishman flashed up before him with new force and meaning. A thousand petty incidents, which he had driven contemptuously from his mind, returned as triumphant evidences; and, with an impetuous determination, he cried out,—

'I see—I see it all, Argemone! We love each other! You are mine, never to be parted!'

What was her womanhood, that it could stand against the energy of his manly will! The almost coarse simplicity of his words silenced her with a delicious violence. She could only bury her face in her hands and sob out,—

'Oh, Lancelot, Lancelot, whither are you forcing me?'

'I am forcing you no whither. God, the Father of spirits, is leading you! You, who believe in Him, how dare you fight against Him?'

'Lancelot, I cannot—I cannot listen to you—read that!' And she handed him the vicar's letter. He read it, tossed it on the carpet, and crushed it with his heel.

'Wretched pedant! Can your intellect be deluded by such barefaced sophistries? "God's will," forsooth! And if your mother's opposition is not a sign that God's will—if it mean anything except your own will, or that— that man's—is against this mad project, and not for it, what sign would you have? So "celibacy is the highest state!" And why? Because "it is the safest and the easiest road to heaven?" A pretty reason, vicar! I should have thought that that was a sign of a lower state and not a higher. Noble spirits show their nobleness by daring the most difficult paths. And even if marriage was but one weed-field of temptations, as these miserable pedants say, who have either never tried it, or misused it to their own shame, it would be a greater deed to conquer its temptations than to flee from them in cowardly longings after ease and safety!'

She did not answer him, but kept her face buried in her hands.

'Again, I say, Argemone, will you fight against Fate—Providence—God—call it what you will? Who made us meet at the chapel? Who made me, by my accident, a guest in your father's house! Who put it into your heart to care for my poor soul? Who gave us this strange attraction towards each other, in spite of our unlikeness? Wonderful that the very chain of circumstances which you seem to fancy the offspring of chance or the devil, should have first taught me to believe that there is a God who guides us! Argemone! speak, tell me, if you will, to go for ever; but tell me first the truth—You love me!'

A strong shudder ran through her frame—the ice of artificial years cracked, and the clear stream of her woman's nature welled up to the light, as pure as when she first lay on her mother's bosom: she lifted up her eyes, and with one long look of passionate tenderness she faltered out,—

'I love you!'

He did not stir, but watched her with clasped hands, like one who in dreams finds himself in some fairy palace, and fears that a movement may break the spell.

'Now, go,' she said; 'go, and let me collect my thoughts. All this has been too much for me. Do not look sad—you may come again to-morrow.'

She smiled and held out her hand. He caught it, covered it with kisses, and pressed it to his heart. She half drew it back, frightened. The sensation was new to her. Again the delicious feeling of being utterly in his power came over her, and she left her hand upon his heart, and blushed as she felt its passionate throbbings.

He turned to go—not as before. She followed with greedy eyes her new-found treasure; and as the door closed behind him, she felt as if Lancelot was the whole world, and there was nothing beside him, and wondered how a moment had made him all in all to her; and then she sank upon her knees, and folded her hands upon her bosom, and her prayers for him were like the prayers of a little child.

CHAPTER XI
THUNDERSTORM THE FIRST

But what had become of the 'bit of writing' which Harry Verney, by the instigation of his evil genius, had put into the squire's fly-book? Tregarva had waited in terrible suspense for many weeks, expecting the explosion which he knew must follow its discovery. He had confided to Lancelot the contents of the paper, and Lancelot had tried many stratagems to get possession of it, but all in vain. Tregarva took this as calmly as he did everything else. Only once, on the morning of the *éclaircissement* between Lancelot and Argemone, he talked to Lancelot of leaving his place, and going out to seek his fortune; but some spell, which he did not explain, seemed to chain him to the Priory. Lancelot thought it was the want of money, and offered to lend him ten pounds whenever he liked; but Tregarva shook his head.

'You have treated me, sir, as no one else has done—like a man and a friend; but I am not going to make a market of your generosity. I will owe no man anything, save to love one another.'

'But how do you intend to live?' asked Lancelot, as they stood together in the cloisters.

'There's enough of me, sir, to make a good navigator if all trades fail.'

'Nonsense! you must not throw yourself away so.'

'Oh, sir, there's good to be done, believe me, among those poor fellows. They wander up and down the land like hogs and heathens, and no one tells them that they have a soul to be saved. Not one parson in a thousand gives a thought to them. They can manage old folks and little children, sir, but, somehow, they never can get hold of the young men—just those who want them most. There's a talk about ragged schools, now. Why don't they try ragged churches, sir, and a ragged service?'

'What do you mean?'

'Why, sir, the parsons are ready enough to save souls, but it must be only according to rule and regulation. Before the Gospel can be preached there must be three thousand pounds got together for a church, and a thousand for an endowment, not to mention the thousand pounds that the clergyman's education costs: I don't think of his own keep, sir; that's little enough, often; and those that work hardest get least pay, it seems to me. But after all that expense, when they've built the church, it's the tradesmen, and the gentry, and the old folk that fill it, and the working men never come near it from one year's end to another.'

'What's the cause, do you think?' asked Lancelot, who had himself remarked the same thing more than once.

'Half of the reason, sir, I do believe, is that same Prayer-book. Not that the Prayer-book ain't a fine book enough, and a true one; but, don't you see, sir, to understand the virtue of it, the poor fellows ought to be already just what you want to make them.'

'You mean that they ought to be thorough Christians already, to appreciate the spirituality of the liturgy.'

'You've hit it, sir. And see what comes of the present plan; how a navvy drops into a church by accident, and there he has to sit like a fish out of water, through that hour's service, staring or sleeping, before he can hear a word that he understands; and, sir, when the sermon does come at last, it's not many of them can make much out of those fine book-words and long sentences. Why don't they have a short simple service, now and then, that might catch the ears of the roughs and the blowens, without tiring out the poor thoughtless creatures' patience, as they do now?'

'Because,' said Lancelot,—'because—I really don't know why.—But I think there is a simpler plan than even a ragged service.'

'What, then, sir?'

'Field-preaching. If the mountain won't come to Mahomet, let Mahomet go to the mountain.'

'Right, sir; right you are. "Go out into the highways and hedges, and compel them to come in." And why are they to speak to them only one by one? Why not by the dozen and the hundred? We Wesleyans know, sir,—for the matter of that, every soldier knows,—what virtue there is in getting a lot of men together; how good and evil spread like wildfire through a crowd; and one man, if you can stir him up, will become leaven to leaven the whole lump. Oh why, sir, are they so afraid of field-preaching? Was not their Master and mine the prince of all field-preachers? Think, if the Apostles had waited to collect subscriptions for a church before they spoke to the poor heathens, where should we have been now?'

Lancelot could not but agree. But at that moment a footman came up, and, with a face half laughing, half terrified, said,—

'Tregarva, master wants you in the study. And please, sir, I think you had better go in too; master knows you're here, and you might speak a word for good, for he's raging like a mad bull.'

'I knew it would come at last,' said Tregarva, quietly, as he followed Lancelot into the house.

It had come at last. The squire was sitting in his study, purple with rage, while his daughters were trying vainly to pacify him. All the men-servants, grooms, and helpers, were drawn up in line along the wall, and greeted Tregarva, whom they all heartily liked, with sly and sorrowful looks of warning,

'Here, you sir; you—, look at this! Is this the way you repay me? I, who have kept you out of the workhouse, treated you like my own child? And then to go and write filthy, rascally, Radical ballads on me and mine! This comes of your Methodism, you canting, sneaking hypocrite!—you viper—you adder—you snake—you—!' And the squire, whose vocabulary was not large, at a loss for another synonym, rounded off his oration by a torrent of oaths; at which Argemone, taking Honoria's hand, walked proudly out of the room, with one glance at Lancelot of mingled shame and love. 'This is your handwriting, you villain! you know it' (and the squire tossed the fatal paper across the table); 'though I suppose you'll lie about it. How can you depend on fellows who speak evil of their betters? But all the servants are ready to swear it's your handwriting.'

'Beg your pardon, sir,' interposed the old butler, 'we didn't quite say that; but we'll all swear it isn't ours.'

'The paper is mine,' said Tregarva.

'Confound your coolness! He's no more ashamed of it than—Read it out, Smith, read it out every word; and let them all hear how this pauper, this ballad-singing vagabond, whom I have bred up to insult me, dares to abuse his own master.'

'I have not abused you, sir,' answered Tregarva. 'I will be heard, sir!' he went on in a voice which made the old man start from his seat and clench his fist but he sat down again. 'Not a word in it is meant for you. You have been a kind and a good master to me. Ask where you will if I was ever heard to say a word against you. I would have cut off my right hand sooner than write about you or yours. But what I had to say about others lies there, and I am not ashamed of it.'

'Not against me? Read it out, Smith, and see if every word of it don't hit at me, and at my daughters, too, by—, worst of all! Read it out, I say!'

Lancelot hesitated; but the squire, who was utterly beside himself, began to swear at him also, as masters of hounds are privileged to do; and Lancelot, to whom the whole scene was becoming every moment more and more intensely ludicrous, thought it best to take up the paper and begin:—

'A ROUGH RHYME ON A ROUGH MATTER.

'The merry brown hares came leaping
  Over the crest of the hill,
Where the clover and corn lay sleeping
  Under the moonlight still.

'Leaping late and early,
  Till under their bite and their tread
The swedes, and the wheat, and the barley,
  Lay cankered, and trampled, and dead.

'A poacher's widow sat sighing
  On the side of the white chalk bank,
Where under the gloomy fir-woods
  One spot in the ley throve rank.

'She watched a long tuft of clover,
  Where rabbit or hare never ran;
For its black sour haulm covered over
  The blood of a murdered man.

'She thought of the dark plantation,
  And the hares and her husband's blood,
And the voice of her indignation
  Rose up to the throne of God.

'"I am long past wailing and whining—
  I have wept too much in my life:
I've had twenty years of pining
  As an English labourer's wife.

'"A labourer in Christian England,
  Where they cant of a Saviour's name,
And yet waste men's lives like the vermin's
  For a few more brace of game.

'"There's blood on your new foreign shrubs, squire;
  There's blood on your pointer's feet;

There's blood on the game you sell, squire,
  And there's blood on the game you eat!"'

'You villain!' interposed the squire, 'when did I ever sell a head of game?'

'"You have sold the labouring man, squire,
  Body and soul to shame,
To pay for your seat in the House, squire,
  And to pay for the feed of your game.

'"You made him a poacher yourself, squire,
  When you'd give neither work nor meat;
And your barley-fed hares robbed the garden
  At our starving children's feet;

'"When packed in one reeking chamber,
  Man, maid, mother, and little ones lay;
While the rain pattered in on the rotting bride-bed,
  And the walls let in the day;

'"When we lay in the burning fever
  On the mud of the cold clay floor,
Till you parted us all for three months, squire,
  At the cursed workhouse door.

'"We quarrelled like brutes, and who wonders?
  What self-respect could we keep,
Worse housed than your hacks and your pointers,
  Worse fed than your hogs and your sheep?"'

'And yet he has the impudence to say he don't mean me!' grumbled the old man. Tregarva winced a good deal—as if he knew what was coming next; and then looked up relieved when he found Lancelot had omitted a stanza—which I shall not omit.

'"Our daughters with base-born babies
  Have wandered away in their shame;
If your misses had slept, squire, where they did,
  Your misses might do the same.

'"Can your lady patch hearts that are breaking
  With handfuls of coals and rice,
Or by dealing out flannel and sheeting
  A little below cost price?

  "'You may tire of the gaol and the workhouse,
   And take to allotments and schools,
  But you've run up a debt that will never
   Be repaid us by penny-club rules.

  '"In the season of shame and sadness,
   In the dark and dreary day
  When scrofula, gout, and madness,
   Are eating your race away;

  "'When to kennels and liveried varlets
   You have cast your daughters' bread;
  And worn out with liquor and harlots,
   Your heir at your feet lies dead;

  "'When your youngest, the mealy-mouthed rector,
   Lets your soul rot asleep to the grave,
  You will find in your God the protector
   Of the freeman you fancied your slave."

  'She looked at the tuft of clover,
   And wept till her heart grew light;
  And at last, when her passion was over,
   Went wandering into the night.

  'But the merry brown hares came leaping
   Over the uplands still,
  Where the clover and corn lay sleeping
   On the side of the white chalk hill.'

 'Surely, sir,' said Lancelot, 'you cannot suppose that this latter part applies to you. or your family?'

 'If it don't, it applies to half the gentlemen in the vale, and that's just as bad. What right has the fellow to speak evil of dignities?' continued he, quoting the only text in the Bible which he was inclined to make a 'rule absolute.' 'What does such an insolent dog deserve? What don't he deserve, I say?'

 'I think,' quoth Lancelot, ambiguously, 'that a man who can write such ballads is not fit to be your gamekeeper, and I think he feels so himself;' and Lancelot stole an encouraging look at Tregarva.

 'And I say, sir,' the keeper answered, with an effort, 'that I leave Mr. Lavington's service here on the spot, once and for all.'

'And that you may do, my fine fellow!' roared the squire. 'Pay the rascal his wages, steward, and then duck him soundly in the weir-pool. He had better have stayed there when he fell in last.'

'So I had, indeed, I think. But I'll take none of your money. The day Harry Verney was buried I vowed that I'd touch no more of the wages of blood. I'm going, sir; I never harmed you, or meant a hard word of all this for you, or dreamt that you or any living soul would ever see it. But what I've seen myself, in spite of myself, I've set down here, and am not ashamed of it. And woe,' he went on with an almost prophetic solemnity in his tone and gesture—'woe to those who do these things! and woe to those also who, though they dare not do them themselves, yet excuse and defend them who dare, just because the world calls them gentlemen, and not tyrants and oppressors.'

He turned to go. The squire, bursting with passion, sprang up with a terrible oath, turned deadly pale, staggered, and dropped senseless on the floor.

They all rushed to lift him up. Tregarva was the first to take him in his arms and place him tenderly in his chair, where he lay back with glassy eyes, snoring heavily in a fit of apoplexy.

'Go; for God's sake, go,' whispered Lancelot to the keeper, 'and wait for me at Lower Whitford. I must see you before you stir.'

The keeper slipped away sadly. The ladies rushed in—a groom galloped off for the doctor—met him luckily in the village, and, in a few minutes, the squire was bled and put to bed, and showed hopeful signs of returning consciousness. And as Argemone and Lancelot leant together over his pillow, her hair touched her lover's, and her fragrant breath was warm upon his cheek; and her bright eyes met his and drank light from them, like glittering planets gazing at their sun.

The obnoxious ballad produced the most opposite effects on Argemone and on Honoria. Argemone, whose reverence for the formalities and the respectabilities of society, never very great, had, of late, utterly vanished before Lancelot's bad counsel, could think of it only as a work of art, and conceived the most romantic longing to raise Tregarva into some station where his talents might have free play. To Honoria, on the other hand, it appeared only as a very fierce, coarse, and impertinent satire, which had nearly killed her father. True, there was not a thought in it which had not at some time or other crossed her own mind; but that made her dislike all the more to see those thoughts put into plain English. That very intense tenderness and excitability which made her toil herself among the poor, and had called out both her admiration of Tregarva and her extravagant passion at his danger, made her also shrink with disgust from anything which thrust on her a painful reality, which she could not remedy. She was a staunch believer, too, in that peculiar creed which allows every one to feel for the poor, except themselves, and considers that to plead the cause of working-men is, in a gentleman, the perfection of virtue, but in a working-man himself, sheer high treason. And so beside her father's sick-bed she thought of the keeper only as a scorpion whom she had helped to warm into life; and sighing assent to her mother, when she said, 'That wretch, and he seemed so pious and so obliging! who would have dreamt that he was such a horrid Radical?' she let him vanish from her mind and out of Whitford Priors, little knowing the sore weight of manly love he bore with him.

As soon as Lancelot could leave the Priory, he hastened home to find Tregarva. The keeper had packed up all his small possessions and brought them down to Lower Whitford, through which the London coach passed. He was determined to go to London and seek his fortune. He talked of turning coal-heaver, Methodist preacher, anything that came to hand, provided that he could but keep independence and a clear conscience. And all the while the man seemed to be struggling with some great purpose,—to feel that he had a work to do, though what it was, and how it was to be done, he did not see.

'I am a tall man,' he said, 'like Saul the son of Kish; and I am going forth, like him, sir, to find my father's asses. I doubt I shan't have to look far for some of them.'

'And perhaps,' said Lancelot, laughing, 'to find a kingdom.'

'May be so, sir. I have found one already, by God's grace, and I'm much mistaken if I don't begin to see my way towards another.'

'And what is that?'

'The kingdom of God on earth, sir, as well as in heaven. Come it must, sir, and come it will some day.'

Lancelot shook his head.

Tregarva lifted up his eyes and said,—

'Are we not taught to pray for the coming of His kingdom, sir? And do you fancy that He who gave the lesson would have set all mankind to pray for what He never meant should come to pass?'

Lancelot was silent. The words gained a new and blessed meaning in his eyes.

'Well,' he said, 'the time, at least, of their fulfilment is far enough off. Union-workhouses and child-murder don't look much like it. Talking of that, Tregarva, what is to become of your promise to take me to a village wake, and show me what the poor are like?'

'I can keep it this night, sir. There is a revel at Bone-sake, about five miles up the river. Will you go with a discharged gamekeeper?'

'I will go with Paul Tregarva, whom I honour and esteem as one of God's own noblemen; who has taught me what a man can be, and what I am not,'—and Lancelot grasped the keeper's hand warmly. Tregarva brushed his hand across his eyes, and answered,—

'"I said in my haste, All men are liars;" and God has just given me the lie back in my own teeth. Well, sir, we will go to-night. You are not ashamed of putting on a smock-frock? For if you go as a gentleman, you will hear no more of them than a hawk does of a covey of partridges.'

So the expedition was agreed on, and Lancelot and the keeper parted until the evening.

But why had the vicar been rambling on all that morning through pouring rain, on the top of the London coach? And why was he so anxious in his inquiries as to the certainty of catching the up-train? Because he had had considerable experience in that wisdom of the serpent, whose combination with the innocence of the dove, in somewhat ultramontane proportions, is recommended by certain late leaders of his school. He had made up his mind, after his conversation with the Irishman, that he must either oust Lancelot at once, or submit to be ousted by him, and he was now on his way to Lancelot's uncle and trustee, the London banker.

He knew that the banker had some influence with his nephew, whose whole property was invested in the bank, and who had besides a deep respect for the kindly and upright practical mind of the veteran Mammonite. And the vicar knew, too, that he himself had some influence with the banker, whose son Luke had been his pupil at college. And when the young man lay sick of a dangerous illness, brought on by debauchery, into which weakness rather than vice had tempted him, the vicar had watched and prayed by his bed, nursed him as tenderly as a mother, and so won over his better heart that he became completely reclaimed, and took holy orders with the most earnest intention to play the man therein, as repentant rakes will often do, half from a mere revulsion to asceticism, half from real gratitude for their deliverance. This good deed had placed the banker in the vicar's debt, and he loved and reverenced him in spite of his dread of 'Popish novelties.' And now the good priest was going to open to him just as much of his heart as should seem fit; and by saying a great deal about Lancelot's evil doings, opinions, and companions, and nothing at all about the heiress of Whitford, persuade the banker to use all his influence in drawing Lancelot up to London, and leaving a clear stage for his plans on Argemone. He caught the up-train, he arrived safe and sound in town, but what he did there must be told in another chapter.

CHAPTER XII
THUNDERSTORM THE SECOND

Weary with many thoughts, the vicar came to the door of the bank. There were several carriages there, and a crowd of people swarming in and out, like bees round a hive-door, entering with anxious faces, and returning with cheerful ones, to stop and talk earnestly in groups round the door. Every moment the mass thickened—there was a run on the bank. An old friend accosted him on the steps,—

'What! have you, too, money here, then?'

'Neither here nor anywhere else, thank Heaven!' said the vicar. 'But is anything wrong?'

'Have not you heard? The house has sustained a frightful blow this week—railway speculations, so they say—and is hardly expected to survive the day. So we are all getting our money out as fast as possible.'

'By way of binding up the bruised reed, eh?'

'Oh! every man for himself. A man is under no obligation to his banker, that I know of.' And the good man bustled off with his pockets full of gold.

The vicar entered. All was hurry and anxiety. The clerks seemed trying to brazen out their own terror, and shovelled the rapidly lessening gold and notes across the counter with an air of indignant nonchalance. The vicar asked to see the principal.

'If you want your money, sir—' answered the official, with a disdainful look.

'I want no money. I must see Mr. Smith on private business, and instantly.'

'He is particularly engaged.'

'I know it, and, therefore, I must see him. Take in my card, and he will not refuse me.' A new vista had opened itself before him.

He was ushered into a private room: and, as he waited for the banker, he breathed a prayer. For what? That his own will might be done—a very common style of petition.

Mr. Smith entered, hurried and troubled. He caught the vicar eagerly by the hand, as if glad to see a face which did not glare on him with the cold selfish stamp of 'business,' and then drew back again, afraid to commit himself by any sign of emotion.

The vicar had settled his plan of attack, and determined boldly to show his knowledge of the banker's distress.

'I am very sorry to trouble you at such an unfortunate moment, sir, and I will be brief; but, as your nephew's spiritual pastor—' (He knew the banker was a stout Churchman.)

'What of my nephew, sir! No fresh misfortunes, I hope?'

'Not so much misfortune, sir, as misconduct—I might say frailty—but frailty which may become ruinous.'

'How? how? Some *mésalliance*?' interrupted Mr. Smith, in a peevish, excited tone. 'I thought there was some heiress on the *tapis*—at least, so I heard from my unfortunate son, who has just gone over to Rome. There's another misfortune.—Nothing but misfortunes; and your teaching, sir, by the bye, I am afraid, has helped me to that one.'

'Gone over to Rome?' asked the vicar, slowly.

'Yes, sir, gone to Rome—to the pope, sir! to the devil, sir! I should have thought you likely to know of it before I did!'

The vicar stared fixedly at him a moment, and burst into honest tears. The banker was moved.

"Pon my honour, sir, I beg your pardon. I did not mean to be rude, but—but—To be plain with a clergyman, sir, so many things coming together have quite unmanned me. Pooh, pooh,' and he shook himself as if to throw off a weight; and, with a face once more quiet and business-like, asked, 'And now, my dear sir, what of my nephew?'

'As for that young lady, sir, of whom you spoke, I can assure you, once for all, as her clergyman, and therefore more or less her confidant, that your nephew has not the slightest chance or hope in that quarter.'

'How, sir? You will not throw obstacles in the way?'

'Heaven, sir, I think, has interposed far more insuperable obstacles—in the young lady's own heart—than I could ever have done. Your nephew's character and opinions, I am sorry to say, are not such as are likely to command the respect and affection of a pure and pious Churchwoman.'

'Opinions, sir? What, is he turning Papist, too?'

'I am afraid, sir, and more than afraid, for he makes no secret of it himself, that his views tend rather in the opposite direction; to an infidelity so subversive of the commonest principles of morality, that I expect, weekly, to hear of some unblushing and disgraceful outrage against decency, committed by him under its fancied sanction. And you know, as well as myself, the double danger of some profligate outbreak, which always attends the miseries of a disappointed earthly passion.'

'True, very true. We must get the boy out of the way, sir. I must have him under my eye.'

'Exactly so, sir,' said the subtle vicar, who had been driving at this very point. 'How much better for him to be here, using his great talents to the advantage of his family in an honourable profession, than to remain where he is, debauching body and mind by hopeless dreams, godless studies, and frivolous excesses.'

'When do you return, sir?'

'An hour hence, if I can be of service to you.'

The banker paused a moment.

'You are a gentleman' (with emphasis on the word), 'and as such I can trust you.'

'Say, rather, as a clergyman.'

'Pardon me, but I have found your cloth give little additional cause for confidence. I have been as much bitten by clergymen—I have seen as sharp practice among them, in money matters as well as in religious squabbles, as I have in any class. Whether it is that their book education leaves them very often ignorant of the plain rules of honour which bind men of the world, or whether their zeal makes them think that the end justifies the means, I cannot tell; but—'

'But,' said the vicar, half smiling, half severely, 'you must not disparage the priesthood before a priest.'

'I know it, I know it; and I beg your pardon: but if you knew the cause I have to complain. The slipperiness, sir, of one staggering parson, has set rolling this very avalanche, which gathers size every moment, and threatens to overwhelm me now, unless that idle dog Lancelot will condescend to bestir himself, and help me.'

The vicar heard, but said nothing.

'Me, at least, you can trust,' he answered proudly; and honestly, too—for he was a gentleman by birth and breeding, unselfish and chivalrous to a fault—and yet, when he heard the banker's words, it was as if the inner voice had whispered to him, 'Thou art the man!'

'When do you go down?' again asked Mr. Smith. 'To tell you the truth, I was writing to Lancelot when you were announced! but the post will not reach him till to-morrow at noon, and we are all so busy here, that I have no one whom I can trust to carry down an express.'

The vicar saw what was coming. Was it his good angel which prompted him to interpose?

'Why not send a parcel by rail?'

'I can trust the rail as far as D—; but I cannot trust those coaches. If you could do me so great a kindness—'

'I will. I can start by the one o'clock train, and by ten o'clock to-night I shall be in Whitford.'

'Are you certain?'

'If God shall please, I am certain.'

'And you will take charge of a letter? Perhaps, too, you could see him yourself; and tell him—you see I trust you with everything—that my fortune, his own fortune, depends on his being here to-morrow morning. He must start to-night, sir—to-night, tell him, if there were twenty Miss Lavingtons in Whitford—or he is a ruined man!'

The letter was written, and put into the vicar's hands, with a hundred entreaties from the terrified banker. A cab was called, and the clergyman rattled off to the railway terminus.

'Well,' said he to himself, 'God has indeed blessed my errand; giving, as always, "exceeding abundantly more than we are able to ask or think!" For some weeks, at least, this poor lamb is safe from the destroyer's clutches. I must improve to the utmost those few precious days in strengthening her in her holy purpose. But, after all, he will return, daring and cunning as ever; and then will not the fascination recommence?'

And, as he mused, a little fiend passed by, and whispered, 'Unless he comes up to-night, he is a ruined man.'

It was Friday, and the vicar had thought it a fit preparation for so important an errand to taste no food that day. Weakness and hunger, joined to the roar and bustle of London, had made him excited, nervous, unable to control his thoughts, or fight against a stupifying headache; and his self-weakened will punished him, by yielding him up an easy prey to his own fancies.

'Ay,' he thought, 'if he were ruined, after all, it would be well for God's cause. The Lavingtons, at least, would find no temptation in his wealth: and Argemone—she is too proud, too luxurious, to marry a beggar. She might embrace a holy poverty for the sake of her own soul; but for the gratification of an earthly passion, never! Base and carnal delights would never tempt her so far.'

Alas, poor pedant! Among all that thy books taught thee, they did not open to thee much of the depths of that human heart which thy dogmas taught thee to despise as diabolic.

Again the little fiend whispered,—

'Unless he comes up to-night, he is a ruined man.'

'And what if he is?' thought the vicar. 'Riches are a curse; and poverty a blessing. Is it not his wealth which is ruining his soul? Idleness and fulness of bread have made him what he is—a luxurious and self-willed dreamer, battening on his own fancies. Were it not rather a boon to him to take from him the root of all evil?'

Most true, vicar. And yet the devil was at that moment transforming himself into an angel of light for thee.

But the vicar was yet honest. If he had thought that by cutting off his right hand he could have saved Lancelot's soul (by canonical methods, of course; for who would wish to save souls in any other?), he would have done it without hesitation.

Again the little fiend whispered,—

'Unless he comes up to-night he is a ruined man.'

A terrible sensation seized him.—Why should he give the letter to-night?

'You promised,' whispered the inner voice.

'No, I did not promise exactly, in so many words; that is, I only said I would be at home to-night, if God pleased. And what if God should not please?—I promised for his good. What if, on second thoughts, it should be better for him not to keep my promise?' A moment afterwards, he tossed the temptation from him indignantly: but back it came. At every gaudy shop, at every smoke-grimed manufactory, at the face of every anxious victim of Mammon, of every sturdy, cheerful artisan, the fiend winked and pointed, crying, 'And what if he be ruined? Look at the thousands who have, and are miserable—at the millions who have not, and are no sadder than their own tyrants.'

Again and again he thrust the thought from him, but more and more weakly. His whole frame shook; the perspiration stood on his forehead. As he took his railway ticket, his look was so haggard and painful that the clerk asked him whether he were ill. The train was just starting; he threw himself into a carriage—he would have locked himself in if he could; and felt an inexpressible relief when he found himself rushing past houses and market-gardens, whirled onward, whether he would or not, in the right path—homeward.

But was it the right path? for again the temptation flitted past him. He threw himself back, and tried to ask counsel of One above; but there was no answer, nor any that regarded. His heart was silent, and dark as midnight fog. Why should there have been an answer? He had not listened to the voice within. Did he wish for a miracle to show him his duty?

'Not that I care for detection,' he said to himself. 'What is shame to me? Is it not a glory to be evil-spoken of in the cause of God? How can the world appreciate the motives of those who are not of the world?—the divine wisdom of the serpent—at once the saint's peculiar weapon, and a part of his peculiar cross, when men call him a deceiver, because they confound, forsooth, his spiritual subtlety with their earthly cunning. Have I not been called "liar," "hypocrite," "Jesuit," often enough already, to harden me towards bearing that name once again?'

That led him into sad thoughts of his last few years' career,—of the friends and pupils whose secession to Rome had been attributed to his hypocrisy, his 'disguised Romanism;' and then the remembrance of poor Luke Smith flashed across him for the first time since he left the bank.

'I must see him,' he said to himself; 'I must argue with him face to face. Who knows but that it may be given even to my unworthiness to snatch him from this accursed slough?'

And then he remembered that his way home lay through the city in which the new convert's parish was—that the coach stopped there to change horses; and again the temptation leapt up again, stronger than ever, under the garb of an imperative call of duty.

He made no determination for or against it. He was too weak in body and mind to resist; and in a half sleep, broken with an aching, terrified sense of something wanting which he could not find, he was swept down the line, got on the coach, and mechanically, almost without knowing it, found himself set down at the city of A—, and the coach rattling away down the street.

He sprang from his stupor, and called madly after it—ran a few steps—

'You might as well try to catch the clouds, sir,' said the ostler. 'Gemmen should make up their minds afore they gets down.'

Alas! so thought the vicar. But it was too late; and, with a heavy heart, he asked the way to the late curate's house.

Thither he went. Mr. Luke Smith was just at dinner, but the vicar was, nevertheless, shown into the bachelor's little dining-room. But what was his disgust and disappointment at finding his late pupil *tête-à-tête* over a comfortable fish-dinner, opposite a burly, vulgar, cunning-eyed man, with a narrow rim of muslin turned down over his stiff cravat, of whose profession there could be no doubt.

'My dearest sir,' said the new convert, springing up with an air of extreme *empressement*, 'what an unexpected pleasure! Allow me to introduce you to my excellent friend, Padre Bugiardo!'

The padre rose, bowed obsequiously, 'was overwhelmed with delight at being at last introduced to one of whom he had heard so much,' sat down again, and poured himself out a bumper of sherry; while the vicar commenced making the best of a bad matter by joining in the now necessary business of eating.

He had not a word to say for himself. Poor Luke was particularly jovial and flippant, and startlingly unlike his former self. The padre went on staring out of the window, and talking in a loud forced tone about the astonishing miracles of the 'Ecstatica' and 'Addolorata;' and the poor vicar, finding the purpose for which he had sacrificed his own word of honour utterly frustrated by the priest's presence, sat silent and crestfallen the whole evening.

The priest had no intention of stirring. The late father-confessor tried to outstay his new rival, but in vain; the padre deliberately announced his intention of taking a bed, and the vicar, with a heavy heart, rose to go to his inn.

As he went out at the door, he caught an opportunity of saying one word to the convert.

'My poor Luke! and are you happy? Tell me honestly, in God's sight tell me!'

'Happier than ever I was in my life! No more self-torture, physical or mental, now. These good priests thoroughly understand poor human nature, I can assure you.'

The vicar sighed, for the speech was evidently meant as a gentle rebuke to himself. But the young man ran on, half laughing,—

'You know how you and the rest used to tell us what a sad thing it was that we were all cursed with consciences,—what a fearful miserable burden moral responsibility was; but that we must submit to it as an inevitable evil. Now that burden is gone, thank God. We of the True Church have some one to keep our consciences for us. The padre settles all about what is right or wrong, and we slip on as easily as—'

'A hog or a butterfly!' said the vicar, bitterly.

'Exactly,' answered Luke. 'And, on your own showing, are clean gainers of a happy life here, not to mention heaven hereafter. God bless you! We shall soon see you one of us.'

'Never, so help me God!' said the vicar; all the more fiercely because he was almost at that moment of the young man's opinion.

The vicar stepped out into the night. The rain, which had given place during the afternoon to a bright sun and clear chilly evening, had returned with double fury. The wind was sweeping and howling down the lonely streets, and lashed the rain into his face, while gray clouds were rushing past the moon like terrified ghosts across the awful void of the black heaven. Above him gaunt poplars groaned and bent, like giants cowering from the wrath of Heaven, yet rooted by grim necessity to their place of torture. The roar and tumult without him harmonised strangely with the discord within. He staggered and strode along the plashy pavement, muttering to himself at intervals,—

'Rest for the soul? peace of mind? I have been promising them all my life to others—have I found them myself? And here is this poor boy saying that he has gained them—in the very barbarian superstition which I have been anathematising to him! What is true, at this rate? What is false? Is anything right or wrong? except in as far as men feel it to be right or wrong. Else whence does this poor fellow's peace come, or the peace of many a convert more? They have all, one by one, told me the same story. And is not a religion to be known by its fruits? Are they not right in going where they can get peace of mind?'

Certainly, vicar. If peace of mind be the *summum bonum*, and religion is merely the science of self-satisfaction, they are right; and your wisest plan will be to follow them at once, or failing that, to apply to the next best substitute that can be discovered—alcohol and opium.

As he went on, talking wildly to himself, he passed the Union Workhouse. Opposite the gate, under the lee of a wall, some twenty men, women, and children, were huddled together on the bare ground. They had been refused lodging in the workhouse, and were going to pass the night in that situation. As he came up to them, coarse jests, and snatches of low drinking-songs, ghastly as the laughter of lost spirits in the pit, mingled with the feeble wailings of some child of shame. The vicar recollected how he had seen the same sight at the door of Kensington Workhouse, walking home one night in company with Luke Smith; and how, too, he had commented to him on that fearful sign of the times, and had somewhat unfairly drawn a contrast between the niggard cruelty of 'popular Protestantism,' and the fancied 'liberality of the middle age.' What wonder if his pupil had taken him at his word?

Delighted to escape from his own thoughts by anything like action, he pulled out his purse to give an alms. There was no silver in it, but only some fifteen or twenty sovereigns, which he that day received as payment for some bitter reviews in a leading religious periodical. Everything that night seemed to shame and confound him more. As he touched the money, there sprang up in his mind in an instant the thought of the articles which had procured it; by one of those terrible, searching inspirations, in which the light which lighteth every man awakes as a lightning-flash of judgment, he saw them, and his own heart, for one moment, as they were;—their blind prejudice; their reckless imputations of motives; their wilful concealment of any palliating clauses; their party nicknames, given without a shudder at the terrible accusations which they conveyed. And then the indignation, the shame, the reciprocal bitterness which those articles would excite, tearing still wider the bleeding wounds of that Church which they professed to defend! And then, in this case, too, the thought rushed across him, 'What if I should have been wrong and my adversary right? What if I have made the heart of the righteous sad whom God has not made sad? I! to have been dealing out Heaven's thunders, as if I were infallible! I! who am certain at this moment of no fact in heaven or earth, except my own untruth! God! who am I that I should judge another?' And the coins seemed to him like the price of blood—he fancied that he felt them red-hot to his hand, and, in his eagerness to get rid of the accursed thing, he dealt it away fiercely to the astonished group, amid whining and flattery, wrangling and ribaldry; and then, not daring to wait and see the use to which his money would be put, hurried off to the inn, and tried in uneasy slumbers to forget the time, until the mail passed through at daybreak on its way to Whitford.

CHAPTER XIII
THE VILLAGE REVEL

At dusk that same evening the two had started for the village fair. A velveteen shooting-jacket, a pair of corduroy trousers, and a waistcoat, furnished by Tregarva, covered with flowers of every imaginable hue, tolerably disguised Lancelot, who was recommended by his conductor to keep his hands in his pockets as much as possible, lest their delicacy, which was, as it happened, not very remarkable, might betray him. As they walked together along the plashy turnpike road, overtaking, now and then, groups of two or three who were out on the same errand as themselves, Lancelot could not help remarking to the keeper how superior was the look of comfort in the boys and young men, with their ruddy cheeks and smart dresses, to the worn and haggard appearance of the elder men.

'Let them alone, poor fellows,' said Tregarva; 'it won't last long. When they've got two or three children at their heels, they'll look as thin and shabby as their own fathers.'

'They must spend a great deal of money on their clothes.'

'And on their stomachs, too, sir. They never lay by a farthing; and I don't see how they can, when their club-money's paid, and their insides are well filled.'

'Do you mean to say that they actually have not as much to eat after they marry?'

'Indeed and I do, sir. They get no more wages afterwards round here, and have four or five to clothe and feed off the same money that used to keep one; and that sum won't take long to work out, I think.'

'But do they not in some places pay the married men higher wages than the unmarried?'

'That's a worse trick still, sir; for it tempts the poor thoughtless boys to go and marry the first girl they can get hold of; and it don't want much persuasion to make them do that at any time.'

'But why don't the clergymen teach them to put into the savings banks?'

'One here and there, sir, says what he can, though it's of very little use. Besides, every one is afraid of savings banks now; not a year but one reads of some breaking and the lawyers going off with the earnings of the poor. And if they didn't, youth's a foolish time at best; and the carnal man will be hankering after amusement, sir—amusement.'

'And no wonder,' said Lancelot; 'at all events, I should not think they got much of it. But it does seem strange that no other amusement can be found for them than the beer-shop. Can't they read? Can't they practise light and interesting handicrafts at home, as the German peasantry do?'

'Who'll teach 'em, sir? From the plough-tail to the reaping-hook, and back again, is all they know. Besides, sir, they are not like us Cornish; they are a stupid pigheaded generation at the best, these south countrymen. They're grown-up babies who want the parson and the squire to be leading them, and preaching to them, and spurring them on, and coaxing them up, every moment. And as for scholarship, sir, a boy leaves school at nine or ten to follow the horses; and between that time and his wedding-day he forgets every word he ever learnt, and becomes, for the most part, as thorough a heathen savage at heart as those wild Indians in the Brazils used to be.'

'And then we call them civilised Englishmen!' said Lancelot. 'We can see that your Indian is a savage, because he wears skins and feathers; but your Irish cottar or your English labourer, because he happens to wear a coat and trousers, is to be considered a civilised man.'

'It's the way of the world, sir,' said Tregarva, 'judging carnal judgment, according to the sight of its own eyes; always looking at the outsides of things and men, sir, and never much deeper. But as for reading, sir, it's all very well for me, who have been a keeper and dawdled about like a gentleman with a gun over my arm; but did you ever do a good day's farm-work in your life? If you had, man or boy, you wouldn't have been game for much reading when you got home; you'd do just what these poor fellows do,—tumble into bed at eight o'clock, hardly waiting to take your clothes off, knowing that you must turn up again at five o'clock the next morning to get a breakfast of bread, and, perhaps, a dab of the squire's dripping, and then back to work again; and so on, day after day, sir, week after week, year after year, without a hope or a chance of being anything but what you are, and only too thankful if you can get work to break your back, and catch the rheumatism over.'

'But do you mean to say that their labour is so severe and incessant?'

'It's only God's blessing if it is incessant, sir, for if it stops, they starve, or go to the house to be worse fed than the thieves in gaol. And as for its being severe, there's many a boy, as their mothers will tell you, comes home night after night, too tired to eat their suppers, and tumble, fasting, to bed in the same foul shirt which they've been working in all the day, never changing their rag of calico from week's end to week's end, or washing the skin that's under it once in seven years.'

'No wonder,' said Lancelot, 'that such a life of drudgery makes them brutal and reckless.'

'No wonder, indeed, sir: they've no time to think; they're born to be machines, and machines they must be; and I think, sir,' he added bitterly, 'it's God's mercy that they daren't think. It's God's mercy that they don't feel. Men that write books and talk at elections call this a free country, and say that the poorest and meanest has a free opening to rise and become prime minister, if he can. But you see, sir, the misfortune is, that in practice he can't; for one who gets into a gentleman's family, or into a little shop, and so saves a few pounds, fifty know that they've no chance before them, but day-labourer born, day-labourer live, from hand to mouth, scraping and pinching to get not meat and beer even, but bread and potatoes; and then, at the end of it all, for a worthy reward, half-a-crown a-week of parish pay—or the workhouse. That's a lively hopeful prospect for a Christian man!'

'But,' said Lancelot, 'I thought this New Poor-law was to stir them up to independence?'

'Oh, sir, the old law has bit too deep: it made them slaves and beggars at heart. It taught them not to be ashamed of parish pay—to demand it as a right.'

'And so it is their right,' said Lancelot. 'In God's name, if a country is so ill-constituted that it cannot find its own citizens in work, it is bound to find them in food.'

'Maybe, sir, maybe. God knows I don't grudge it them. It's a poor pittance at best, when they have got it. But don't you see, sir, how all poor-laws, old or new either, suck the independent spirit out of a man; how they make the poor wretch reckless; how they tempt him to spend every extra farthing in amusement?'

'How then?'

'Why, he is always tempted to say to himself, "Whatever happens to me, the parish must keep me. If I am sick it must doctor me; if I am worn out it must feed me; if I die it must bury me; if I leave my children paupers the parish must look after them, and they'll be as well off with the parish as they were with me. Now they've only got just enough to keep body and soul together, and the parish can't give them less than that. What's the use of cutting myself off from sixpenny-worth of pleasure here, and sixpenny-worth there. I'm not saving money for my children, I'm only saving the farmers' rates." There it is, sir,' said Tregarva; 'that's the bottom of it, sir,— "I'm only saving the farmers' rates. Let us eat and drink, for to-morrow we die!"'

'I don't see my way out of it,' said Lancelot.

'So says everybody, sir. But I should have thought those members of parliament, and statesmen, and university scholars have been set up in the high places, out of the wood where we are all struggling and scrambling, just that they might see their way out of it; and if they don't, sir, and that soon, as sure as God is in heaven, these poor fellows will cut their way out of it.'

'And blindfolded and ignorant as they are,' said Lancelot, 'they will be certain to cut their way out just in the wrong direction.'

'I'm not so sure of that, sir,' said Tregarva, lowering his voice. 'What is written'? That there is One who hears the desire of the poor. "Lord, Thou preparest their hearts and Thine ear hearkeneth thereto, to help the fatherless and poor unto their right, that the man of the earth be no more exalted against them."'

'Why, you are talking like any Chartist, Tregarva!'

'Am I, sir? I haven't heard much Scripture quoted among them myself, poor fellows; but to tell you the truth, sir, I don't know what I am becoming. I'm getting half mad with all I see going on and not going on; and you will agree, sir, that what's happened this day can't have done much to cool my temper or brighten my hopes; though, God's my witness, there's no spite in me for my own sake. But what makes me maddest of all, sir, is to see that everybody sees these evils, except just the men who can cure them—the squires and the clergy.'

'Why surely, Tregarva, there are hundreds, if not thousands, of clergymen and landlords working heart and soul at this moment, to better the condition of the labouring classes!'

'Ay, sir, they see the evils, and yet they don't see them. They do not see what is the matter with the poor man; and the proof of it is, sir, that the poor have no confidence in them. They'll take their alms, but they'll hardly take their schooling, and their advice they won't take at all. And why is it, sir? Because the poor have got in their heads in these days a strange confused fancy, maybe, but still a deep and a fierce one, that they haven't got what they call their rights. If you were to raise the wages of every man in this country from nine to twelve shillings a-week to-morrow, you wouldn't satisfy them; at least, the only ones whom you would satisfy would be the mere hogs among them, who, as long as they can get a full stomach, care for nothing else.'

'What, in Heaven's name, do they want?' asked Lancelot.

'They hardly know yet, sir; but they know well what they don't want. The question with them, sir, believe me, is not so much, How shall we get better fed and better housed, but whom shall we depend upon for our food and for our house? Why should we depend on the will and fancy of any man for our rights? They are asking ugly questions among themselves, sir, about what those two words, rent and taxes, mean, and about what that same strange word, freedom, means. Right or wrong, they've got the thought into their heads, and it's growing there, and they will find an answer for it. Depend upon it, sir, I tell you a truth, and they expect a change. You will hear them talk of it to-night, sir, if you've luck.'

'We all expect a change, for that matter,' said Lancelot. 'That feeling is common to all classes and parties just now.'

Tregarva took off his hat.

'"For the word of the Lord hath spoken it." Do you know, sir, I long at times that I did agree with those Chartists? If I did, I'd turn lecturer to-morrow. How a man could speak out then! If he saw any door of hope, any way of salvation for these poor fellows, even if it was nothing better than salvation by Act of Parliament!'

'But why don't you trust the truly worthy among the clergy and the gentry to leaven their own ranks and bring all right in time?'

'Because, sir, they seem to be going the way only to make things worse. The people have been so dependent on them heretofore, that they have become thorough beggars. You can have no knowledge, sir, of the whining, canting, deceit, and lies which those poor miserable labourers' wives palm on charitable ladies. If they weren't angels, some of them, they'd lock up their purses and never give away another farthing. And, sir, these free-schools, and these penny-clubs, and clothing clubs, and these heaps of money which are given away, all make the matter worse and worse. They make the labourer fancy that he is not to depend upon God and his own right hand, but on what his wife can worm out of the good nature of the rich. Why, sir, they growl as insolently now at the parson or the squire's wife if they don't get as much money as their neighbours, as they used to at the parish vestrymen under the old law. Look at that Lord Vieuxbois, sir, as sweet a gentleman as ever God made. It used to do me good to walk behind him when he came over here shooting, just to hear the gentle kind-hearted way in which he used to speak to every old soul he met. He spends his whole life and time about the poor, I hear. But, sir, as sure as you live he's making his people slaves and humbugs. He doesn't see, sir, that they want to be raised bodily out of this miserable hand-to-mouth state, to be brought nearer up to him, and set on a footing where they can shift for themselves. Without meaning it, sir, all his boundless charities are keeping the people down, and telling them they must stay down, and not help themselves, but wait for what he gives them. He fats prize-labourers, sir, just as Lord Minchampstead fats prize-oxen and pigs.'

Lancelot could not help thinking of that amusingly inconsistent, however well-meant, scene in *Coningsby*, in which Mr. Lyle is represented as trying to restore 'the independent order of peasantry,' by making them the receivers of public alms at his own gate, as if they had been middle-age serfs or vagabonds, and not citizens of modern England.

'It may suit the Mr. Lyles of this age,' thought Lancelot, 'to make the people constantly and visibly comprehend that property is their protector and their friend, but I question whether it will suit the people themselves, unless they can make property understand that it owes them something more definite than protection.'

Saddened by this conversation, which had helped to give another shake to the easy-going complacency with which Lancelot had been used to contemplate the world below him, and look on its evils as necessaries, ancient and fixed as the universe, he entered the village fair, and was a little disappointed at his first glimpse of the village-green. Certainly his expectations had not been very exalted; but there had run through them a hope of something melodramatic, dreams of May-pole dancing and athletic games, somewhat of village-belle rivalry, of the Corin and Sylvia school; or, failing that, a few Touchstones and Audreys, some genial earnest buffo humour here and there. But there did not seem much likelihood of it. Two or three apple and gingerbread stalls, from which draggled children were turning slowly and wistfully away to go home; a booth full of trumpery fairings, in front of which tawdry girls were coaxing maudlin youths, with faded southernwood in their button-holes; another long low booth, from every crevice of which reeked odours of stale beer and smoke, by courtesy denominated tobacco, to the treble accompaniment of a jigging fiddle and a tambourine, and the bass one of grumbled oaths and curses within—these were the means of relaxation which the piety, freedom, and civilisation of fourteen centuries, from Hengist to Queen Victoria, had devised and made possible for the English peasant!

'There seems very little here to see,' said Lancelot, half peevishly.

'I think, sir,' quoth Tregarva, 'that very thing is what's most worth seeing.'

Lancelot could not help, even at the risk of detection, investing capital enough in sugar-plums and gingerbread, to furnish the urchins around with the material for a whole carnival of stomach-aches; and he felt a great inclination to clear the fairing-stall in a like manner, on behalf of the poor bedizened sickly-looking girls round, but he was afraid of the jealousy of some beer-bemuddled swain. The ill-looks of the young girls surprised him much. Here and there smiled a plump rosy face enough; but the majority seemed under-sized, under-fed, utterly wanting in grace, vigour, and what the penny-a-liners call 'rude health.' He remarked it to Tregarva. The keeper smiled mournfully.

'You see those little creatures dragging home babies in arms nearly as big as themselves, sir. That and bad food, want of milk especially, accounts for their growing up no bigger than they do; and as for their sad countenances, sir, most of them must carry a lighter conscience before they carry a brighter face.'

'What do you mean?' asked Lancelot.

'The clergyman who enters the weddings and the baptisms knows well enough what I mean, sir. But we'll go into that booth, if you want to see the thick of it, sir; that's to say, if you're not ashamed.'

'I hope we need neither of us do anything to be ashamed of there; and as for seeing, I begin to agree with you, that what makes the whole thing most curious is its intense dulness.'

'What upon earth is that?'

'I say, look out there!'

'Well, you look out yourself!'

This was caused by a violent blow across the shins with a thick stick, the deed of certain drunken wiseacres who were persisting in playing in the dark the never very lucrative game of three sticks a penny, conducted by a couple of gipsies. Poor fellows! there was one excuse for them. It was the only thing there to play at, except a set of skittles; and on those they had lost their money every Saturday night for the last seven years each at his own village beer-shop.

So into the booth they turned; and as soon as Lancelot's eyes were accustomed to the reeking atmosphere, he saw seated at two long temporary tables of board, fifty or sixty of 'My Brethren,' as clergymen call them in their sermons, wrangling, stupid, beery, with sodden eyes and drooping lips—interspersed with more girls and brazen-faced women, with dirty flowers in their caps, whose whole business seemed to be to cast jealous looks at each other, and defend themselves from the coarse overtures of their swains.

Lancelot had been already perfectly astonished at the foulness of language which prevailed; and the utter absence of anything like chivalrous respect, almost of common decency, towards women. But lo! the language of the elder women was quite as disgusting as that of the men, if not worse. He whispered a remark on the point to Tregarva, who shook his head.

'It's the field-work, sir—the field-work, that does it all. They get accustomed there from their childhood to hear words whose very meanings they shouldn't know; and the older teach the younger ones, and the married ones are worst of all. It wears them out in body, sir, that field-work, and makes them brutes in soul and in manners.'

'Why don't they give it up? Why don't the respectable ones set their faces against it?'

'They can't afford it, sir. They must go a-field, or go hungered, most of them. And they get to like the gossip and scandal, and coarse fun of it, while their children are left at home to play in the roads, or fall into the fire, as plenty do every year.'

'Why not at school?'

'The big ones are kept at home, sir, to play at nursing those little ones who are too young to go. Oh, sir,' he added, in a tone of deep feeling, 'it is very little of a father's care, or a mother's love, that a labourer's child knows in these days!'

Lancelot looked round the booth with a hopeless feeling. There was awkward dancing going on at the upper end. He was too much sickened to go and look at it. He began examining the faces and foreheads of the company, and was astonished at the first glance by the lofty and ample development of brain in at least one half. There were intellects there— or rather capacities of intellect, capable, surely, of anything, had not the promise of the brow been almost always belied by the loose and sensual lower features. They were evidently rather a degraded than an undeveloped race. 'The low forehead of the Kabyle and Koord,' thought Lancelot, 'is compensated by the grim sharp lip, and glittering eye, which prove that all the small capabilities of the man have been called out into clear and vigorous action: but here the very features themselves, both by what they have and what they want, testify against that society which carelessly wastes her most precious wealth, the manhood of her masses! Tregarva! you have observed a good many things—did you ever observe whether the men with the large foreheads were better than the men with the small ones?'

'Ay, sir, I know what you are driving at. I've heard of that new-fangled notion of scholars, which, if you'll forgive my plain speaking, expects man's brains to do the work of God's grace.'

'But what have you remarked?'

'All I ever saw was, that the stupid-looking ones were the greatest blackguards, and the clever-looking ones the greatest rogues.'

Lancelot was rebuked, but not surprised. He had been for some time past suspecting, from the bitter experience of his own heart, the favourite modern theory which revives the Neo-Platonism of Alexandria, by making intellect synonymous with virtue, and then jumbling, like poor bewildered Proclus, the 'physical understanding' of the brain with the pure 'intellect' of the spirit.

'You'll see something, if you look round, sir, a great deal easier to explain—and, I should have thought, a great deal easier to cure—than want of wits.'

'And what is that?'

'How different-looking the young ones are from their fathers, and still more from their grandfathers! Look at those three or four old grammers talking together there. For all their being shrunk with age and weather, you won't see such fine-grown men anywhere else in this booth.'

It was too true. Lancelot recollected now having remarked it before when at church; and having wondered why almost all the youths were so much smaller, clumsier, lower-brained, and weaker-jawed than their elders.

'Why is it, Tregarva?'

'Worse food, worse lodging, worse nursing—and, I'm sore afraid, worse blood. There was too much filthiness and drunkenness went on in the old war-times, not to leave a taint behind it, for many a generation. The prosperity of fools shall destroy them!'

'Oh!' thought Lancelot, 'for some young sturdy Lancashire or Lothian blood, to put new life into the old frozen South Saxon veins! Even a drop of the warm enthusiastic Celtic would be better than none. Perhaps this Irish immigration may do some good, after all.'

Perhaps it may, Lancelot. Let us hope so, since it is pretty nearly inevitable.

Sadder and sadder, Lancelot tried to listen to the conversation of the men round him. To his astonishment he hardly understood a word of it. It was half articulate, nasal, guttural, made up almost entirely of vowels, like the speech of savages. He had never before been struck with the significant contrast between the sharp, clearly-defined articulation, the vivid and varied tones of the gentleman, or even of the London street-boy when compared with the coarse, half-formed growls, as of a company of seals, which he heard round him. That single fact struck him, perhaps, more deeply than any; it connected itself with many of his physiological fancies; it was the parent of many thoughts and plans of his after-life. Here and there he could distinguish a half sentence. An old shrunken man opposite him was drawing figures in the spilt beer with his pipe-stem, and discoursing of the glorious times before the great war, 'when there was more food than there were mouths, and more work than there were hands.' 'Poor human nature!' thought Lancelot, as he tried to follow one of those unintelligible discussions about the relative prices of the loaf and the bushel of flour, which ended, as usual, in more swearing, and more quarrelling, and more beer to make it up—'Poor human nature! always looking back, as the German sage says, to some fancied golden age, never looking forward to the real one which is coming!'

'But I say, vather,' drawled out some one, 'they say there's a sight more money in England now, than there was afore the war-time.'

'Eees, booy,' said the old man; 'but *its got into too few hands.*'

'Well,' thought Lancelot, 'there's a glimpse of practical sense, at least.' And a pedlar who sat next him, a bold, black-whiskered bully, from the Potteries, hazarded a joke,—

'It's all along of this new sky-and-tough-it farming. They used to spread the money broadcast, but now they drills it all in one place, like bone-dust under their fancy plants, and we poor self-sown chaps gets none.'

This garland of fancies was received with great applause; whereat the pedlar, emboldened, proceeded to observe, mysteriously, that 'donkeys took a beating, but horses kicked at it; and that they'd found out that in Staffordshire long ago. You want a good Chartist lecturer down here, my covies, to show you donkeys of labouring men that you have got iron on your heels, if you only know'd how to use it.'

'And what's the use of rioting?' asked some one, querulously.

'Why, if you don't riot, the farmers will starve you.'

'And if we do, they'd turn sodgers—yeomanry, as they call it, though there ain't a yeoman among them in these parts; and then they takes sword and kills us. So, riot or none, they has it all their own way.'

Lancelot heard many more scraps of this sort. He was very much struck with their dread of violence. It did not seem cowardice. It was not loyalty—the English labourer has fallen below the capability of so spiritual a feeling; Lancelot had found out that already. It could not be apathy, for he heard nothing but complaint upon complaint bandied from mouth to mouth the whole evening. They seemed rather sunk too low in body and mind,—too stupefied and spiritless, to follow the example of the manufacturing districts; above all, they were too ill-informed. It is not mere starvation which goads the Leicester weaver to madness. It is starvation with education,—an empty stomach and a cultivated, even though miscultivated, mind.

At that instant, a huge hulking farm-boy rolled into the booth, roaring, dolefully, the end of a song, with a punctuation of his own invention—

'He'll maak me a lady. Zo. Vine to be zyure.
And, vaithfully; love me. Although; I; be-e; poor-r-r-r.'

Lancelot would have laughed heartily at him anywhere else; but the whole scene was past a jest; and a gleam of pathos and tenderness seemed to shine even from that doggerel,—a vista, as it were, of true genial nature, in the far distance. But as he looked round again, 'What hope,' he thought, 'of its realisation? Arcadian dreams of pastoral innocence and graceful industry, I suppose, are to be henceforth monopolised by the stage or the boudoir? Never, so help me, God!'

The ursine howls of the new-comer seemed to have awakened the spirit of music in the party.

'Coom, Blackburd, gi' us zong, Blackburd, bo'!' cried a dozen voices to an impish, dark-eyed gipsy boy, of some thirteen years old.

'Put 'n on taable. Now, then, pipe up!'

'What will 'ee ha'?'

'Mary; gi' us Mary.'

'I shall make a' girls cry,' quoth Blackbird, with a grin.

'Do'n good, too; they likes it: zing away.'

And the boy began, in a broad country twang, which could not overpower the sad melody of the air, or the rich sweetness of his flute-like voice,—

'Young Mary walked sadly down through the green clover,
   And sighed as she looked at the babe at her breast;
"My roses are faded, my false love a rover,
   The green graves they call me, 'Come home to your rest.'"

'Then by rode a soldier in gorgeous arraying,
  And "Where is your bride-ring, my fair maid?" he cried;
"I ne'er had a bride-ring, by false man's betraying,
  Nor token of love but this babe at my side.

'"Tho' gold could not buy me, sweet words could deceive me;
  So faithful and lonely till death I must roam."
"Oh, Mary, sweet Mary, look up and forgive me,
  With wealth and with glory your true love comes home;

'"So give me my own babe, those soft arms adorning,
  I'll wed you and cherish you, never to stray;
For it's many a dark and a wild cloudy morning,
  Turns out by the noon-time a sunshiny day."'

'A bad moral that, sir,' whispered Tregarva.

'Better than none,' answered Lancelot.

'It's well if you are right, sir, for you'll hear no other.'

The keeper spoke truly; in a dozen different songs, more or less coarsely, but, in general, with a dash of pathetic sentiment, the same case of lawless love was embodied. It seemed to be their only notion of the romantic. Now and then there was a poaching song; then one of the lowest flash London school—filth and all—was roared in chorus in presence of the women.

'I am afraid that you do not thank me for having brought you to any place so unfit for a gentleman,' said Tregarva, seeing Lancelot's sad face.

'Because it is so unfit for a gentleman, therefore I do thank you. It is right to know what one's own flesh and blood are doing.'

'Hark to that song, sir! that's an old one. I didn't think they'd get on to singing that.'

The Blackbird was again on the table, but seemed this time disinclined to exhibit.

'Out wi' un, boy; it wain't burn thy mouth!'

'I be afeard.'

'O' who?'

'Keeper there.'

He pointed to Tregarva; there was a fierce growl round the room.

'I am no keeper,' shouted Tregarva, starting up. 'I was turned off this morning for speaking my mind about the squires, and now I'm one of you, to live and die.'

This answer was received with a murmur of applause; and a fellow in a scarlet merino neckerchief, three waistcoats, and a fancy shooting-jacket, who had been eyeing Lancelot for some time, sidled up behind them, and whispered in Tregarva's ear,—

'Perhaps you'd like an engagement in our line, young man, and your friend there, he seems a sporting gent too.—We could show him very pretty shooting.'

Tregarva answered by the first and last oath Lancelot ever heard from him, and turning to him, as the rascal sneaked off,—

'That's a poaching crimp from London, sir; tempting these poor boys to sin, and deceit, and drunkenness, and theft, and the hulks.'

'I fancy I saw him somewhere the night of our row—you understand?'

'So do I, sir, but there's no use talking of it.'

Blackbird was by this time prevailed on to sing, and burst out as melodious as ever, while all heads were cocked on one side in delighted attention.

> 'I zeed a vire o' Monday night,
>   A vire both great and high;
> But I wool not tell you where, my boys,
>   Nor wool not tell you why.
> The varmer he comes screeching out,
>   To zave 'uns new brood mare;
> Zays I, "You and your stock may roast,
>   Vor aught us poor chaps care."

'Coorus, boys, coorus!'

And the chorus burst out,—

> 'Then here's a curse on varmers all
>   As rob and grind the poor;
> To re'p the fruit of all their works
>   In **** for evermoor-r-r.

> 'A blind owld dame come to the vire,
>   Zo near as she could get;

Yeast: A Problem | 159

Zays, "Here's a luck I warn't asleep
To lose this blessed hett.

'"They robs us of our turfing rights,
Our bits of chips and sticks,
Till poor folks now can't warm their hands,
Except by varmer's ricks."
'Then, etc.'

And again the boy's delicate voice rung out the ferocious chorus, with something, Lancelot fancied, of fiendish exultation, and every worn face lighted up with a coarse laugh, that indicated no malice—but also no mercy.

Lancelot was sickened, and rose to go.

As he turned, his arm was seized suddenly and firmly. He looked round, and saw a coarse, handsome, showily-dressed girl, looking intently into his face. He shook her angrily off.

'You needn't be so proud, Mr. Smith; I've had my hand on the arm of as good as you. Ah, you needn't start! I know you—I know you, I say, well enough. You used to be with him. Where is he?'

'Whom do you mean?'

'He!' answered the girl, with a fierce, surprised look, as if there could be no one else in the world.

'Colonel Bracebridge,' whispered Tregarva.

'Ay, he it is! And now walk further off, bloodhound! and let me speak to Mr. Smith. He is in Norway,' she ran on eagerly. 'When will he be back? When?'

'Why do you want to know?' asked Lancelot.

'When will he be back?'—she kept on fiercely repeating the question; and then burst out,—'Curse you gentlemen all! Cowards! you are all in a league against us poor girls! You can hunt alone when you betray us, and lie fast enough then? But when we come for justice, you all herd together like a flock of rooks; and turn so delicate and honourable all of a sudden—to each other! When will he be back, I say?'

'In a month,' answered Lancelot, who saw that something really important lay behind the girl's wildness.

'Too late!' she cried, wildly, clapping her hands together; 'too late! Here—tell him you saw me; tell him you saw Mary; tell him where and in what a pretty place, too, for maid, master, or man! What are you doing here?'

'What is that to you, my good girl?'

'True. Tell him you saw me here; and tell him, when next he hears of me, it will be in a very different place.'

She turned and vanished among the crowd. Lancelot almost ran out into the night,—into a triad of fights, two drunken men, two jealous wives, and a brute who struck a poor, thin, worn-out woman, for trying to coax him home. Lancelot rushed up to interfere, but a man seized his uplifted arm.

'He'll only beat her all the more when he getteth home.'

'She has stood that every Saturday night for the last seven years, to my knowledge,' said Tregarva; 'and worse, too, at times.'

'Good God! is there no escape for her from her tyrant?'

'No, sir. It's only you gentlefolks who can afford such luxuries; your poor man may be tied to a harlot, or your poor woman to a ruffian, but once done, done for ever.'

'Well,' thought Lancelot, 'we English have a characteristic way of proving the holiness of the marriage tie. The angel of Justice and Pity cannot sever it, only the stronger demon of Money.'

Their way home lay over Ashy Down, a lofty chalk promontory, round whose foot the river made a sudden bend. As they paced along over the dreary hedgeless stubbles, they both started, as a ghostly 'Ha! ha! ha!' rang through the air over their heads, and was answered by a like cry, faint and distant, across the wolds.

'That's those stone-curlews—at least, so I hope,' said Tregarva. 'He'll be round again in a minute.'

And again, right between them and the clear, cold moon, 'Ha! ha! ha!' resounded over their heads. They gazed up into the cloudless star-bespangled sky, but there was no sign of living thing.

'It's an old sign to me,' quoth Tregarva; 'God grant that I may remember it in this black day of mine.'

'How so!' asked Lancelot; 'I should not have fancied you a superstitious man.'

'Names go for nothing, sir, and what my forefathers believed in I am not going to be conceited enough to disbelieve in a hurry. But if you heard my story you would think I had reason enough to remember that devil's laugh up there.'

'Let me hear it then.'

'Well, sir, it may be a long story to you, but it was a short one to me, for it was the making of me, out of hand, there and then, blessed be God! But if you will have it—'

'And I will have it, friend Tregarva,' quoth Lancelot, lighting his cigar.

'I was about sixteen years old, just after I came home from the Brazils—'

'What! have you been in the Brazils?'

'Indeed and I have, sir, for three years; and one thing I learnt there, at least, that's worth going for.'

'What's that?'

'What the Garden of Eden must have been like. But those Brazils, under God, were the cause of my being here; for my father, who was a mine-captain, lost all his money there, by no man's fault but his own, and not his either, the world would say, and when we came back to Cornwall he could not stand the bal work, nor I neither. Out of that burning sun, sir, to come home here, and work in the levels, up to our knees in warm water, with the thermometer at 85°, and then up a thousand feet of ladder to grass, reeking wet with heat, and find the easterly sleet driving across those open furze-crofts—he couldn't stand it, sir—few stand it long, even of those who stay in Cornwall. We miners have a short lease of life; consumption and strains break us down before we're fifty.'

'But how came you here?'

'The doctor told my father, and me too, sir, that we must give up mining, or die of decline: so he came up here, to a sister of his that was married to the squire's gardener, and here he died; and the squire, God bless him and forgive him, took a fancy to me, and made me under-keeper. And I loved the life, for it took me among the woods and the rivers, where I could think of the Brazils, and fancy myself back again. But mustn't talk of that—where God wills is all right. And it is a fine life for reading and thinking, a gamekeeper's, for it's an idle life at best. Now that's over,' he added, with a sigh, 'and the Lord has fulfilled His words to me, that He spoke the first night that ever I heard a stone-plover cry.'

'What on earth can you mean?' asked Lancelot, deeply interested.

'Why, sir, it was a wild, whirling gray night, with the air full of sleet and rain, and my father sent me over to Redruth town to bring home some trade or other. And as I came back I got blinded with the sleet, and I lost my way across the moors. You know those Cornish furze-moors, sir?'

'No.'

'Well, then, they are burrowed like a rabbit-warren with old mine-shafts. You can't go in some places ten yards without finding great, ghastly black holes, covered in with furze, and weeds, and bits of rotting timber; and when I was a boy I couldn't keep from them. Something seemed to draw me to go and peep down, and drop pebbles in, to hear them rattle against the sides, fathoms below, till they plumped into the ugly black still water at the bottom. And I used to be always after them in my dreams, when I was young, falling down them, down, down, all night long, till I woke screaming; for I fancied they were hell's mouth, every one of them. And it stands to reason, sir; we miners hold that the lake of fire can't be far below. For we find it grow warmer, and warmer, and warmer, the farther we sink a shaft; and the learned gentlemen have proved, sir, that it's not the blasting powder, nor the men's breaths, that heat the mine.'

Lancelot could but listen.

'Well, sir, I got into a great furze-croft, full of deads (those are the earth-heaps they throw out of the shafts), where no man in his senses dare go forward or back in the dark, for fear of the shafts; and the wind and the snow were so sharp, they made me quite stupid and sleepy; and I knew if I stayed there I should be frozen to death, and if I went on, there were the shafts ready to swallow me up: and what with fear and the howling and raging of the wind, I was like a mazed boy, sir. And I knelt down and tried to pray; and then, in one moment, all the evil things I'd ever done, and the bad words and thoughts that ever crossed me, rose up together as clear as one page of a print-book; and I knew that if I died that minute I should go to hell. And then I saw through the ground all the water in the shafts glaring like blood, and all the sides of the shafts fierce red-hot, as if hell was coming up. And I heard the knockers knocking, or thought I heard them, as plain as I hear that grasshopper in the hedge now.'

'What are the knockers?'

'They are the ghosts, the miners hold, of the old Jews, sir, that crucified our Lord, and were sent for slaves by the Roman emperors to work the mines; and we find their old smelting-houses, which we call Jews' houses, and their blocks of tin, at the bottom of the great bogs, which we call Jews' tin; and there's a town among us, too, which we call Market-Jew—but the old name was Marazion; that means the Bitterness of Zion, they tell me. Isn't it so, sir?'

'I believe it is,' said Lancelot, utterly puzzled in this new field of romance.

'And bitter work it was for them, no doubt, poor souls! We used to break into the old shafts and adits which they had made, and find old stags'-horn pickaxes, that crumbled to pieces when we brought them to grass; and they say, that if a man will listen, sir, of a still night, about those old shafts, he may hear the ghosts of them at working, knocking, and picking, as clear as if there was a man at work in the next level. It may be all an old fancy. I suppose it is. But I believed it when I was a boy; and it helped the work in me that night. But I'll go on with my story.'

'Go on with what you like,' said Lancelot.

'Well, sir, I was down on my knees among the furze-bushes, and I tried to pray; but I was too frightened, for I felt the beast I had been, sir; and I expected the ground to open and let me down every moment; and then there came by over my head a rushing, and a cry. "Ha! ha! ha! Paul!" it said; and it seemed as if all the devils and witches were out on the wind, a-laughing at my misery. "Oh, I'll mend—I'll repent," I said, "indeed I will:" and again it came back,—"Ha! ha! ha! Paul!" it said. I knew afterwards that it was a bird; but the Lord sent it to me for a messenger, no less, that night. And I shook like a reed in the water; and then, all at once a thought struck me. "Why should I be a coward? Why should I be afraid of shafts, or devils, or hell, or anything else? If I am a miserable sinner, there's One died for me—I owe him love, not fear at all. I'll not be frightened into doing right—that's a rascally reason for repentance." And so it was, sir, that I rose up like a man, and said to the Lord Jesus, right out into the black, dumb air,—"If you'll be on my side this night, good Lord, that died for me, I'll be on your side for ever, villain as I am, if I'm worth making any use of." And there and then, sir, I saw a light come over the bushes, brighter, and brighter, up to me; and there rose up a voice within me, and spoke to me, quite soft and sweet,—"Fear not, Paul, for I will send thee far hence unto the Gentiles." And what more happened I can't tell, for when I woke I was safe at home. My father and his folk had been out with lanterns after me; and there they found me, sure enough, in a dead faint on the ground. But this I know, sir, that those words have never left my mind since for a day together; and I know that they will be fulfilled in me this tide, or never.'

Lancelot was silent a few minutes.

'I suppose, Tregarva, that you would call this your conversion?'

'I should call it one, sir, because it was one.'

'Tell me now, honestly, did any real, practical change in your behaviour take place after that night?'

'As much, sir, as if you put a soul into a hog, and told him that he was a gentleman's son; and, if every time he remembered that, he got spirit enough to conquer his hoggishness, and behave like a man, till the hoggishness died out of him, and the manliness grew up and bore fruit in him, more and more each day.'

Lancelot half understood him, and sighed.

A long silence followed, as they paced on past lonely farmyards, from which the rich manure-water was draining across the road in foul black streams, festering and steaming in the chill night air. Lancelot sighed as he saw the fruitful materials of food running to waste, and thought of the 'over-population' cry; and then he looked across to the miles of brown moorland on the opposite side of the valley, that lay idle and dreary under the autumn moon, except where here and there a squatter's cottage and rood of fruitful garden gave the lie to the laziness and ignorance of man, who pretends that it is not worth his while to cultivate the soil which God has given him. 'Good heavens!' he thought, 'had our forefathers had no more enterprise than modern landlords, where should we all have been at this moment? Everywhere waste? Waste of manure, waste of land, waste of muscle, waste of brain, waste of population—and we call ourselves the workshop of the world!'

As they passed through the miserable hamlet-street of Ashy, they saw a light burning in window. At the door below, a haggard woman was looking anxiously down the village.

'What's the matter, Mistress Cooper?' asked Tregarva.

'Here's Mrs. Grane's poor girl lying sick of the fever—the Lord help her! and the boy died of it last week. We sent for the doctor this afternoon, and he's busy with a poor soul that's in her trouble; and now we've sent down to the squire's, and the young ladies, God bless them! sent answer they'd come themselves straightway.'

'No wonder you have typhus here,' said Lancelot, 'with this filthy open drain running right before the door. Why can't you clean it out?'

'Why, what harm does that do?' answered the woman, peevishly. 'Besides, here's my master gets up to his work by five in the morning, and not back till seven at night, and by then he ain't in no humour to clean out gutters. And where's the water to come from to keep a place clean? It costs many a one of us here a shilling a week the summer through to pay fetching water up the hill. We've work enough to fill our kettles. The muck must just lie in the road, smell or none, till the rain carries it away.'

Lancelot sighed again.

'It would be a good thing for Ashy, Tregarva, if the weir-pool did, some fine morning, run up to Ashy Down, as poor Harry Verney said on his deathbed.'

'There won't be much of Ashy left by that time, sir, if the landlords go on pulling down cottages at their present rate; driving the people into the towns, to herd together there like hogs, and walk out to their work four or five miles every morning.'

'Why,' said Lancelot, 'wherever one goes one sees commodious new cottages springing up.'

'Wherever you go, sir; but what of wherever you don't go? Along the roadsides, and round the gentlemen's parks, where the cottages are in sight, it's all very smart; but just go into the outlying hamlets—a whited sepulchre, sir, is many a great estate; outwardly swept and garnished, and inwardly full of all uncleanliness, and dead men's bones.'

At this moment two cloaked and veiled figures came up to the door, followed by a servant. There was no mistaking those delicate footsteps, and the two young men drew back with fluttering hearts, and breathed out silent blessings on the ministering angels, as they entered the crazy and reeking house.

'I'm thinking, sir,' said Tregarva, as they walked slowly and reluctantly away, 'that it is hard of the gentlemen to leave all God's work to the ladies, as nine-tenths of them do.'

'And I am thinking, Tregarva, that both for ladies and gentlemen, prevention is better than cure.'

'There's a great change come over Miss Argemone, sir. She used not to be so ready to start out at midnight to visit dying folk. A blessed change!'

Lancelot thought so too, and he thought that he knew the cause of it.

Argemone's appearance, and their late conversation, had started a new covey of strange fancies. Lancelot followed them over hill and dale, glad to escape a moment from the mournful lessons of that evening; but even over them there was a cloud of sadness. Harry Verney's last words, and Argemone's accidental whisper about 'a curse upon the Lavingtons,' rose to his mind. He longed to ask Tregarva, but he was afraid—not of the man, for there was a delicacy in his truthfulness which encouraged the most utter confidence; but of the subject itself; but curiosity conquered.

'What did Old Harry mean about the Nun-pool?' he said at last. 'Every one seemed to understand him.'

'Ah, sir, he oughtn't to have talked of it! But dying men, at times, see over the dark water into deep things—deeper than they think themselves. Perhaps there's one speaks through them. But I thought every one knew the story.'

'I do not, at least.'

'Perhaps it's so much the better, sir.'

'Why? I must insist on knowing. It is necessary—proper, that is—that I should hear everything that concerns—'

'I understand, sir; so it is; and I'll tell you. The story goes, that in the old Popish times, when the nuns held Whitford Priors, the first Mr. Lavington that ever was came from the king with a warrant to turn them all out, poor souls, and take the lands for his own. And they say the head lady of them—prioress, or abbess, as they called her—withstood him, and cursed him, in the name of the Lord, for a hypocrite who robbed harmless women under the cloak of punishing them for sins they'd never committed (for they say, sir, he went up to court, and slandered the nuns there for drunkards and worse). And she told him, "That the curse of the nuns of Whitford should be on him and his, till they helped the poor in the spirit of the nuns of Whitford, and the Nun-pool ran up to Ashy Down."'

'That time is not come yet,' said Lancelot.

'But the worst is to come, sir. For he or his, sir, that night, said or did something to the lady, that was more than woman's heart could bear: and the next morning she was found dead and cold, drowned in that weir-pool. And there the gentleman's eldest son was drowned, and more than one Lavington beside. Miss Argemone's only brother, that was the heir, was drowned there too, when he was a little one.'

'I never heard that she had a brother.'

'No, sir, no one talks of it. There are many things happen in the great house that you must go to the little house to hear of. But the country-folk believe, sir, that the nun's curse holds true; and they say, that Whitford folks have been getting poorer and wickeder ever since that time, and will, till the Nun-pool runs up to Ashy, and the Lavingtons' name goes out of Whitford Priors.'

Yeast: A Problem | 167

Lancelot said nothing. A presentiment of evil hung over him. He was utterly down-hearted about Tregarva, about Argemone, about the poor. The truth was, he could not shake off the impression of the scene he had left, utterly disappointed and disgusted with the 'revel.' He had expected, as I said before, at least to hear something of pastoral sentiment, and of genial frolicsome humour; to see some innocent, simple enjoyment: but instead, what had he seen but vanity, jealousy, hoggish sensuality, dull vacuity? drudges struggling for one night to forget their drudgery. And yet withal, those songs, and the effect which they produced, showed that in these poor creatures, too, lay the germs of pathos, taste, melody, soft and noble affections. 'What right have we,' thought he, 'to hinder their development? Art, poetry, music, science,—ay, even those athletic and graceful exercises on which we all pride ourselves, which we consider necessary to soften and refine ourselves, what God has given us a monopoly of them?—what is good for the rich man is good for the poor. Over-education? And what of that? What if the poor be raised above "their station"? What right have we to keep them down? How long have they been our born thralls in soul, as well as in body? What right have we to say that they shall know no higher recreation than the hogs, because, forsooth, if we raised them, they might refuse to work—*for us*? Are *we* to fix how far their minds may be developed? Has not God fixed it for us, when He gave them the same passions, talents, tastes, as our own?'

Tregarva's meditations must have been running in a very different channel, for he suddenly burst out, after a long silence—

'It's a pity these fairs can't be put down. They do a lot of harm; ruin all the young girls round, the Dissenters' children especially, for they run utterly wild; their parents have no hold on them at all.'

'They tell them that they are children of the devil,' said Lancelot. 'What wonder if the children take them at their word, and act accordingly?'

'The parson here, sir, who is a God-fearing man enough, tried hard to put down this one, but the innkeepers were too strong for him.'

'To take away their only amusement, in short. He had much better have set to work to amuse them himself.'

'His business is to save souls, sir, and not to amuse them. I don't see, sir, what Christian people want with such vanities.'

Lancelot did not argue the point, for he knew the prejudices of Dissenters on the subject; but it did strike him that if Tregarva's brain had been a little less preponderant, he, too, might have found the need of some recreation besides books and thought.

By this time they were at Lancelot's door. He bid the keeper a hearty good-night, made him promise to see him next day, and went to bed and slept till nearly noon.

When he walked into his breakfast-room, he found a note on the table in his uncle's handwriting. The vicar's servant had left it an hour before. He opened it listlessly, rang the bell furiously, ordered out his best horse, and, huddling on his clothes, galloped to the nearest station, caught the train, and arrived at his uncle's bank—it had stopped payment two hours before.

CHAPTER XIV
WHAT'S TO BE DONE?

Yes! the bank had stopped. The ancient firm of Smith, Brown, Jones, Robinson, and Co., which had been for some years past expanding from a solid golden organism into a cobweb-tissue and huge balloon of threadbare paper, had at last worn through and collapsed, dropping its car and human contents miserably into the Thames mud. Why detail the pitiable post-mortem examination resulting? Lancelot sickened over it for many a long day; not, indeed, mourning at his private losses, but at the thorough hollowness of the system which it exposed, about which he spoke his mind pretty freely to his uncle, who bore it good-humouredly enough. Indeed, the discussions to which it gave rise rather comforted the good man, by turning his thought from his own losses to general principles. 'I have ruined you, my poor boy,' he used to say; 'so you may as well take your money's worth out of me in bullying.' Nothing, indeed, could surpass his honest and manly sorrow for having been the cause of Lancelot's beggary; but as for persuading him that his system was wrong, it was quite impossible. Not that Lancelot was hard upon him; on the contrary, he assured him, repeatedly, of his conviction, that the precepts of the Bible had nothing to do with the laws of commerce; that though the Jews were forbidden to take interest of Jews, Christians had a perfect right to be as hard as they liked on 'brother' Christians; that there could not be the least harm in share-jobbing, for though it did, to be sure, add nothing to the wealth of the community—only conjure money out of your neighbour's pocket into your own—yet was not that all fair in trade? If a man did not know the real value of the shares he sold you, you were not bound to tell him. Again, Lancelot quite agreed with his uncle, that though covetousness might be idolatry, yet money-making could not be called covetousness; and that, on the whole, though making haste to be rich was denounced as a dangerous and ruinous temptation in St. Paul's times, that was not the slightest reason why it should be so now. All these concessions were made with a freedom which caused the good banker to suspect at times that his shrewd nephew was laughing at him in his sleeve, but he could not but subscribe to them for the sake of consistency; though as a staunch Protestant, it puzzled him a little at times to find it necessary to justify himself by getting his 'infidel' nephew to explain away so much of the Bible for him. But men are accustomed to do that now-a-days, and so was he.

Once only did Lancelot break out with his real sentiments when the banker was planning how to re-establish his credit; to set to work, in fact, to blow over again the same bubble which had already burst under him.

'If I were a Christian,' said Lancelot, 'like you, I would call this credit system of yours the devil's selfish counterfeit of God's order of mutual love and trust; the child of that miserable dream, which, as Dr. Chalmers well said, expects universal selfishness to do the work of universal love. Look at your credit system, how—not in its abuse, but in its very essence—it carries the seeds of self-destruction. In the first place, a man's credit depends, not upon his real worth and property, but upon his reputation for property; daily and hourly he is tempted, he is forced, to puff himself, to pretend to be richer than he is.'

The banker sighed and shrugged his shoulders. 'We all do it, my dear boy.'

'I know it. You must do it, or be more than human. There is lie the first, and look at lie the second. This credit system is founded on the universal faith and honour of men towards men. But do you think faith and honour can be the children of selfishness? Men must be chivalrous and disinterested to be honourable. And you expect them all to join in universal faith—each for his own selfish interest? You forget that if that is the prime motive, men will be honourable only as long as it suits that same self-interest.'

The banker shrugged his shoulders again.

'Yes, my dear uncle,' said Lancelot, 'you all forget it, though you suffer for it daily and hourly; though the honourable men among you complain of the stain which has fallen on the old chivalrous good faith of English commerce, and say that now, abroad as well as at home, an Englishman's word is no longer worth other men's bonds. You see the evil, and you deplore it in disgust. Ask yourself honestly, how can you battle against it, while you allow in practice, and in theory too, except in church on Sundays, the very falsehood from which it all springs?—that a man is bound to get wealth, not for his country, but for himself; that, in short, not patriotism, but selfishness, is the bond of all society. Selfishness can collect, not unite, a herd of cowardly wild cattle, that they may feed together, breed together, keep off the wolf and bear together. But when one of your wild cattle falls sick, what becomes of the corporate feelings of the herd then? For one man of your class who is nobly helped by his fellows, are not the thousand left behind to perish? Your Bible talks of society, not as a herd, but as a living tree, an organic individual body, a holy brotherhood, and kingdom of God. And here is an idol which you have set up instead of it!'

But the banker was deaf to all arguments. No doubt he had plenty, for he was himself a just and generous—ay, and a God-fearing man in his way, only he regarded Lancelot's young fancies as too visionary to deserve an answer; which they most probably are; else, having been broached as often as they have been, they would surely, ere now, have provoked the complete refutation which can, no doubt, be given to them by hundreds of learned votaries of so-called commerce. And here I beg my readers to recollect that I am in no way answerable for the speculations, either of Lancelot or any of his acquaintances; and that these papers have been, from beginning to end, as in name, so in nature, Yeast—an honest sample of the questions, which, good or bad, are fermenting in the minds of the young of this day, and are rapidly leavening the minds of the rising generation. No doubt they are all as full of fallacies as possible, but as long as the saying of the German sage stands true, that 'the destiny of any nation, at any given moment, depends on the opinions of its young men under five-and-twenty,' so long it must be worth while for those who wish to preserve the present order of society to justify its acknowledged evils somewhat, not only to the few young men who are interested in preserving them, but also to the many who are not.

Though, therefore, I am neither Plymouth Brother nor Communist, and as thoroughly convinced as the newspapers can make me, that to assert the duties of property is only to plot its destruction, and that a community of goods must needs imply a community of wives (as every one knows was the case with the apostolic Christians), I shall take the liberty of narrating Lancelot's fanatical conduct, without execratory comment, certain that he will still receive his just reward of condemnation; and that, if I find facts, a sensible public will find abhorrence for them. His behaviour was, indeed, most singular; he absolutely refused a good commercial situation which his uncle procured him. He did not believe in being 'cured by a hair of the dog that bit him;' and he refused, also, the really generous offers of the creditors, to allow him a sufficient maintenance.

'No,' he said, 'no more pay without work for me. I will earn my bread or starve. It seems God's will to teach me what poverty is—I will see that His intention is not left half fulfilled. I have sinned, and only in the stern delight of a just penance can I gain self-respect.'

'But, my dear madman,' said his uncle, 'you are just the innocent one among us all. You, at least, were only a sleeping partner.'

'And therein lies my sin; I took money which I never earned, and cared as little how it was gained as how I spent it. Henceforth I shall touch no farthing which is the fruit of a system which I cannot approve. I accuse no one. Actions may vary in rightfulness, according to the age and the person. But what may be right for you, because you think it right, is surely wrong for me because I think it wrong.'

So, with grim determination, he sent to the hammer every article he possessed, till he had literally nothing left but the clothes in which he stood. 'He could not rest,' he said, 'till he had pulled out all his borrowed peacock's feathers. When they were gone he should be able to see, at last, whether he was jackdaw or eagle.' And wonder not, reader, at this same strength of will. The very genius, which too often makes its possessor self-indulgent in common matters, from the intense capability of enjoyment which it brings, may also, when once his whole being is stirred into motion by some great object, transform him into a hero.

And he carried a letter, too, in his bosom, night and day, which routed all coward fears and sad forebodings as soon as they arose, and converted the lonely and squalid lodging to which he had retired, into a fairy palace peopled with bright phantoms of future bliss. I need not say from whom it came.

'Beloved!' (it ran) 'Darling! you need not pain yourself to tell me anything. I know all; and I know, too (do not ask me how), your noble determination to drink the wholesome cup of poverty to the very dregs.

'Oh that I were with you! Oh that I could give you my fortune! but that is not yet, alas! in my own power. No! rather would I share that poverty with you, and strengthen you in your purpose. And yet, I cannot bear the thought of you, lonely—perhaps miserable. But, courage! though you have lost all, you have found me; and now you are knitting me to you for ever—justifying my own love to me by your nobleness; and am I not worth all the world to you? I dare say this to you; you will not think me conceited. Can we misunderstand each other's hearts? And all this while you are alone! Oh! I have mourned for you! Since I heard of your misfortune I have not tasted pleasure. The light of heaven has been black to me, and I have lived only upon love. I will not taste comfort while you are wretched. Would that I could be poor like you! Every night upon the bare floor I lie down to sleep, and fancy you in your little chamber, and nestle to you, and cover that dear face with kisses. Strange! that I should dare to speak thus to you, whom a few months ago I had never heard of! Wonderful simplicity of love! How all that is prudish and artificial flees before it! I seem to have begun a new life. If I could play now, it would be only with little children. Farewell! be great—a glorious future is before you and me in you!'

Lancelot's answer must remain untold; perhaps the veil has been already too far lifted which hides the sanctuary of such love. But, alas! to his letter no second had been returned; and he felt—though he dared not confess it to himself—a gloomy presentiment of evil flit across him, as he thought of his fallen fortunes, and the altered light in which his suit would be regarded by Argemone's parents. Once he blamed himself bitterly for not having gone to Mr. Lavington the moment he discovered Argemone's affection, and insuring—as he then might have done—his consent. But again he felt that no sloth had kept him back, but adoring reverence for his God-given treasure, and humble astonishment at his own happiness; and he fled from the thought into renewed examination into the state of the masses, the effect of which was only to deepen his own determination to share their lot.

But at the same time it seemed to him but fair to live, as long as it would last, on that part of his capital which his creditors would have given nothing for—namely, his information; and he set to work to write. But, alas! he had but a 'small literary connection;' and the *entrée* of the initiated ring is not obtained in a day. . . . Besides, he would not write trash.—He was in far too grim a humour for that; and if he wrote on important subjects, able editors always were in the habit of entrusting them to old contributors,—men, in short, in whose judgment they had confidence—not to say anything which would commit the magazine to anything but its own little party-theory. And behold! poor Lancelot found himself of no party whatsoever. He was in a minority of one against the whole world, on all points, right or wrong. He had the unhappiest knack (as all geniuses have) of seeing connections, humorous or awful, between the most seemingly antipodal things; of illustrating every subject from three or four different spheres which it is anathema to mention in the same page. If he wrote a physical-science article, able editors asked him what the deuce a scrap of high-churchism did in the middle of it? If he took the same article to a high-church magazine, the editor could not commit himself to any theory which made the earth more than six thousand years old, and was afraid that the public taste would not approve of the allusions to free-masonry and Soyer's soup. . . . And worse than that, one and all—Jew, Turk, infidel, and heretic, as well as the orthodox—joined in pious horror at his irreverence;—the shocking way he had of jumbling religion and politics—the human and the divine—the theories of the pulpit with the facts of the exchange. . . . The very atheists, who laughed at him for believing in a God, agreed that that, at least, was inconsistent with the dignity of the God—who did not exist. . . . It was Syncretism . . . Pantheism. . . .

'Very well, friends,' quoth Lancelot to himself, in bitter rage, one day, 'if you choose to be without God in the world, and to honour Him by denying

Him . . . do so! You shall have your way; and go to the place whither it seems leading you just now, at railroad pace. But I must live. . . . Well, at least, there is some old college nonsense of mine, written three years ago, when I believed, like you, that all heaven and earth was put together out of separate bits, like a child's puzzle, and that each topic ought to have its private little pigeon-hole all to itself in a man's brain, like drugs in a chemist's shop. Perhaps it will suit you, friends; perhaps it will be system-frozen, and narrow, and dogmatic, and cowardly, and godless enough for you.' . . . So he went forth with them to market; and behold! they were bought forthwith. There was verily a demand for such; . . . and in spite of the ten thousand ink-fountains which were daily pouring out similar Stygian liquors, the public thirst remained unslaked. 'Well,' thought Lancelot, 'the negro race is not the only one which is afflicted with manias for eating dirt. . . . By the bye, where is poor Luke?'

Ah! where was poor Luke? Lancelot had received from him one short and hurried note, blotted with tears, which told how he had informed his father; and how his father had refused to see him, and had forbid him the house; and how he had offered him an allowance of fifty pounds a year (it should have been five hundred, he said, if he had possessed it), which Luke's director, sensibly enough, had compelled him to accept. . . . And there the letter ended, abruptly, leaving the writer evidently in lower depths than he had either experienced already, or expected at all.

Lancelot had often pleaded for him with his father; but in vain. Not that the good man was hard-hearted: he would cry like a child about it all to Lancelot when they sat together after dinner. But he was utterly beside himself, what with grief, shame, terror, and astonishment. On the whole, the sorrow was a real comfort to him: it gave him something beside his bankruptcy to think of; and, distracted between the two different griefs, he could brood over neither. But of the two, certainly his son's conversion was the worst in his eyes. The bankruptcy was intelligible—measurable; it was something known and classified—part of the ills which flesh (or, at least, commercial flesh) is heir to. But going to Rome!—

'I can't understand it. I won't believe it. It's so foolish, you see, Lancelot—so foolish—like an ass that eats thistles! . . . There must be some reason;—there must be—something we don't know, sir! Do you think they could have promised to make him a cardinal?'

Lancelot quite agreed that there were reasons for it, that they—or, at least, the banker—did not know. . . .

'Depend upon it, they promised him something—some prince-bishopric, perhaps. Else why on earth could a man go over! It's out of the course of nature!'

Lancelot tried in vain to make him understand that a man might sacrifice everything to conscience, and actually give up all worldly weal for what he thought right. The banker turned on him with angry resignation—

'Very well—I suppose he's done right then! I suppose you'll go next! Take up a false religion, and give up everything for it! Why, then, he must be honest; and if he's honest, he's in the right; and I suppose I'd better go too!'

Lancelot argued: but in vain. The idea of disinterested sacrifice was so utterly foreign to the good man's own creed and practice, that he could but see one pair of alternatives.

'Either he is a good man, or he's a hypocrite. Either he's right, or he's gone over for some vile selfish end; and what can that be but money?'

Lancelot gently hinted that there might be other selfish ends besides pecuniary ones—saving one's soul, for instance.

'Why, if he wants to save his soul, he's right. What ought we all to do, but try to save our souls? I tell you there's some sinister reason. They've told him that they expect to convert England—I should like to see them do it!—and that he'll be made a bishop. Don't argue with me, or you'll drive me mad. I know those Jesuits!'

And as soon as he began upon the Jesuits, Lancelot prudently held his tongue. The good man had worked himself up into a perfect frenzy of terror and suspicion about them. He suspected concealed Jesuits among his footmen and his housemaids; Jesuits in his counting-house, Jesuits in his duns....

'Hang it, sir! how do I know that there ain't a Jesuit listening to us now behind the curtain?'

'I'll go and look,' quoth Lancelot, and suited the action to the word.

'Well, if there ain't there might be. They're everywhere, I tell you. That vicar of Whitford was a Jesuit. I was sure of it all along; but the man seemed so pious; and certainly he did my poor dear boy a deal of good. But he ruined you, you know. And I'm convinced—no, don't contradict me; I tell you, I won't stand it—I'm convinced that this whole mess of mine is a plot of those rascals;—I'm as certain of it as if they'd told me!'

'For what end?'

'How the deuce can I tell? Am I a Jesuit, to understand their sneaking, underhand—pah! I'm sick of life! Nothing but rogues wherever one turns!'

And then Lancelot used to try to persuade him to take poor Luke back again. But vague terror had steeled his heart.

'What! Why, he'd convert us all! He'd convert his sisters! He'd bring his priests in here, or his nuns disguised as ladies' maids, and we should all go over, every one of us, like a set of nine-pins!'

'You seem to think Protestantism a rather shaky cause, if it is so easy to be upset.'

'Sir! Protestantism is the cause of England and Christianity, and civilisation, and freedom, and common sense, sir! and that's the very reason why it's so easy to pervert men from it; and the very reason why it's a lost cause, and popery, and Antichrist, and the gates of hell are coming in like a flood to prevail against it!'

'Well,' thought Lancelot, 'that is the very strangest reason for it's being a lost cause! Perhaps if my poor uncle believed it really to be the cause of God Himself, he would not be in such extreme fear for it, or fancy it required such a hotbed and greenhouse culture. . . . Really, if his sisters were little girls of ten years old, who looked up to him as an oracle, there would be some reason in it. . . . But those tall, ball-going, flirting, self-satisfied cousins of mine—who would have been glad enough, either of them, two months ago, to snap up me, infidelity, bad character, and all, as a charming rich young *roué*—if they have not learnt enough Protestantism in the last five-and-twenty years to take care of themselves, Protestantism must have very few allurements, or else be very badly carried out in practice by those who talk loudest in favour of it. . . . I heard them praising O'Blareaway's "ministry," by the bye, the other day. So he is up in town at last—at the summit of his ambition. Well, he may suit them. I wonder how many young creatures like Argemone and Luke he would keep from Popery!'

But there was no use arguing with a man in such a state of mind; and gradually Lancelot gave it up, in hopes that time would bring the good man to his sane wits again, and that a father's feelings would prove themselves stronger, because more divine, than a so-called Protestant's fears, though that would have been, in the banker's eyes, and in the Jesuit's also—so do extremes meet—the very reason for expecting them to be the weaker; for it is the rule with all bigots, that the right cause is always a lost cause, and therefore requires—God's weapons of love, truth, and reason being well known to be too weak—to be defended, if it is to be saved, with the devil's weapons of bad logic, spite, and calumny.

At last, in despair of obtaining tidings of his cousin by any other method, Lancelot made up his mind to apply to a certain remarkable man, whose 'conversion' had preceded Luke's about a year, and had, indeed, mainly caused it.

He went, . . . and was not disappointed. With the most winning courtesy and sweetness, his story and his request were patiently listened to.

'The outcome of your speech, then, my dear sir, as I apprehend it, is a request to me to send back the fugitive lamb into the jaws of the well-meaning, but still lupine wolf?'

This was spoken with so sweet and arch a smile, that it was impossible to be angry.

'On my honour, I have no wish to convert him. All I want is to have human speech of him—to hear from his own lips that he is content. Whither should I convert him? Not to my own platform—for I am nowhere. Not to that which he has left, . . . for if he could have found standing ground there, he would not have gone elsewhere for rest.'

'Therefore they went out from you, because they were not of you,' said the 'Father,' half aside.

'Most true, sir. I have felt long that argument was bootless with those whose root-ideas of Deity, man, earth, and heaven, were as utterly different from my own, as if we had been created by two different beings.'

'Do you include in that catalogue those ideas of truth, love, and justice, which are Deity itself? Have you no common ground in them?'

'You are an elder and a better man than I. . . . It would be insolent in me to answer that question, except in one way, . . . and—'

'In that you cannot answer it. Be it so. . . . You shall see your cousin. You may make what efforts you will for his re-conversion. The Catholic Church,' continued he, with one of his arch, deep-meaning smiles, 'is not, like popular Protestantism, driven into shrieking terror at the approach of a foe. She has too much faith in herself, and in Him who gives to her the power of truth, to expect every gay meadow to allure away her lambs from the fold.'

'I assure you that your gallant permission is unnecessary. I am beginning, at least, to believe that there is a Father in Heaven who educates His children; and I have no wish to interfere with His methods. Let my cousin go his way . . . he will learn something which he wanted, I doubt not, on his present path, even as I shall on mine. "Se tu segui la tua stella" is my motto. . . . Let it be his too, wherever the star may guide him. If it be a will-o'-the-wisp, and lead to the morass, he will only learn how to avoid morasses better for the future.'

'Ave Maris stella! It is the star of Bethlehem which he follows . . . the star of Mary, immaculate, all-loving!' . . . And he bowed his head reverently. 'Would that you, too, would submit yourself to that guidance! . . . You, too, would seem to want some loving heart whereon to rest.' . . .

Lancelot sighed. 'I am not a child, but a man; I want not a mother to pet, but a man to rule me.'

Slowly his companion raised his thin hand, and pointed to the crucifix, which stood at the other end of the apartment.

'Behold him!' and he bowed his head once more . . . and Lancelot, he knew not why, did the same . . . and yet in an instant he threw his head up proudly, and answered with George Fox's old reply to the Puritans,—

'I want a live Christ, not a dead one. . . . That is noble . . . beautiful . . . it may be true. . . . But it has no message for me.'

'He died for you.'

'I care for the world, and not myself.'

'He died for the world.'

'And has deserted it, as folks say now, and become—an absentee, performing His work by deputies. . . . Do not start; the blasphemy is not mine, but those who preach it. No wonder that the owners of the soil think it no shame to desert their estates, when preachers tell them that He to whom they say, all power is given in heaven and earth, has deserted His.'

'What would you have, my dear sir?' asked the father.

'What the Jews had. A king of my nation, and of the hearts of my nation, who would teach soldiers, artists, craftsmen, statesmen, poets, priests, if priests there must be. I want a human lord, who understands me and the millions round me, pities us, teaches us, orders our history, civilisation, development for us. I come to you, full of manhood, and you send me to a woman. I go to the Protestants, full of desires to right the world—and they begin to talk of the next life, and give up this as lost!'

A quiet smile lighted up the thin wan face, full of unfathomable thoughts; and he replied, again half to himself,—

'Am I God, to kill or to make alive, that thou sendest to me to recover a man of his leprosy? Farewell. You shall see your cousin here at noon tomorrow. You will not refuse my blessing, or my prayers, even though they be offered to a mother?'

'I will refuse nothing in the form of human love.' And the father blessed him fervently, and he went out. . . .

'What a man!' said he to himself, 'or rather the wreck of what a man! Oh, for such a heart, with the thews and sinews of a truly English brain!'

Next day he met Luke in that room. Their talk was short and sad. Luke was on the point of entering an order devoted especially to the worship of the Blessed Virgin.

'My father has cast me out . . . I must go to her feet. She will have mercy, though man has none.'

'But why enter the order? Why take an irrevocable step?'

'Because it is irrevocable; because I shall enter an utterly new life, in which old things shall pass away, and all things become new, and I shall forget the very names of Parent, Englishman, Citizen,—the very existence of that strange Babel of man's building, whose roar and moan oppress me every time I walk the street. Oh, for solitude, meditation, penance! Oh, to make up by bitter self-punishment my ingratitude to her who has been leading me unseen, for years, home to her bosom!—The all-prevailing mother, daughter of Gabriel, spouse of Deity, flower of the earth, whom I have so long despised! Oh, to follow the example of the blessed Mary of Oignies, who every day inflicted on her most holy person eleven hundred stripes in honour of that all-perfect maiden!'

'Such an honour, I could have thought, would have pleased better Kali, the murder-goddess of the Thugs,' thought Lancelot to himself; but he had not the heart to say it, and he only replied,—

'So torture propitiates the Virgin? That explains the strange story I read lately, of her having appeared in the Cevennes, and informed the peasantry that she had sent the potato disease on account of their neglecting her shrines; that unless they repented, she would next year destroy their cattle; and the third year, themselves.'

'Why not?' asked poor Luke.

'Why not, indeed? If God is to be capricious, proud, revengeful, why not the Son of God? And if the Son of God, why not His mother?'

'You judge spiritual feelings by the carnal test of the understanding; your Protestant horror of asceticism lies at the root of all you say. How can you comprehend the self-satisfaction, the absolute delight, of self-punishment?'

'So far from it, I have always had an infinite respect for asceticism, as a noble and manful thing—the only manful thing to my eyes left in popery;

and fast dying out of that under Jesuit influence. You recollect the quarrel between the Tablet and the Jesuits, over Faber's unlucky honesty about St. Rose of Lima? . . . But, really, as long as you honour asceticism as a means of appeasing the angry deities, I shall prefer to St. Dominic's cuirass or St. Hedwiga's chilblains, John Mytton's two hours' crawl on the ice in his shirt, after a flock of wild ducks. They both endured like heroes; but the former for a selfish, if not a blasphemous end; the latter, as a man should, to test and strengthen his own powers of endurance. . . . There, I will say no more. Go your way, in God's name. There must be lessons to be learnt in all strong and self-restraining action. . . . So you will learn something from the scourge and the hair-shirt. We must all take the bitter medicine of suffering, I suppose.'

'And, therefore, I am the wiser, in forcing the draught on myself.'

'Provided it be the right draught, and do not require another and still bitterer one to expel the effects of the poison. I have no faith in people's doctoring themselves, either physically or spiritually.'

'I am not my own physician; I follow the rules of an infallible Church, and the examples of her canonised saints.'

'Well . . . perhaps they may have known what was best for themselves. . . . But as for you and me here, in the year 1849. . . . However, we shall argue on for ever. Forgive me if I have offended you.'

'I am not offended. The Catholic Church has always been a persecuted one.'

'Then walk with me a little way, and I will persecute you no more.'

'Where are you going?'

'To . . . To—' Lancelot had not the heart to say whither.

'To my father's! Ah! what a son I would have been to him now, in his extreme need! . . . And he will not let me! Lancelot, is it impossible to move him? I do not want to go home again . . . to live there . . . I could not face that, though I longed but this moment to do it. I cannot face the self-satisfied, pitying looks . . . the everlasting suspicion that they suspect me to be speaking untruths, or proselytising in secret. . . . Cruel and unjust!'

Lancelot thought of a certain letter of Luke's . . . but who was he, to break the bruised reed?

'No; I will not see him. Better thus; better vanish, and be known only according to the spirit by the spirits of saints and confessors, and their successors upon earth. No! I will die, and give no sign.'

'I must see somewhat more of you, indeed.'

'I will meet you here, then, two hours hence. Near that house—even along the way which leads to it—I cannot go. It would be too painful: too painful to think that you were walking towards it,—the old house where I was born and bred . . . and I shut out,—even though it be for the sake of the kingdom of heaven!'

'Or for the sake of your own share therein, my poor cousin!' thought Lancelot to himself, 'which is a very different matter.'

'Whither, after you have been—?' Luke could not get out the word home.

'To Claude Mellot's.'

'I will walk part of the way thither with you. But he is a very bad companion for you.'

'I can't help that. I cannot live; and I am going to turn painter. It is not the road in which to find a fortune; but still, the very sign-painters live somehow, I suppose. I am going this very afternoon to Claude Mellot, and enlist. I sold the last of my treasured MSS. to a fifth-rate magazine this morning, for what it would fetch. It has been like eating one's own children—but, at least, they have fed me. So now "to fresh fields and pastures new."'

CHAPTER XV
DEUS E MACHINÂ

When Lancelot reached the banker's a letter was put into his hand; it bore the Whitford postmark, and Mrs. Lavington's handwriting. He tore it open; it contained a letter from Argemone, which, it is needless to say, he read before her mother's:—

'My beloved! my husband!—Yes—though you may fancy me fickle and proud—I will call you so to the last; for were I fickle, I could have saved myself the agony of writing this; and as for pride, oh! how that darling vice has been crushed out of me! I have rolled at my mother's feet with bitter tears, and vain entreaties—and been refused; and yet I have obeyed her after all. We must write to each other no more. This one last letter must explain the forced silence which has been driving me mad with fears that you would suspect me. And now you may call me weak; but it is your love which has made me strong to do this—which has taught me to see with new intensity my duty, not only to you, but to every human being—to my parents. By this self-sacrifice alone can I atone to them for all my past undutifulness. Let me, then, thus be worthy of you. Hope that by this submission we may win even her to change. How calmly I write! but it is only my hand that is calm. As for my heart, read Tennyson's Fatima, and then know how I feel towards you! Yes, I love you—madly, the world would say. I seem to understand now how women have died of love. Ay, that indeed would be blessed; for then my spirit would seek out yours, and hover over it for ever! Farewell, beloved! and let me hear of you through your deeds. A feeling at my heart, which should not be, although it is, a sad one, tells me that we shall meet soon—soon.'

Stupefied and sickened, Lancelot turned carelessly to Mrs. Lavington's cover, whose blameless respectability thus uttered itself:—

'I cannot deceive you or myself by saying I regret that providential circumstances should have been permitted to break off a connection which I always felt to be most unsuitable; and I rejoice that the intercourse my dear child has had with you has not so far undermined her principles as to prevent her yielding the most filial obedience to my wishes on the point of her future correspondence with you. Hoping that all that has occurred will be truly blessed to you, and lead your thoughts to another world, and to a true concern for the safety of your immortal soul,

'I remain, yours truly,

'C. LAVINGTON.'

'Another world!' said Lancelot to himself. 'It is most merciful of you, certainly, my dear madame, to put one in mind of the existence of another world, while such as you have their own way in this one!' and thrusting the latter epistle into the fire, he tried to collect his thoughts.

What had he lost? The oftener he asked himself, the less he found to unman him. Argemone's letters were so new a want, that the craving for them was not yet established. His intense imagination, resting on the delicious certainty of her faith, seemed ready to fill the silence with bright hopes and noble purposes. She herself had said that he would see her soon. But yet—but yet—why did that allusion to death strike chilly through him? They were but words,—a melancholy fancy, such as women love at times to play with. He would toss it from him. At least here was another reason for bestirring himself at once to win fame in the noble profession he had chosen.

And yet his brain reeled as he went upstairs to his uncle's private room.

There, however, he found a person closeted with the banker, whose remarkable appearance drove everything else out of his mind. He was a huge, shaggy, toil-worn man, the deep melancholy earnestness of whose rugged features reminded him almost ludicrously of one of Land-seer's bloodhounds. But withal there was a tenderness—a genial, though covert humour playing about his massive features, which awakened in Lancelot at first sight a fantastic longing to open his whole heart to him. He was dressed like a foreigner, but spoke English with perfect fluency. The banker sat listening, quite crestfallen, beneath his intense and melancholy gaze, in which, nevertheless, there twinkled some rays of kindly sympathy.

'It was all those foreign railways,' said Mr. Smith pensively.

'And it serves you quite right,' answered the stranger. 'Did I not warn you of the folly and sin of sinking capital in foreign countries while English land was crying out for tillage, and English poor for employment?'

'My dear friend' (in a deprecatory tone), 'it was the best possible investment I could make.'

'And pray, who told you that you were sent into the world to make investments?'

'But—'

'But me no buts, or I won't stir a finger towards helping you. What are you going to do with this money if I procure it for you?'

'Work till I can pay back that poor fellow's fortune,' said the banker, earnestly pointing to Lancelot. 'And if I could clear my conscience of that, I would not care if I starved myself, hardly if my own children did.'

'Spoken like a man!' answered the stranger; 'work for that and I'll help you. Be a new man, once and for all, my friend. Don't even make this younker your first object. Say to yourself, not "I will invest this money where it shall pay me most, but I will invest it where it shall give most employment to English hands, and produce most manufactures for English bodies." In short, seek first the kingdom of God and His justice with this money of yours, and see if all other things, profits and suchlike included, are not added unto you.'

'And you are certain you can obtain the money?'

'My good friend the Begum of the Cannibal Islands has more than she knows what to do with; and she owes me a good turn, you know.'

'What are you jesting about now?'

'Did I never tell you? The new king of the Cannibal Islands, just like your European ones, ran away, and would neither govern himself nor let any one else govern; so one morning his ministers, getting impatient, ate him, and then asked my advice. I recommended them to put his mother on the throne, who, being old and tough, would run less danger; and since then everything has gone on smoothly as anywhere else.'

'Are you mad?' thought Lancelot to himself, as he stared at the speaker's matter-of-fact face.

'No, I am not mad, my young friend,' quoth he, facing right round upon him, as if he had divined his thoughts.

'I—I beg your pardon, I did not speak,' stammered Lancelot, abashed at a pair of eyes which could have looked down the boldest mesmerist in three seconds.

'I am perfectly well aware that you did not. I must have some talk with you: I've heard a good deal about you. You wrote those articles in the --- Review about George Sand, did you not?'

'I did.'

'Well, there was a great deal of noble feeling in them, and a great deal of abominable nonsense. You seem to be very anxious to reform society?'

'I am.'

'Don't you think you had better begin by reforming yourself?'

'Really, sir,' answered Lancelot, 'I am too old for that worn-out quibble. The root of all my sins has been selfishness and sloth. Am I to cure them by becoming still more selfish and slothful? What part of myself can I reform except my actions? and the very sin of my actions has been, as I take it, that I've been doing nothing to reform others; never fighting against the world, the flesh, and the devil, as your Prayer-book has it.'

'*My* Prayer-book?' answered the stranger, with a quaint smile.

'Upon my word, Lancelot,' interposed the banker, with a frightened look, 'you must not get into an argument: you must be more respectful: you don't know to whom you are speaking.'

'And I don't much care,' answered he. 'Life is really too grim earnest in these days to stand on ceremony. I am sick of blind leaders of the blind, of respectable preachers to the respectable, who drawl out second-hand trivialities, which they neither practise nor wish to see practised. I've had enough all my life of Scribes and Pharisees in white cravats, laying on man heavy burdens, and grievous to be borne, and then not touching them themselves with one of their fingers.'

'Silence, sir!' roared the banker, while the stranger threw himself into a chair, and burst into a storm of laughter.

'Upon my word, friend Mammon, here's another of Hans Andersen's ugly ducks!'

'I really do not mean to be rude,' said Lancelot, recollecting himself, 'but I am nearly desperate. If your heart is in the right place, you will understand me! if not, the less we talk to each other the better.'

'Most true,' answered the stranger; 'and I do understand you; and if, as I hope, we see more of each other henceforth, we will see if we cannot solve one or two of these problems between us.'

At this moment Lancelot was summoned downstairs, and found, to his great pleasure, Tregarva waiting for him. That worthy personage bowed to Lancelot reverently and distantly.

'I am quite ashamed to intrude myself upon you, sir, but I could not rest without coming to ask whether you have had any news.'—He broke down at this point in the sentence, but Lancelot understood him.

'I have no news,' he said. 'But what do you mean by standing off in that way, as if we were not old and fast friends? Remember, I am as poor as you are now; you may look me in the face and call me your equal, if you will, or your inferior; I shall not deny it.'

'Pardon me, sir,' answered Tregarva; 'but I never felt what a real substantial thing rank is, as I have since this sad misfortune of yours.'

'And I have never till now found out its worthlessness.'

'You're wrong, sir, you are wrong; look at the difference between yourself and me. When you've lost all you have, and seven times more, you're still a gentleman. No man can take that from you. You may look the proudest duchess in the land in the face, and claim her as your equal; while I, sir,—I don't mean, though, to talk of myself—but suppose that you had loved a pious and a beautiful lady, and among all your worship of her, and your awe of her, had felt that you were worthy of her, that you could become her comforter, and her pride, and her joy, if it wasn't for that accursed gulf that men had put between you, that you were no gentleman; that you didn't know how to walk, and how to pronounce, and when to speak, and when to be silent, not even how to handle your own knife and fork without disgusting her, or how to keep your own body clean and sweet—Ah, sir, I see it now as I never did before, what a wall all these little defects build up round a poor man; how he longs and struggles to show himself as he is at heart, and cannot, till he feels sometimes as if he was enchanted, pent up, like folks in fairy tales, in the body of some dumb beast. But, sir,' he went on, with a concentrated bitterness which Lancelot had never seen in him before, 'just because this gulf which rank makes is such a deep one, therefore it looks to me all the more devilish; not that I want to pull down any man to my level; I despise my own level too much; I want to rise; I want those like me to rise with me. Let the rich be as rich as they will.—I, and those like me, covet not money, but manners. Why should not the workman be a gentleman, and a workman still? Why are they to be shut out from all that is beautiful, and delicate, and winning, and stately?'

'Now perhaps,' said Lancelot, 'you begin to understand what I was driving at on that night of the revel?'

'It has come home to me lately, sir, bitterly enough. If you knew what had gone on in me this last fortnight, you would know that I had cause to curse the state of things which brings a man up a savage against his will, and cuts him off, as if he were an ape or a monster, from those for whom the same Lord died, and on whom the same Spirit rests. Is that God's will, sir? No, it is the devil's will. "Those whom God hath joined, let no man put asunder."'

Lancelot coloured, for he remembered with how much less reason he had been lately invoking in his own cause those very words. He was at a loss for an answer; but seeing, to his relief, that Tregarva had returned to his usual impassive calm, he forced him to sit down, and began questioning him as to his own prospects and employment.

About them Tregarva seemed hopeful enough. He had found out a Wesleyan minister in town who knew him, and had, by his means, after assisting for a week or two in the London City Mission, got some similar appointment in a large manufacturing town. Of the state of things he spoke more sadly than ever. 'The rich cannot guess, sir, how high ill-feeling is rising in these days. It's not only those who are outwardly poorest who long for change; the middling people, sir, the small town shopkeepers especially, are nearly past all patience. One of the City Mission assured me that he has been watching them these several years past, and that nothing could beat their fortitude and industry, and their determination to stand peaceably by law and order; but yet, this last year or two, things are growing too bad to bear. Do what they will, they cannot get their bread; and when a man cannot get that, sir—'

'But what do you think is the reason of it?'

'How should I tell, sir? But if I had to say, I should say this—just what they say themselves—that there are too many of them. Go where you will, in town or country, you'll find half-a-dozen shops struggling for a custom that would only keep up one, and so they're forced to undersell one another. And when they've got down prices all they can by fair means, they're forced to get them down lower by foul—to sand the sugar, and sloe-leave the tea, and put—Satan only that prompts 'em knows what—into the bread; and then they don't thrive—they can't thrive; God's curse must be on them. They begin by trying to oust each other, and eat each other up; and while they're eating up their neighbours, their neighbours eat up them; and so they all come to ruin together.'

'Why, you talk like Mr. Mill himself, Tregarva; you ought to have been a political economist, and not a City missionary. By the bye, I don't like that profession for you.'

'It's the Lord's work, sir. It's the very sending to the Gentiles that the Lord promised me.'

'I don't doubt it, Paul; but you are meant for other things, if not better. There are plenty of smaller men than you to do that work. Do you think that God would have given you that strength, that brain, to waste on a work which could be done without them? Those limbs would certainly be good capital for you, if you turned a live model at the Academy. Perhaps you'd better be mine; but you can't even be that if you go to Manchester.'

The giant looked hopelessly down at his huge limbs. 'Well! God only knows what use they are of just now. But as for the brains, sir—in much learning is much sorrow. One had much better work than read, I find. If I read much more about what men might be, and are not, and what English soil might be, and is not, I shall go mad. And that puts me in mind of one thing I came here for, though, like a poor rude country fellow as I am, I clean forgot it a thinking of—Look here, sir; you've given me a sight of books in my time, and God bless you for it. But now I hear that—that you are determined to be a poor man like us; and that you shan't be, while Paul Tregarva has ought of yours. So I've just brought all the books back, and there they lie in the hall; and may God reward you for the loan of them to his poor child! And so, sir, farewell;' and he rose to go.

'No, Paul; the books and you shall never part.'

'And I say, sir, the books and you shall never part.'

'Then we two can never part'—and a sudden impulse flashed over him—'and we will not part, Paul! The only man whom I utterly love, and trust, and respect on the face of God's earth, is you; and I cannot lose sight of you. If we are to earn our bread, let us earn it together; if we are to endure poverty, and sorrow, and struggle to find out the way of bettering these wretched millions round us, let us learn our lesson together, and help each other to spell it out.'

'Do you mean what you say?' asked Paul slowly.

'I do.'

'Then I say what you say. Where thou goest, I will go; and where thou lodgest, I will lodge. Come what will, I will be your servant, for good luck or bad, for ever.'

'My equal, Paul, not my servant.'

'I know my place, sir. When I am as learned and as well-bred as you, I shall not refuse to call myself your equal; and the sooner that day comes, the better I shall be pleased. Till then I am your friend and your brother; but I am your scholar too, and I shall not set up myself against my master.'

'I have learnt more of you, Paul, than ever you have learnt of me. But be it as you will; only whatever you may call yourself, we must eat at the same table, live in the same room, and share alike all this world's good things—or we shall have no right to share together this world's bad things. If that is your bargain, there is my hand on it.'

'Amen!' quoth Tregarva; and the two young men joined hands in that sacred bond—now growing rarer and rarer year by year—the utter friendship of two equal manful hearts.

'And now, sir, I have promised—and you would have me keep my promise—to go and work for the City Mission in Manchester—at least, for the next month, till a young man's place who has just left, is filled up. Will you let me go for that time? and then, if you hold your present mind, we will join home and fortunes thenceforth, and go wherever the Lord shall send us. There's work enough of His waiting to be done. I don't doubt but if we are willing and able, He will set us about the thing we're meant for.'

As Lancelot opened the door for him, he lingered on the steps, and grasping his hand, said, in a low, earnest voice: 'The Lord be with you, sir. Be sure that He has mighty things in store for you, or He would not have brought you so low in the days of your youth.'

'And so,' as John Bunyan has it, 'he went on his way;' and Lancelot saw him no more till—but I must not outrun the order of time.

After all, this visit came to Lancelot timely. It had roused him to hope, and turned off his feelings from the startling news he had just heard. He stepped along arm in arm with Luke, cheerful, and fate-defiant, and as he thought of Tregarva's complaints,—

'The beautiful?' he said to himself, 'they shall have it! At least they shall be awakened to feel their need of it, their right to it. What a high destiny, to be the artist of the people! to devote one's powers of painting, not to mimicking obsolete legends, Pagan or Popish, but to representing to the working men of England the triumphs of the Past and the yet greater triumphs of the Future!'

Luke began at once questioning him about his father.

'And is he contrite and humbled? Does he see that he has sinned?'

'In what?'

'It is not for us to judge; but surely it must have been some sin or other of his which has drawn down such a sore judgment on him.'

Lancelot smiled; but Luke went on, not perceiving him.

'Ah! we cannot find out for him. Nor has he, alas! as a Protestant, much likelihood of finding out for himself. In our holy church he would have been compelled to discriminate his faults by methodic self-examination, and lay them one by one before his priest for advice and pardon, and so start a new and free man once more.'

'Do you think,' asked Lancelot with a smile, 'that he who will not confess his faults either to God or to himself, would confess them to man? And would his priest honestly tell him what he really wants to know? which sin of his has called down this so-called judgment? It would be imputed, I suppose, to some vague generality, to inattention to religious duties, to idolatry of the world, and so forth. But a Romish priest would be the last person, I should think, who could tell him fairly, in the present case, the cause of his affliction; and I question whether he would give a patient hearing to any one who told it him.'

'How so? Though, indeed, I have remarked that people are perfectly willing to be told they are miserable sinners, and to confess themselves such, in a general way; but if the preacher once begins to specify, to fix on any particular act or habit, he is accused of personality or uncharitableness; his hearers are ready to confess guilty to any sin but the very one with which he charges them. But, surely, this is just what I am urging against you Protestants—just what the Catholic use of confession obviates.'

'Attempts to do so, you mean!' answered Lancelot. 'But what if your religion preaches formally that which only remains in our religion as a fast-dying superstition?—That those judgments of God, as you call them, are not judgments at all in any fair use of the word, but capricious acts of punishment on the part of Heaven, which have no more reference to the fault which provokes them, than if you cut off a man's finger because he made a bad use of his tongue. That is part, but only a part, of what I meant just now, by saying that people represent God as capricious, proud, revengeful.'

'But do not Protestants themselves confess that our sins provoke God's anger?'

'Your common creed, when it talks rightly of God as one "who has no passions," ought to make you speak more reverently of the possibility of any act of ours disturbing the everlasting equanimity of the absolute Love. Why will men so often impute to God the miseries which they bring upon themselves?'

'Because, I suppose, their pride makes them more willing to confess themselves sinners than fools.'

'Right, my friend; they will not remember that it is of "their pleasant vices that God makes whips to scourge them." Oh, I at least have felt the deep wisdom of that saying of Wilhelm Meister's harper, that it is

"Voices from the depth of *Nature* borne
Which woe upon the guilty head proclaim."

Of nature—of those eternal laws of hers which we daily break. Yes! it is not because God's temper changes, but because God's universe is unchangeable, that such as I, such as your poor father, having sown the wind, must reap the whirlwind. I have fed my self-esteem with luxuries and not with virtue, and, losing them, have nothing left. He has sold himself to a system which is its own punishment. And yet the last place in which he will look for the cause of his misery is in that very money-mongering to which he now clings as frantically as ever. But so it is throughout the world. Only look down over that bridge-parapet, at that huge black-mouthed sewer, vomiting its pestilential riches across the mud. There it runs, and will run, hurrying to the sea vast stores of wealth, elaborated by Nature's chemistry into the ready materials of food; which proclaim, too, by their own foul smell, God's will that they should be buried out of sight in the fruitful all-regenerating grave of earth: there it runs, turning them all into the seeds of pestilence, filth, and drunkenness.—And then, when it obeys the laws which we despise, and the pestilence is come at last, men will pray against it, and confess it to be "a judgment for their sins;" but if you ask *what* sin, people will talk about "les voiles d'airain," as Fourier says, and tell you that it is presumptuous to pry into God's secret counsels, unless, perhaps, some fanatic should inform you that the cholera has been drawn down on the poor by the endowment of Maynooth by the rich.'

'It is most fearful, indeed, to think that these diseases should be confined to the poor—that a man should be exposed to cholera, typhus, and a host of attendant diseases, simply because he is born into the world an artisan; while the rich, by the mere fact of money, are exempt from such curses, except when they come in contact with those whom they call on Sunday "their brethren," and on week days the "masses."'

'Thank Heaven that you do see that,—that in a country calling itself civilised and Christian, pestilence should be the peculiar heritage of the poor! It is past all comment.'

'And yet are not these pestilences a judgment, even on them, for their dirt and profligacy?'

'And how should they be clean without water? And how can you wonder if their appetites, sickened with filth and self-disgust, crave after the gin-shop for temporary strength, and then for temporary forgetfulness? Every London doctor knows that I speak the truth; would that every London preacher would tell that truth from his pulpit!'

'Then would you too say, that God punishes one class for the sins of another?'

'Some would say,' answered Lancelot, half aside, 'that He may be punishing them for not demanding their *right* to live like human beings, to all those social circumstances which shall not make their children's life one long disease. But are not these pestilences a judgment on the rich, too, in the truest sense of the word? Are they not the broad, unmistakable seal to God's opinion of a state of society which confesses its economic relations to be so utterly rotten and confused, that it actually cannot afford to save yearly millions of pounds' worth of the materials of food, not to mention thousands of human lives? Is not every man who allows such things hastening the ruin of the society in which he lives, by helping to foster the indignation and fury of its victims? Look at that group of stunted, haggard artisans, who are passing us. What if one day they should call to account the landlords whose coveteousness and ignorance make their dwellings hells on earth?'

By this time they had reached the artist's house.

Luke refused to enter.... 'He had done with this world, and the painters of this world.' ... And with a tearful last farewell, he turned away up the street, leaving Lancelot to gaze at his slow, painful steps, and abject, earth-fixed mien.

'Ah!' thought Lancelot, 'here is the end of *your* anthropology! At first, your ideal man is an angel. But your angel is merely an unsexed woman; and so you are forced to go back to the humanity after all—but to a woman, not a man? And this, in the nineteenth century, when men are telling us that the poetic and enthusiastic have become impossible, and that the only possible state of the world henceforward will be a universal good-humoured hive, of the Franklin-Benthamite religion ... a vast prosaic Cockaigne of steam mills for grinding sausages—for those who can get at them. And all the while, in spite of all Manchester schools, and high and dry orthodox schools, here are the strangest phantasms, new and old, sane and insane, starting up suddenly into live practical power, to give their prosaic theories the lie—Popish conversions, Mormonisms, Mesmerisms, Californias, Continental revolutions, Paris days of June ... Ye hypocrites! ye can discern the face of the sky, and yet ye cannot discern the signs of this time!'

He was ushered upstairs to the door of his studio, at which he knocked, and was answered by a loud 'Come in.' Lancelot heard a rustle as he entered, and caught sight of a most charming little white foot retreating hastily through the folding doors into the inner room.

The artist, who was seated at his easel, held up his brush as a signal of silence, and did not even raise his eyes till he had finished the touches on which he was engaged.

'And now—what do I see!—the last man I should have expected! I thought you were far down in the country. And what brings you to me with such serious and business-like looks?'

'I am a penniless youth—'

'What?'

'Ruined to my last shilling, and I want to turn artist.'

'Oh, ye gracious powers! Come to my arms, brother at last with me in the holy order of those who must work or starve. Long have I wept in secret over the pernicious fulness of your purse!'

'Dry your tears, then, now,' said Lancelot, 'for I neither have ten pounds in the world, nor intend to have till I can earn them.'

'Artist!' ran on Mellot; 'ah! you shall be an artist, indeed! You shall stay with me and become the English Michael Angelo; or, if you are fool enough, go to Rome, and utterly eclipse Overbeck, and throw Schadow for ever into the shade.'

'I fine you a supper,' said Lancelot, 'for that execrable attempt at a pun.'

'Agreed! Here, Sabina, send to Covent Garden for huge nosegays, and get out the best bottle of Burgundy. We will pass an evening worthy of Horace, and with garlands and libations honour the muse of painting.'

'Luxurious dog!' said Lancelot, 'with all your cant about poverty.'

As he spoke, the folding doors opened, and an exquisite little brunette danced in from the inner room, in which, by the bye, had been going on all the while a suspicious rustling, as of garments hastily arranged. She was dressed gracefully in a loose French morning-gown, down which Lancelot's eye glanced towards the little foot, which, however, was now hidden in a tiny velvet slipper. The artist's wife was a real beauty, though without a single perfect feature, except a most delicious little mouth, a skin like velvet, and clear brown eyes, from which beamed earnest simplicity and arch good humour. She darted forward to her husband's friend, while her rippling brown hair, fantastically arranged, fluttered about her neck, and seizing Lancelot's hands successively in both of hers, broke out in an accent prettily tinged with French,—

'Charming!—delightful! And so you are really going to turn painter! And I have longed so to be introduced to you! Claude has been raving about you these two years; you already seem to me the oldest friend in the world. You must not go to Rome. We shall keep you, Mr. Lancelot; positively you must come and live with us—we shall be the happiest trio in London. I will make you so comfortable: you must let me cater for you—cook for you.'

'And be my study sometimes?' said Lancelot, smiling.

'Ah,' she said, blushing, and shaking her pretty little fist at Claude, 'that madcap! how he has betrayed me! When he is at his easel, he is so in the seventh heaven, that he sees nothing, thinks of nothing, but his own dreams.'

At this moment a heavy step sounded on the stairs, the door opened, and there entered, to Lancelot's astonishment, the stranger who had just puzzled him so much at his uncle's.

Claude rose reverentially, and came forward, but Sabina was beforehand with him, and running up to her visitor, kissed his hand again and again, almost kneeling to him.

'The dear master!' she cried; 'what a delightful surprise! we have not seen you this fortnight past, and gave you up for lost.'

'Where do you come from, my dear master?' asked Claude.

'From going to and fro in the earth, and from walking up and down in it,' answered he, smiling, and laying his finger on his lips, 'my dear pupils. And you are both well and happy?'

'Perfectly, and doubly delighted at your presence to-day, for your advice will come in a providential moment for my friend here.'

'Ah!' said the strange man, 'well met once more! So you are going to turn painter?'

He bent a severe and searching look on Lancelot.

'You have a painter's face, young man,' he said; 'go on and prosper. What branch of art do you intend to study?'

'The ancient Italian painters, as my first step.'

'Ancient? it is not four hundred years since Perugino died. But I should suppose you do not intend to ignore classic art?'

'You have divined rightly. I wish, in the study of the antique, to arrive at the primeval laws of unfallen human beauty.'

'Were Phidias and Praxiteles, then, so primeval? the world had lasted many a thousand years before their turn came. If you intend to begin at the beginning, why not go back at once to the garden of Eden, and there study the true antique?'

'If there were but any relics of it,' said Lancelot, puzzled, and laughing.

'You would find it very near you, young man, if you had but eyes to see it.'

Claude Mellot laughed significantly, and Sabina clapped her little hands.

'Yet till you take him with you, master, and show it to him, he must needs be content with the Royal Academy and the Elgin marbles.'

'But to what branch of painting, pray,' said the master to Lancelot, 'will you apply your knowledge of the antique? Will you, like this foolish fellow here' (with a kindly glance at Claude), 'fritter yourself away on Nymphs and Venuses, in which neither he nor any one else believes?'

'Historic art, as the highest,' answered Lancelot, 'is my ambition.'

'It is well to aim at the highest, but only when it is possible for us. And how can such a school exist in England now? You English must learn to understand your own history before you paint it. Rather follow in the steps of your Turners, and Landseers, and Standfields, and Creswicks, and add your contribution to the present noble school of naturalist painters. That is the niche in the temple which God has set you English to fill up just now. These men's patient, reverent faith in Nature as they see her, their knowledge that the ideal is neither to be invented nor abstracted, but found and left where God has put it, and where alone it can be represented, in actual and individual phenomena;—in these lies an honest development of the true idea of Protestantism, which is paving the way to the mesothetic art of the future.'

'Glorious!' said Sabina: 'not a single word that we poor creatures can understand!'

But our hero, who always took a virtuous delight in hearing what he could not comprehend, went on to question the orator.

'What, then, is the true idea of Protestantism?' said he.

'The universal symbolism and dignity of matter, whether in man or nature.'

'But the Puritans—?'

'Were inconsistent with themselves and with Protestantism, and therefore God would not allow them to proceed. Yet their repudiation of all art was better than the Judas-kiss which Romanism bestows on it, in the meagre eclecticism of the ancient religious schools, and of your modern Overbecks and Pugins. The only really wholesome designer of great power whom I have seen in Germany is Kaulbach; and perhaps every one would not agree with my reasons for admiring him, in this whitewashed age. But you, young sir, were meant for better things than art. Many young geniuses have an early hankering, as Goethe had, to turn painters. It seems the shortest and easiest method of embodying their conceptions in visible form; but they get wiser afterwards, when they find in themselves thoughts that cannot be laid upon the canvas. Come with me—I like striking while the iron is hot; walk with me towards my lodgings, and we will discuss this weighty matter.'

And with a gay farewell to the adoring little Sabina, he passed an iron arm through Lancelot's, and marched him down into the street.

Lancelot was surprised and almost nettled at the sudden influence which he found this quaint personage was exerting over him. But he had, of late, tasted the high delight of feeling himself under the guidance of a superior mind, and longed to enjoy it once more. Perhaps they were reminiscences of this kind which stirred in him the strange fancy of a connection, almost of a likeness, between his new acquaintance and Argemone. He asked, humbly enough, why Art was to be a forbidden path to him?

'Besides you are an Englishman, and a man of uncommon talent, unless your physiognomy belies you; and one, too, for whom God has strange things in store, or He would not have so suddenly and strangely overthrown you.'

Lancelot started. He remembered that Tregarva had said just the same thing to him that very morning, and the (to him) strange coincidence sank deep into his heart.

'You must be a politician,' the stranger went on. 'You are bound to it as your birthright. It has been England's privilege hitherto to solve all political questions as they arise for the rest of the world; it is her duty now. Here, or nowhere, must the solution be attempted of those social problems which are convulsing more and more all Christendom. She cannot afford to waste brains like yours, while in thousands of reeking alleys, such as that one opposite us, heathens and savages are demanding the rights of citizenship. Whether they be right or wrong, is what you, and such as you, have to find out at this day.'

Silent and thoughtful, Lancelot walked on by his side.

'What is become of your friend Tregarva? I met him this morning after he parted from you, and had some talk with him. I was sorely minded to enlist him. Perhaps I shall; in the meantime, I shall busy myself with you.'

'In what way,' asked Lancelot, 'most strange sir, of whose name, much less of whose occupation, I can gain no tidings.'

'My name for the time being is Barnakill. And as for business, as it is your English fashion to call new things obstinately by old names, careless whether they apply or not, you may consider me as a recruiting-sergeant; which trade, indeed, I follow, though I am no more like the popular red-coated ones than your present "glorious constitution" is like William the Third's, or Overbeck's high art like Fra Angelico's. Farewell! When I want you, which will be most likely when you want me, I shall find you again.'

The evening was passed, as Claude had promised, in a truly Horatian manner. Sabina was most piquante, and Claude interspersed his genial and enthusiastic eloquence with various wise saws of 'the prophet.'

'But why on earth,' quoth Lancelot, at last, 'do you call him a prophet?'

'Because he is one; it's his business, his calling. He gets his living thereby, as the showman did by his elephant.'

'But what does he foretell?'

'Oh, son of the earth! And you went to Cambridge—are reported to have gone in for the thing, or phantom, called the tripos, and taken a first class! . . . Did you ever look out the word "prophetes" in Liddell and Scott?'

'Why, what do you know about Liddell and Scott?'

'Nothing, thank goodness; I never had time to waste over the crooked letters. But I have heard say that prophetes means, not a foreteller, but an out-teller—one who declares the will of a deity, and interprets his oracles. Is it not so?'

'Undeniably.'

'And that he became a foreteller among heathens at least—as I consider, among all peoples whatsoever—because knowing the real bearing of what had happened, and what was happening, he could discern the signs of the times, and so had what the world calls a shrewd guess—what I, like a Pantheist as I am denominated, should call a divine and inspired foresight—of what was going to happen.'

'A new notion, and a pleasant one, for it looks something like a law.'

'I am no scollard, as they would say in Whitford, you know; but it has often struck me, that if folks would but believe that the Apostles talked not such very bad Greek, and had some slight notion of the received meaning of the words they used, and of the absurdity of using the same term to express nineteen different things, the New Testament would be found to be a much simpler and more severely philosophic book than "Theologians" ("Anthropo-sophists" I call them) fancy.'

'Where on earth did you get all this wisdom, or foolishness?'

'From the prophet, a fortnight ago.'

'Who is this prophet? I will know.'

'Then you will know more than I do. Sabina—light my meerschaum, there's a darling; it will taste the sweeter after your lips.' And Claude laid his delicate woman-like limbs upon the sofa, and looked the very picture of luxurious nonchalance.

'What is he, you pitiless wretch?'

'Fairest Hebe, fill our Prometheus Vinctus another glass of Burgundy, and find your guitar, to silence him.'

'It was the ocean nymphs who came to comfort Prometheus—and unsandalled, too, if I recollect right,' said Lancelot, smiling at Sabina. 'Come, now, if he will not tell me, perhaps you will?'

Sabina only blushed, and laughed mysteriously.

'You surely are intimate with him, Claude? When and where did you meet him first?'

'Seventeen years ago, on the barricades of the three days, in the charming little pandemonium called Paris, he picked me out of a gutter, a boy of fifteen, with a musket-ball through my body; mended me, and sent me to a painter's studio. . . . The next séjour I had with him began in sight of the Demawend. Sabina, perhaps you might like to relate to Mr. Smith that interview, and the circumstances under which you made your first sketch of that magnificent and little-known volcano?'

Sabina blushed again—this time scarlet; and, to Lancelot's astonishment, pulled off her slipper, and brandishing it daintily, uttered some unintelligible threat, in an Oriental language, at the laughing Claude.

'Why, you must have been in the East?'

'Why not! Do you think that figure and that walk were picked up in stay-ridden, toe-pinching England? . . . Ay, in the East; and why not elsewhere? Do you think I got my knowledge of the human figure from the live-model in the Royal Academy?'

'I certainly have always had my doubts of it. You are the only man I know who can paint muscle in motion.'

'Because I am almost the only man in England who has ever seen it. Artists should go to the Cannibal Islands for that. . . . J'ai fait le grand tour. I should not wonder if the prophet made you take it.'

'That would be very much as I chose.'

'Or otherwise.'

'What do you mean?'

'That if he wills you to go, I defy you to stay. Eh, Sabina!'

'Well, you are a very mysterious pair,—and a very charming one.'

'So we think ourselves—as to the charmingness. . . . and as for the mystery . . . "Omnia exeunt in mysterium," says somebody, somewhere—or if he don't, ought to, seeing that it is so. You will be a mystery some day, and a myth, and a thousand years hence pious old ladies will be pulling caps as to whether you were a saint or a devil, and whether you did really work miracles or not, as corroborations of your ex-supra-lunar illumination on social questions. . . . Yes . . . you will have to submit, and see Bogy, and enter the Eleusinian mysteries. Eh, Sabina?'

'My dear Claude, what between the Burgundy and your usual foolishness, you seem very much inclined to divulge the Eleusinian mysteries.'

'I can't well do that, my beauty, seeing that, if you recollect, we were both turned back at the vestibule, for a pair of naughty children as we are.'

'Do be quiet! and let me enjoy, for once, my woman's right to the last word!'

And in this hopeful state of mystification, Lancelot went home, and dreamt of Argemone.

His uncle would, and, indeed, as it seemed, could, give him very little information on the question which had so excited his curiosity. He had met the man in India many years before, had received there from him most important kindnesses, and considered him, from experience, of oracular wisdom. He seemed to have an unlimited command of money, though most frugal in his private habits; visited England for a short time every few years, and always under a different appellation; but as for his real name, habitation, or business, here or at home, the good banker knew nothing, except that whenever questioned on them, he wandered off into Pantagruelist jokes, and ended in Cloud-land. So that Lancelot was fain to give up his questions and content himself with longing for the reappearance of this inexplicable sage.

CHAPTER XVI
ONCE IN A WAY

A few mornings afterwards, Lancelot, as he glanced his eye over the columns of *The Times*, stopped short at the beloved name of Whitford. To his disgust and disappointment, it only occurred in one of those miserable cases, now of weekly occurrence, of concealing the birth of a child. He was turning from it, when he saw Bracebridge's name. Another look sufficed to show him that he ought to go at once to the colonel, who had returned the day before from Norway.

A few minutes brought him to his friend's lodging, but *The Times* had arrived there before him. Bracebridge was sitting over his untasted breakfast, his face buried in his hands.

'Do not speak to me,' he said, without looking up. 'It was right of you to come—kind of you; but it is too late.'

He started, and looked wildly round him, as if listening for some sound which he expected, and then laid his head down on the table. Lancelot turned to go.

'No—do not leave me! Not alone, for God's sake, not alone!'

Lancelot sat down. There was a fearful alteration in Bracebridge. His old keen self-confident look had vanished. He was haggard, life-weary, shame-stricken, almost abject. His limbs looked quite shrunk and powerless, as he rested his head on the table before him, and murmured incoherently from time to time,—

'My own child! And I never shall have another! No second chance for those who—Oh Mary! Mary! you might have waited—you might have trusted me! And why should you?—ay, why, indeed? And such a pretty baby, too!—just like his father!'

Lancelot laid his hand kindly on his shoulder.

'My dearest Bracebridge, the evidence proves that the child was born dead.'

'They lie!' he said, fiercely, starting up. 'It cried twice after it was born!'

Lancelot stood horror-struck.

'I heard it last night, and the night before that, and the night before that again, under my pillow, shrieking—stifling—two little squeaks, like a caught hare; and I tore the pillows off it—I did; and once I saw it, and it had beautiful black eyes—just like its father—just like a little miniature that used to lie on my mother's table, when I knelt at her knee, before they sent me out "to see life," and Eton, and the army, and Crockford's, and Newmarket, and fine gentlemen, and fine ladies, and luxury, and flattery, brought me to this! Oh, father! father! was that the only way to make a gentleman of your son?—There it is again! Don't you hear it?—under the sofa cushions! Tear them off! Curse you! Save it!'

And, with a fearful oath, the wretched man sent Lancelot staggering across the room, and madly tore up the cushions.

A long postman's knock at the door.—He suddenly rose up quite collected.

'The letter! I knew it would come. She need not have written it: I know what is in it.'

The servant's step came up the stairs. Poor Bracebridge turned to Lancelot with something of his own stately determination.

'I must be alone when I receive this letter. Stay here.' And with compressed lips and fixed eyes he stalked out at the door, and shut it.

Lancelot heard him stop; then the servant's footsteps down the stairs; then the colonel's treading, slowly and heavily, went step by step up to the room above. He shut that door too. A dead silence followed. Lancelot stood in fearful suspense, and held his breath to listen. Perhaps he had fainted? No, for then he would have heard a fall. Perhaps he had fallen on the bed? He would go and see. No, he would wait a little longer. Perhaps he was praying? He had told Lancelot to pray once—he dared not interrupt him now. A slight stir—a noise as of an opening box. Thank God, he was, at least, alive! Nonsense! Why should he not be alive? What could happen to him? And yet he knew that something was going to happen. The silence was ominous—unbearable; the air of the room felt heavy and stifling, as if a thunderstorm were about to burst. He longed to hear the man raging and stamping. And yet he could not connect the thought of one so gay and full of gallant life, with the terrible dread that was creeping over him—with the terrible scene which he had just witnessed. It must be all a temporary excitement—a mistake—a hideous dream, which the next post would sweep away. He would go and tell him so. No, he could not stir. His limbs seemed leaden, his feet felt rooted to the ground, as in long nightmare. And still the intolerable silence brooded overhead.

What broke it? A dull, stifled report, as of a pistol fired against the ground; a heavy fall; and again the silence of death.

He rushed upstairs. A corpse lay on its face upon the floor, and from among its hair, a crimson thread crept slowly across the carpet. It was all over. He bent over the head, but one look was sufficient. He did not try to lift it up.

On the table lay the fatal letter. Lancelot knew that he had a right to read it. It was scrawled, mis-spelt—but there were no tear-blots on the paper:—

'Sir—I am in prison—and where are you? Cruel man! Where were you all those miserable weeks, while I was coming nearer and nearer to my shame? Murdering dumb beasts in foreign lands. You have murdered more than them. How I loved you once! How I hate you now! But I have my revenge. *Your baby cried twice after it was born*!'

Lancelot tore the letter into a hundred pieces, and swallowed them, for every foot in the house was on the stairs.

So there was terror, and confusion, and running in and out: but there were no wet eyes there except those of Bracebridge's groom, who threw himself on the body, and would not stir. And then there was a coroner's inquest; and it came out in the evidence how 'the deceased had been for several days very much depressed, and had talked of voices and apparitions;' whereat the jury—as twelve honest, good-natured Christians were bound to do—returned a verdict of temporary insanity; and in a week more the penny-a-liners grew tired; and the world, too, who never expects anything, not even French revolutions, grew tired also of repeating,—'Dear me! who would have expected it?' and having filled up the colonel's place, swaggered on as usual, arm-in-arm with the flesh and the devil.

Bracebridge's death had, of course, a great effect on Lancelot's spirit. Not in the way of warning, though—such events seldom act in that way, on the highest as well as on the lowest minds. After all, your 'Rakes' Progresses,' and 'Atheists' Deathbeds,' do no more good than noble George Cruikshank's 'Bottle' will, because every one knows that they are the exception, and not the rule; that the Atheist generally dies with a conscience as comfortably callous as a rhinocerous-hide; and the rake, when old age stops his power of sinning, becomes generally rather more respectable than his neighbours. The New Testament deals very little in appeals *ad terrorem*; and it would be well if some, who fancy that they follow it, would do the same, and by abstaining from making 'hell-fire' the chief incentive to virtue, cease from tempting many a poor fellow to enlist on the devil's side the only manly feeling he has left—personal courage.

But yet Lancelot was affected. And when, on the night of the colonel's funeral, he opened, at hazard, Argemone's Bible, and his eyes fell on the passage which tells how 'one shall be taken and another left,' great honest tears of gratitude dropped upon the page; and he fell on his knees, and in bitter self-reproach thanked the new found Upper Powers, who, as he began to hope, were leading him not in vain,—that he had yet a life before him wherein to play the man.

And now he felt that the last link was broken between him and all his late frivolous companions. All had deserted him in his ruin but this one—and he was silent in the grave. And now, from the world and all its toys and revelry, he was parted once and for ever; and he stood alone in the desert, like the last Arab of a plague-stricken tribe, looking over the wreck of ancient cities, across barren sands, where far rivers gleamed in the distance, that seemed to beckon him away into other climes, other hopes, other duties. Old things had passed away—when would all things become new?

Not yet, Lancelot. Thou hast still one selfish hope, one dream of bliss, however impossible, yet still cherished. Thou art a changed man—but for whose sake? For Argemone's. Is she to be thy god, then? Art thou to live for her, or for the sake of One greater than she? All thine idols are broken—swiftly the desert sands are drifting over them, and covering them in.—All but one—must that, too, be taken from thee?

One morning a letter was put into Lancelot's hands, bearing the Whitford postmark. Tremblingly he tore it open. It contained a few passionate words from Honoria. Argemone was dying of typhus fever, and entreating to see him once again; and Honoria had, with some difficulty, as she hinted, obtained leave from her parents to send for him. His last bank note carried him down to Whitford; and, calm and determined, as one who feels that he has nothing more to lose on earth, and whose torment must henceforth become his element, he entered the Priory that evening.

He hardly spoke or looked at a soul; he felt that he was there on an errand which none understood; that he was moving towards Argemone through a spiritual world, in which he and she were alone; that, in his utter poverty and hopelessness, he stood above all the luxury, even above all the sorrow, around him; that she belonged to him, and to him alone; and the broken-hearted beggar followed the weeping Honoria towards his lady's chamber, with the step and bearing of a lord. He was wrong; there were pride and fierceness enough in his heart, mingled with that sense of nothingness of rank, money, chance and change, yea, death itself, of all but

Love;—mingled even with that intense belief that his sorrows were but his just deserts, which now possessed all his soul. And in after years he knew that he was wrong; but so he felt at the time; and even then the strength was not all of earth which bore him manlike through that hour.

He entered the room; the darkness, the silence, the cool scent of vinegar, struck a shudder through him. The squire was sitting half idiotic and helpless, in his arm-chair. His face lighted up as Lancelot entered, and he tried to hold out his palsied hand. Lancelot did not see him. Mrs. Lavington moved proudly and primly back from the bed, with a face that seemed to say through its tears, 'I at least am responsible for nothing that occurs from this interview.' Lancelot did not see her either: he walked straight up towards the bed as if he were treading on his own ground. His heart was between his lips, and yet his whole soul felt as dry and hard as some burnt-out volcano-crater.

A faint voice—oh, how faint, how changed!—called him from within the closed curtains.

'He is there! I know it is he! Lancelot! my Lancelot!'

Silently still he drew aside the curtain; the light fell full upon her face. What a sight! Her beautiful hair cut close, a ghastly white handkerchief round her head, those bright eyes sunk and lustreless, those ripe lips baked, and black and drawn; her thin hand fingering uneasily the coverlid.—It was too much for him. He shuddered and turned his face away. Quick-sighted that love is, even to the last! slight as the gesture was, she saw it in an instant.

'You are not afraid of infection?' she said, faintly. 'I was not.'

Lancelot laughed aloud, as men will at strangest moments, sprung towards her with open arms, and threw himself on his knees beside the bed. With sudden strength she rose upright, and clasped him in her arms.

'Once more!' she sighed, in a whisper to herself, 'Once more on earth!' And the room, and the spectators, and disease itself faded from around them like vain dreams, as she nestled closer and closer to him, and gazed into his eyes, and passed her shrunken hand over his cheeks, and toyed with his hair, and seemed to drink in magnetic life from his embrace.

No one spoke or stirred. They felt that an awful and blessed spirit overshadowed the lovers, and were hushed, as if in the sanctuary of God.

Suddenly again she raised her head from his bosom, and in a tone, in which her old queenliness mingled strangely with the saddest tenderness,—

'All of you go away now; I must talk to my husband alone.'

They went, leading out the squire, who cast puzzled glances toward the pair, and murmured to himself that 'she was sure to get well now Smith was come: everything went right when he was in the way.'

So they were left alone.

'I do not look so very ugly, my darling, do I? Not so very ugly? though they have cut off all my poor hair, and I told them so often not! But I kept a lock for you;' and feebly she drew from under the pillow a long auburn tress, and tried to wreathe it round his neck, but could not, and sunk back.

Poor fellow! he could bear no more. He hid his face in his hands, and burst into a long low weeping.

'I am very thirsty, darling; reach me—No, I will drink no more, except from your dear lips.'

He lifted up his head, and breathed his whole soul upon her lips; his tears fell on her closed eyelids.

'Weeping? No.—You must not cry. See how comfortable I am. They are all so kind—soft bed, cool room, fresh air, sweet drinks, sweet scents. Oh, so different from *that* room!'

'What room?—my own!'

'Listen, and I will tell you. Sit down—put your arm under my head—so. When I am on your bosom I feel so strong. God! let me last to tell him all. It was for that I sent for him.'

And then, in broken words, she told him how she had gone up to the fever patient at Ashy, on the fatal night on which Lancelot had last seen her. Shuddering, she hinted at the horrible filth and misery she had seen, at the foul scents which had sickened her. A madness of remorse, she said, had seized her. She had gone, in spite of her disgust, to several houses which she found open. There were worse cottages there than even her father's; some tradesmen in a neighbouring town had been allowed to run up a set of rack rent hovels.—Another shudder seized her when she spoke of them; and from that point in her story all was fitful, broken, like the images of a hideous dream. 'Every instant those foul memories were defiling her nostrils. A horrible loathing had taken possession of her, recurring from time to time, till it ended in delirium and fever. A scent-fiend was haunting her night and day,' she said. 'And now the curse of the Lavingtons had truly come upon her. To perish by the people whom they made. Their neglect, cupidity, oppression, are avenged on me! Why not? Have I not wantoned in down and perfumes, while they, by whose labour my luxuries were bought, were pining among scents and sounds,—one day of which would have driven me mad! And then they wonder why men turn Chartists! There are those horrible scents again! Save me from them! Lancelot—darling! Take me to the fresh air! I choke! I am festering away! The Nun-pool! Take all the water, every drop, and wash Ashy clean again! Make a great fountain in it—beautiful marble—to bubble and gurgle, and trickle and foam, for ever and ever, and wash away the sins of the Lavingtons, that the little rosy children may play round it, and the poor toil-bent woman may wash—and wash—and drink—Water! water! I am dying of thirst!'

He gave her water, and then she lay back and babbled about the Nun-pool sweeping 'all the houses of Ashy into one beautiful palace, among great flower-gardens, where the school children will sit and sing such merry hymns, and never struggle with great pails of water up the hill of Ashy any more.'

'You will do it! darling! Strong, wise, noble-hearted that you are! Why do you look at me? You will be rich some day. You will own land, for you are worthy to own it. Oh that I could give you Whitford! No! It was mine too long—therefore I die! because I—Lord Jesus! have I not repented of my sin?'

Then she grew calm once more. A soft smile crept over her face, as it grew sharper and paler every moment. Faintly she sank back on the pillows, and faintly whispered to him to kneel and pray. He obeyed her mechanically. . . . 'No—not for me, for them—for them, and for yourself—that you may save them whom I never dreamt that I was bound to save!'

And he knelt and prayed . . . what, he alone and those who heard his prayer, can tell. . . .

When he lifted up his head at last, he saw that Argemone lay motionless. For a moment he thought she was dead, and frantically sprang to the bell. The family rushed in with the physician. She gave some faint token of life, but none of consciousness. The doctor sighed, and said that her end was near. Lancelot had known that all along.

'I think, sir, you had better leave the room,' said Mrs. Lavington; and followed him into the passage.

What she was about to say remained unspoken; for Lancelot seized her hand in spite of her, with frantic thanks for having allowed him this one interview, and entreaties that he might see her again, if but for one moment.

Mrs. Lavington, somewhat more softly than usual, said,—'That the result of this visit had not been such as to make a second desirable—that she had no wish to disturb her daughter's mind at such a moment with earthly regrets.'

'Earthly regrets!' How little she knew what had passed there! But if she had known, would she have been one whit softened? For, indeed, Argemone's spirituality was not in her mother's language. And yet the good woman had prayed, and prayed, and wept bitter tears, by her daughter's bedside, day after day; but she had never heard her pronounce the talismanic formula of words, necessary in her eyes to ensure salvation; and so she was almost without hope for her. Oh, Bigotry! Devil, who turnest God's love into man's curse! are not human hearts hard and blind enough of themselves, without thy cursed help?

For one moment a storm of unutterable pride and rage convulsed Lancelot—the next instant love conquered; and the strong proud man threw himself on his knees at the feet of the woman he despised, and with wild sobs entreated for one moment more—one only!

At that instant a shriek from Honoria resounded from the sick chamber. Lancelot knew what it meant, and sprang up, as men do when shot through the heart.—In a moment he was himself again. A new life had begun for him—alone.

'You will not need to grant my prayer, madam,' he said, calmly: 'Argemone is dead.'

CHAPTER XVII
THE VALLEY OF THE SHADOW OF DEATH

Let us pass over the period of dull, stupefied misery that followed, when Lancelot had returned to his lonely lodging, and the excitement of his feelings had died away. It is impossible to describe that which could not be separated into parts, in which there was no foreground, no distance, but only one dead, black, colourless present. After a time, however, he began to find that fancies, almost ridiculously trivial, arrested and absorbed his attention; even as when our eyes have become accustomed to darkness, every light-coloured mote shows luminous against the void blackness of night. So we are tempted to unseemly frivolity in churches, and at funerals, and all most solemn moments; and so Lancelot found his imagination fluttering back, half amused, to every smallest circumstance of the last few weeks, as objects of mere curiosity, and found with astonishment that they had lost their power of paining him. Just as victims on the rack have fallen, it is said, by length of torture, into insensibility, and even calm repose, his brain had been wrought until all feeling was benumbed. He began to think what an interesting autobiography his life might make; and the events of the last few years began to arrange themselves in a most attractive dramatic form. He began even to work out a scene or two, and where 'motives' seemed wanting, to invent them here and there. He sat thus for hours silent over his fire, playing with his old self, as though it were a thing which did not belong to him—a suit of clothes which he had put off, and which,

> 'For that it was too rich to hang by the wall,
> It must be ripped,'

and then pieced and dizened out afresh as a toy. And then again he started away from his own thoughts, at finding himself on the edge of that very gulf, which, as Mellot had lately told him, Barnakill denounced as the true hell of genius, where Art is regarded as an end and not a means, and objects are interesting, not in as far as they form our spirits, but in proportion as they can be shaped into effective parts of some beautiful whole. But whether it was a temptation or none, the desire recurred to him again and again. He even attempted to write, but sickened at the sight of the first words. He turned to his pencil, and tried to represent with it one scene at least; and with the horrible calmness of some self-torturing ascetic, he sat down to sketch a drawing of himself and Argemone on her dying day, with her head upon his bosom for the last time—and then tossed it angrily into the fire, partly because he felt just as he had in his attempts to write, that there was something more in all these events than he could utter by pen or pencil, than he could even understand; principally because he could not arrange the attitudes gracefully enough. And now, in front of the stern realities of sorrow and death, he began to see a meaning in another mysterious saying of Barnakill's, which Mellot was continually quoting, that 'Art was never Art till it was more than Art; that the Finite only existed as a body of the Infinite; and that the man of genius must first know the Infinite, unless he wished to become not a poet, but a maker of idols.' Still he felt in himself a capability, nay, an infinite longing to speak; though what he should utter, or how—whether as poet, social theorist, preacher, he could not yet decide. Barnakill had forbidden him painting, and though he hardly knew why, he dared not disobey him. But Argemone's dying words lay on him as a divine command to labour. All his doubts, his social observations, his dreams of the beautiful and the blissful, his intense perception of social evils, his new-born hope—faith it could not yet be called—in a ruler and deliverer of the world, all urged him on to labour: but at what? He felt as if he were the demon in the legend, condemned to twine endless ropes of sand. The world, outside which he now stood for good and evil, seemed to him like some frantic whirling waltz; some serried struggling crowd, which rushed past him in aimless confusion, without allowing him time or opening to take his place among their ranks: and as for wings to rise above, and to look down upon the uproar, where were they? His melancholy paralysed him more and more. He was too listless even to cater for his daily bread by writing his articles for the magazines. Why should he? He had nothing to say. Why should he pour out words and empty sound, and add one more futility to the herd of 'prophets that had become wind, and had no truth in them'? Those who could write without a conscience, without an object except that of seeing their own fine words, and filling their own pockets—let them do it: for his part he would have none of it. But his purse was empty, and so was his stomach; and as for asking assistance of his uncle, it was returning like the dog to his vomit. So one day he settled all bills with his last shilling, tied up his remaining clothes in a bundle, and stoutly stepped forth into the street to find a job—to hold a horse, if nothing better offered; when, behold! on the threshold he met Barnakill himself.

'Whither away?' said that strange personage. 'I was just going to call on you.'

'To earn my bread by the labour of my hands. So our fathers all began.'

'And so their sons must all end. Do you want work?'

'Yes, if you have any.'

'Follow me, and carry a trunk home from a shop to my lodgings.'

He strode off, with Lancelot after him; entered a mathematical instrument maker's shop in the neighbouring street, and pointed out a heavy corded case to Lancelot, who, with the assistance of the shopman, got it on his shoulders; and trudging forth through the streets after his employer, who walked before him silent and unregarding, felt himself for the first time in his life in the same situation as nine hundred and ninety-nine out of every thousand of Adam's descendants, and discovered somewhat to his satisfaction that when he could once rid his mind of its old superstition that every one was looking at him, it mattered very little whether the burden carried were a deal trunk or a Downing Street despatch-box.

His employer's lodgings were in St. Paul's Churchyard. Lancelot set the trunk down inside the door.

'What do you charge?'

'Sixpence.'

Barnakill looked him steadily in the face, gave him the sixpence, went in, and shut the door.

Lancelot wandered down the street, half amused at the simple test which had just been applied to him, and yet sickened with disappointment; for he had cherished a mysterious fancy that with this strange being all his hopes of future activity were bound up. Tregarva's month was nearly over, and yet no tidings of him had come. Mellot had left London on some mysterious errand of the prophet's, and for the first time in his life he seemed to stand utterly alone. He was at one pole, and the whole universe at the other. It was in vain to tell himself that his own act had placed him there; that he had friends to whom he might appeal. He would not, he dare not, accept outward help, even outward friendship, however hearty and sincere, at that crisis of his existence. It seemed a desecration of its awfulness to find comfort in anything but the highest and the deepest. And the glimpse of that which he had attained seemed to have passed away from him again,—seemed to be something which, as it had arisen with Argemone, was lost with her also,—one speck of the far blue sky which the rolling clouds had covered in again. As he passed under the shadow of the huge soot-blackened cathedral, and looked at its grim spiked railings and closed doors, it seemed to him a symbol of the spiritual world, clouded and barred from him. He stopped and looked up, and tried to think. The rays of the setting sun lighted up in clear radiance the huge cross on the summit. Was it an omen? Lancelot thought so; but at that instant he felt a hand on his shoulder, and looked round. It was that strange man again.

'So far well,' said he. 'You are making a better day's work than you fancy, and earning more wages. For instance, here is a packet for you.'

Lancelot seized it, trembling, and tore it open. It was directed in Honoria's handwriting.

'Whence had you this?' said he.

'Through Mellot, through whom I can return your answer, if one be needed.'

The letter was significant of Honoria's character. It busied itself entirely about facts, and showed the depth of her sorrow by making no allusion to it. 'Argemone, as Lancelot was probably aware, had bequeathed to him the whole of her own fortune at Mrs. Lavington's death, and had directed that various precious things of hers should be delivered over to him immediately. Her mother, however, kept her chamber under lock and key, and refused to allow an article to be removed from its accustomed place. It was natural in the first burst of her sorrow, and Lancelot would pardon.' All his drawings and letters had been, by Argemone's desire, placed with her in her coffin. Honoria had been only able to obey her in sending a favourite ring of hers, and with it the last stanzas which she had composed before her death:—

> 'Twin stars, aloft in ether clear,
>   Around each other roll away,
> Within one common atmosphere
>   Of their own mutual light and day.
>
> 'And myriad happy eyes are bent
>   Upon their changeless love alway;
> As, strengthened by their one intent,
>   They pour the flood of life and day,
>
> 'So we, through this world's waning night,
>   Shall, hand in hand, pursue our way;
> Shed round us order, love, and light,
>   And shine unto the perfect day.'

The precious relic, with all its shattered hopes, came at the right moment to soften his hard-worn heart. The sight, the touch of it, shot like an electric spark through the black stifling thunder-cloud of his soul, and dissolved it in refreshing showers of tears.

Barnakill led him gently within the area of the railings, where he might conceal his emotion, and it was but a few seconds before Lancelot had recovered his self-possession and followed him up the steps through the wicket door.

They entered. The afternoon service was proceeding. The organ droned sadly in its iron cage to a few musical amateurs. Some nursery maids and foreign sailors stared about within the spiked felon's dock which shut off the body of the cathedral, and tried in vain to hear what was going on inside the choir. As a wise author—a Protestant, too—has lately said, 'the scanty service rattled in the vast building, like a dried kernel too small for its shell.' The place breathed imbecility, and unreality, and sleepy life-in-death, while the whole nineteenth century went roaring on its way outside. And as Lancelot thought, though only as a *dilettante*, of old St. Paul's, the morning star and focal beacon of England through centuries and dynasties, from old Augustine and Mellitus, up to those Paul's Cross sermons whose thunders shook thrones, and to noble Wren's masterpiece of art, he asked, 'Whither all this? Coleridge's dictum, that a cathedral is a petrified religion, may be taken to bear more meanings than one. When will life return to this cathedral system?'

'When was it ever a living system?' answered the other. 'When was it ever anything but a transitionary makeshift since the dissolution of the monasteries?'

'Why, then, not away with it at once?'

'You English have not done with it yet. At all events, it is keeping your cathedrals rain-proof for you, till you can put them to some better use than now.'

'And in the meantime?'

'In the meantime there is life enough in them; life that will wake the dead some day. Do you hear what those choristers are chanting now?'

'Not I,' said Lancelot; 'nor any one round us, I should think.'

'That is our own fault, after all; for we were not good churchmen enough to come in time for vespers.'

'Are you a churchman then?'

'Yes, thank God. There may be other churches than those of Europe or Syria, and right Catholic ones, too. But, shall I tell you what they are singing? "He hath put down the mighty from their seat, and hath exalted the humble and meek. He hath filled the hungry with good things, and the rich He hath sent empty away." Is there no life, think you, in those words, spoken here every afternoon in the name of God?'

'By hirelings, who neither care nor understand—'

'Hush. Be not hasty with imputations of evil, within walls dedicated to and preserved by the All-good. Even should the speakers forget the meaning of their own words, to my sense, perhaps, that may just now leave the words more entirely God's. At all events, confess that whatever accidental husks may have clustered round it, here is a germ of Eternal Truth. No, I dare not despair of you English, as long as I hear your priesthood forced by Providence, even in spite of themselves, thus to speak God's words about an age in which the condition of the poor, and the rights and duties of man, are becoming the rallying-point for all thought and all organisation.'

'But does it not make the case more hopeless that such words have been spoken for centuries, and no man regards them?'

'You have to blame for that the people, rather than the priest. As they are, so will he be, in every age and country. He is but the index which the changes of their spiritual state move up and down the scale: and as they will become in England in the next half century, so will he become also.'

'And can these dry bones live?' asked Lancelot, scornfully.

'Who are you to ask? What were you three months ago? for I know well your story. But do you remember what the prophet saw in the Valley of Vision? How first that those same dry bones shook and clashed together, as if uneasy because they were disorganised; and how they then found flesh and stood upright: and yet there was no life in them, till at last the Spirit came down and entered into them? Surely there is shaking enough among the bones now! It is happening to the body of your England as it did to Adam's after he was made. It lay on earth, the rabbis say, forty days before the breath of life was put into it, and the devil came and kicked it; and it sounded hollow, as England is doing now; but that did not prevent the breath of life coming in good time, nor will it in England's case.'

Lancelot looked at him with a puzzled face.

'You must not speak in such deep parables to so young a learner.'

'Is my parable so hard, then? Look around you and see what is the characteristic of your country and of your generation at this moment. What a yearning, what an expectation, amid infinite falsehoods and confusions, of some nobler, more chivalrous, more godlike state! Your very costermonger trolls out his belief that "there's a good time coming," and the hearts of *gamins*, as well as millenarians, answer, "True!" Is not that a clashing among the dry bones? And as for flesh, what new materials are springing up among you every month, spiritual and physical, for a state such as "eye hath not seen nor ear heard?"—railroads, electric telegraphs, associate-lodging-houses, club-houses, sanitary reforms, experimental schools, chemical agriculture, a matchless school of inductive science, an equally matchless school of naturalist painters,—and all this in the very workshop of the world! Look, again, at the healthy craving after religious art and ceremonial,—the strong desire to preserve that which has stood the test of time; and on the other hand, at the manful resolution of your middle classes to stand or fall by the Bible alone,—to admit no innovations in worship which are empty of instinctive meaning. Look at the enormous amount of practical benevolence which now struggles in vain against evil, only because it is as yet private, desultory, divided. How dare you, young man, despair of your own nation, while its nobles can produce a Carlisle, an Ellesmere, an Ashley, a Robert Grosvenor,—while its middle classes can beget a Faraday, a Stephenson, a Brooke, an Elizabeth Fry? See, I say, what a chaos of noble materials is here,—all confused, it is true,—polarised, jarring, and chaotic,—here bigotry, there self-will, superstition, sheer Atheism often, but only waiting for the one inspiring Spirit to organise, and unite, and consecrate this chaos into the noblest polity the world ever saw realised! What a destiny may be that of your land, if you have but the faith to see your own honour! Were I not of my own country, I would be an Englishman this day.'

'And what is your country?' asked Lancelot. 'It should be a noble one which breeds such men as you.'

The stranger smiled.

'Will you go thither with me?'

'Why not? I long for travel, and truly I am sick of my own country. When the Spirit of which you speak,' he went on, bitterly, 'shall descend, I may return; till then England is no place for the penniless.'

'How know you that the Spirit is not even now poured out? Must your English Pharisees and Sadducees, too, have signs and wonders ere they believe? Will man never know that "the kingdom of God comes not by observation"? that now, as ever, His promise stands true,—"Lo! I am with you alway, even unto the end of the world"? How many inspired hearts even now may be cherishing in secret the idea which shall reform the age, and fulfil at once the longings of every sect and rank?'

'Name it to me, then!'

'Who can name it? Who can even see it, but those who are like Him from whom it comes? Them a long and stern discipline awaits. Would you be of them, you must, like the Highest who ever trod this earth, go fasting into the wilderness, and, among the wild beasts, stand alone face to face with the powers of Nature.'

'I will go where you shall bid me. I will turn shepherd among the Scottish mountains—live as an anchorite in the solitudes of Dartmoor. But to what purpose? I have listened long to Nature's voice, but even the whispers of a spiritual presence which haunted my childhood have died away, and I hear nothing in her but the grinding of the iron wheels of mechanical necessity.'

'Which is the will of God. Henceforth you shall study, not Nature, but Him. Yet as for place—I do not like your English primitive formations, where earth, worn out with struggling, has fallen wearily asleep. No, you shall rather come to Asia, the oldest and yet the youngest continent,—to our volcanic mountain ranges, where her bosom still heaves with the creative energy of youth, around the primeval cradle of the most ancient race of men. Then, when you have learnt the wondrous harmony between man and his dwelling-place, I will lead you to a land where you shall see the highest spiritual cultivation in triumphant contact with the fiercest energies of matter; where men have learnt to tame and use alike the volcano and the human heart, where the body and the spirit, the beautiful and the useful, the human and the divine, are no longer separate, and men have embodied to themselves on earth an image of the "city not made with hands, eternal in the heavens."'

'Where is this land?' said Lancelot eagerly.

'Poor human nature must have its name for everything. You have heard of the country of Prester John, that mysterious Christian empire, rarely visited by European eye?'

'There are legends of two such,' said Lancelot, 'an Ethiopian and an Asiatic one; and the Ethiopian, if we are to believe Colonel Harris's Journey to Shoa, is a sufficiently miserable failure.'

'True; the day of the Chamitic race is past; you will not say the same of our Caucasian empire. To our race the present belongs,—to England, France, Germany, America,—to us. Will you see what we have done, and, perhaps, bring home, after long wanderings, a message for your country which may help to unravel the tangled web of this strange time?'

'I will,' said Lancelot, 'now, this moment. And yet, no. There is one with whom I have promised to share all future weal and woe. Without him I can take no step.'

'Tregarva?'

'Yes—he. What made you guess that I spoke of him?'

'Mellot told me of him, and of you, too, six weeks ago. He is now gone to fetch him from Manchester. I cannot trust him here in England yet. The country made him sad; London has made him mad; Manchester may make him bad. It is too fearful a trial even for his faith. I must take him with us.'

'What interest in him—not to say what authority over him—have you?'

'The same which I have over you. You will come with me; so will he. It is my business, as my name signifies, to save the children alive whom European society leaves carelessly and ignorantly to die. And as for my power, I come,' said he, with a smile, 'from a country which sends no one on its errands without first thoroughly satisfying itself as to his power of fulfilling them.'

'If he goes, I go with you.'

'And he will go. And yet, think what you do. It is a fearful journey. They who travel it, even as they came naked out of their mother's womb—even as they return thither, and carry nothing with them of all which they have gotten in this life, so must those who travel to my land.'

'What? Tregarva? Is he, too, to give up all? I had thought that I saw in him a precious possession, one for which I would barter all my scholarship, my talents,—ay—my life itself.'

'A possession worth your life? What then?'

'Faith in an unseen God.'

'Ask him whether he would call that a possession—his own in any sense?'

'He would call it a revelation to him.'

'That is, a taking of the veil from something which was behind the veil already.'

'Yes.'

'And which may therefore just as really be behind the veil in other cases without its presence being suspected.'

'Certainly.'

'In what sense, now, is that a possession? Do you possess the sun because you see it? Did Herschel create Uranus by discovering it; or even increase, by an atom, its attraction on one particle of his own body?'

'Whither is all this tending?'

'Hither. Tregarva does not possess his Father and his Lord; he is possessed by them.'

'But he would say—and I should believe him—that he has seen and known them, not with his bodily eyes, but with his soul, heart, imagination—call it what you will. All I know is, that between him and me there is a great gulf fixed.'

'What! seen and known them utterly? comprehended them? Are they not infinite, incomprehensible? Can the less comprehend the greater?'

'He knows, at least, enough of them to make him what I am not.'

'That is, he knows something of them. And may not you know something of them also?—enough to make you what he is not?'

Lancelot shook his head in silence.

'Suppose that you had met and spoken with your father, and loved him when you saw him, and yet were not aware of the relation in which you stood to him, still you would know him?'

'Not the most important thing of all—that he was my father.'

'Is that the most important thing? Is it not more important that he should know that you were his son? That he should support, guide, educate you, even though unseen? Do you not know that some one has been doing that?'

'That I have been supported, guided, educated, I know full well; but by whom I know not. And I know, too, that I have been punished. And therefore—therefore I cannot free the thought of a Him—of a Person—only of a Destiny, of Laws and Powers, which have no faces wherewith to frown awful wrath upon me! If it be a Person who has been leading me, I must go mad, or know that He has forgiven!'

'I conceive that it is He, and not punishment which you fear?'

Lancelot was silent a moment. . . . 'Yes. He, and not hell at all, is what I fear. He can inflict no punishment on me worse than the inner hell which I have felt already, many and many a time.'

'Bona verba! That is an awful thing to say: but better this extreme than the other. . . . And you would—what?'

'Be pardoned.'

'If He loves you, He has pardoned you already.'

'How do I know that He loves me?'

'How does Tregarva?'

'He is a righteous man, and I—'

'Am a sinner. He would, and rightly, call himself the same.'

'But he knows that God loves him—that he is God's child.'

'So, then, God did not love him till he caused God to love him, by knowing that He loved him? He was not God's child till he made himself one, by believing that he was one when as yet he was not? I appeal to common sense and logic . . . It was revealed to Tregarva that God had been loving him while he was yet a bad man. If He loved him, in spite of his sin, why should He not have loved you?'

'If He had loved me, would He have left me in ignorance of Himself? For if He be, to know Him is the highest good.'

'Had he left Tregarva in ignorance of Himself?'

'No. . . . Certainly, Tregarva spoke of his conversion as of a turning to one of whom he had known all along, and disregarded.'

'Then do you turn like him, to Him whom you have known all along, and disregarded.'

'I?'

'Yes—you! If half I have heard and seen of you be true, He has been telling you more, and not less, of Himself than He does to most men. You, for aught I know, may know more of Him than Tregarva does. The gulf between you and him is this: he has obeyed what he knew—and you have not.' . . .

Lancelot paused a moment, then—

'No!—do not cheat me! You said once that you were a churchman.'

'So I am. A Catholic of the Catholics. What then?'

'Who is He to whom you ask me to turn? You talk to me of Him as my Father; but you talk of Him to men of your own creed as The Father. You have mysterious dogmas of a Three in One. I know them . . . I have admired them. In all their forms—in the Vedas, in the Neo-Platonists, in Jacob Boëhmen, in your Catholic creeds, in Coleridge, and the Germans from whom he borrowed, I have looked at them, and found in them beautiful phantasms of philosophy, . . . all but scientific necessities; . . . but—'

'But what?'

'I do not want cold abstract necessities of logic: I want living practical facts. If those mysterious dogmas speak of real and necessary properties of His being, they must be necessarily interwoven in practice with His revelation of Himself?'

'Most true. But how would you have Him unveil Himself?'

'By unveiling Himself.'

'What? To your simple intuition? That was Semele's ambition.... You recollect the end of that myth. You recollect, too, as you have read the Neo-Platonists, the result of their similar attempt.'

'Idolatry and magic.'

'True; and yet, such is the ambition of man, you who were just now envying Tregarva, are already longing to climb even higher than Saint Theresa.'

'I do not often indulge in such an ambition. But I have read in your Schoolmen tales of a Beatific Vision; how that the highest good for man was to see God.'

'And did you believe that?'

'One cannot believe the impossible—only regret its impossibility.'

'Impossibility? You can only see the Uncreate in the Create—the Infinite in the Finite—the absolute good in that which is like the good. Does Tregarva pretend to more? He sees God in His own thoughts and consciousnesses, and in the events of the world around him, imaged in the mirror of his own mind. Is your mirror, then, so much narrower than his?'

'I have none. I see but myself, and the world, and far above them, a dim awful Unity, which is but a notion.'

'Fool!—and slow of heart to believe! Where else would you see Him but in yourself and in the world? They are all things cognisable to you. Where else, but everywhere, would you see Him whom no man hath seen, or can see?'

'When He shows Himself to me in them, then I may see Him. But now—'

'You have seen Him; and because you do not know the name of what you see—or rather will not acknowledge it—you fancy that it is not there.'

'How in His name? What have I seen?'

'Ask yourself. Have you not seen, in your fancy, at least, an ideal of man, for which you spurned (for Mellot has told me all) the merely negative angelic—the merely receptive and indulgent feminine-ideals of humanity, and longed to be a man, like that ideal and perfect man?'

'I have.'

'And what was your misery all along? Was it not that you felt you ought to be a person with a one inner unity, a one practical will, purpose, and business given to you—not invented by yourself—in the great order and harmony of the universe,—and that you were not one?—That your self-willed fancies, and self-pleasing passions, had torn you in pieces, and left you inconsistent, dismembered, helpless, purposeless? That, in short, you were below your ideal, just in proportion as you were not a person?'

'God knows you speak truth!'

'Then must not that ideal of humanity be a person himself?—Else how can he be the ideal man? Where is your logic? An impersonal ideal of a personal species! . . . And what is the most special peculiarity of man? Is it not that he alone of creation is a son, with a Father to love and to obey? Then must not the ideal man be a son also? And last, but not least, is it not the very property of man that he is a spirit invested with flesh and blood? Then must not the ideal man have, once at least, taken on himself flesh and blood also? Else, how could he fulfil his own idea?'

'Yes . . . Yes . . . That thought, too, has glanced through my mind at moments, like a lightning-flash; till I have envied the old Greeks their faith in a human Zeus, son of Kronos—a human Phoibos, son of Zeus. But I could not rest in them. They are noble. But are they—are any—perfect ideals? The one thing I did, and do, and will believe, is the one which they do not fulfil—that man is meant to be the conqueror of the earth, matter, nature, decay, death itself, and to conquer them, as Bacon says, by obeying them.'

'Hold it fast;—but follow it out, and say boldly, the ideal of humanity must be one who has conquered nature—one who rules the universe—one who has vanquished death itself; and conquered them, as Bacon says, not by violating, but by submitting to them. Have you never heard of one who is said to have done this? How do you know that in this ideal which you have seen, you have not seen the Son—the perfect Man, who died and rose again, and sits for ever Healer, and Lord, and Ruler of the universe? . . . Stay—do not answer me. Have you not, besides, had dreams of an all-Father—from whom, in some mysterious way, all things and beings must derive their source, and that Son—if my theory be true—among the rest, and above all the rest?'

'Who has not? But what more dim or distant—more drearily, hopelessly notional, than that thought?'

'Only the thought that there is none. But the dreariness was only in your own inconsistency. If He be the Father of all, He must be the Father of persons—He Himself therefore a Person. He must be the Father of all in whom dwell personal qualities, power, wisdom, creative energy, love, justice, pity. Can He be their Father, unless all these very qualities are infinitely His? Does He now look so terrible to you?'

'I have had this dream, too; but I turned away from it in dread.'

'Doubtless you did. Some day you will know why. Does that former dream of a human Son relieve this dream of none of its awfulness? May not the type be beloved for the sake of its Antitype, even if the very name of All-Father is no guarantee for His paternal pity! . . . But you have had this dream. How know you, that in it you were not allowed a glimpse, however dim and distant, of Him whom the Catholics call the Father?'

'It may be; but—'

'Stay again. Had you never the sense of a Spirit in you—a will, an energy, an inspiration, deeper than the region of consciousness and reflection, which, like the wind, blew where it listed, and you heard the sound of it ringing through your whole consciousness, and yet knew not whence it came, or whither it went, or why it drove you on to dare and suffer, to love and hate; to be a fighter, a sportsman, an artist—'

'And a drunkard!' added Lancelot, sadly.

'And a drunkard. But did it never seem to you that this strange wayward spirit, if anything, was the very root and core of your own personality? And had you never a craving for the help of some higher, mightier spirit, to guide and strengthen yours; to regulate and civilise its savage and spasmodic self-will; to teach you your rightful place in the great order of the universe around; to fill you with a continuous purpose and with a continuous will to do it? Have you never had a dream of an Inspirer?—a spirit of all spirits?'

Lancelot turned away with a shudder.

'Talk of anything but that! Little you know—and yet you seem to know everything—the agony of craving with which I have longed for guidance; the rage and disgust which possessed me when I tried one pretended teacher after another, and found in myself depths which their spirits could not, or rather would not, touch. I have been irreverent to the false, from very longing to worship the true; I have been a rebel to sham leaders, for very desire to be loyal to a real one; I have envied my poor cousin his Jesuits; I have envied my own pointers their slavery to my whip and whistle; I have fled, as a last resource, to brandy and opium, for the inspiration which neither man nor demon would bestow. . . . Then I found . . . you know my story. . . . And when I looked to her to guide and inspire me, behold! I found myself, by the very laws of humanity, compelled to guide and inspire her;—blind, to lead the blind!—Thank God, for her sake, that she was taken from me!'

'Did you ever mistake these substitutes, even the noblest of them, for the reality? Did not your very dissatisfaction with them show you that the true inspirer ought to be, if he were to satisfy your cravings, a person, truly—else how could he inspire and teach you, a person yourself!—but an utterly infinite, omniscient, eternal person? How know you that in that dream He was not unveiling Himself to you—He, The Spirit, who is the Lord and Giver of Life; The Spirit, who teaches men their duty and relation to those above, around, beneath them; the Spirit of order, obedience, loyalty, brotherhood, mercy, condescension?'

'But I never could distinguish these dreams from each other; the moment that I essayed to separate them, I seemed to break up the thought of an absolute one ground of all things, without which the universe would have seemed a piecemeal chaos; and they receded to infinite distance, and became transparent, barren, notional shadows of my own brain, even as your words are now.'

'How know you that you were meant to distinguish them? How know you that that very impossibility was not the testimony of fact and experience to that old Catholic dogma, for the sake of which you just now shrank from my teaching? I say that this is so. How do you know that it is not?'

'But how do I know that it is? I want proof.'

'And you are the man who was, five minutes ago, crying out for practical facts, and disdaining cold abstract necessities of logic! Can you prove that your body exists?'

'No.'

'Can you prove that your spirit exists?'

'No.'

'And yet know that they both exist. And how?'

'Solvitur ambulando.'

'Exactly. When you try to prove either of them without the other, you fail. You arrive, if at anything, at some barren polar notion. By action alone you prove the mesothetic fact which underlies and unites them.'

'Quorsum hæc?'

'Hither. I am not going to demonstrate the indemonstrable—to give you intellectual notions which, after all, will be but reflexes of my own peculiar brain, and so add the green of my spectacles to the orange of yours, and make night hideous by fresh monsters. I may help you to think yourself into a theoretical Tritheism, or a theoretical Sabellianism; I cannot make you think yourself into practical and living Catholicism. As you of anthropology, so I say of theology,—Solvitur ambulando. Don't believe

Catholic doctrine unless you like; faith is free. But see if you can reclaim either society or yourself without it; see if He will let you reclaim them. Take Catholic doctrine for granted; act on it; and see if you will not reclaim them!'

'Take for granted? Am I to come, after all, to implicit faith?'

'Implicit fiddlesticks! Did you ever read the *Novum Organum*? Mellot told me that you were a geologist.'

'Well?'

'You took for granted what you read in geological books, and went to the mine and the quarry afterwards, to verify it in practice; and according as you found fact correspond to theory, you retained or rejected. Was that implicit faith, or common sense, common humility, and sound induction?'

'Sound induction, at least.'

'Then go now, and do likewise. Believe that the learned, wise, and good, for 1800 years, may possibly have found out somewhat, or have been taught somewhat, on this matter, and test their theory by practice. If a theory on such a point is worth anything at all, it is omnipotent and all-explaining. If it will not work, of course there is no use keeping it a moment. Perhaps it will work. I say it will.'

'But I shall not work it; I still dread my own spectacles. I dare not trust myself alone to verify a theory of Murchison's or Lyell's. How dare I trust myself in this?'

'Then do not trust yourself alone: come and see what others are doing. Come, and become a member of a body which is verifying, by united action, those universal and eternal truths, which are too great for the grasp of any one time-ridden individual. Not that we claim the gift of infallibility, any more than I do that of perfect utterance of the little which we do know.'

'Then what do you promise me in asking me to go with you?'

'Practical proof that these my words are true,—practical proof that they can make a nation all that England might be and is not,—the sight of what a people might become who, knowing thus far, do what they know. We believe no more than you, but we believe it. Come and see!—and yet you will not see; facts, and the reasons of them, will be as impalpable to you there as here, unless you can again obey your Novum Organum.'

'How then?'

'By renouncing all your idols—the idols of the race and of the market, of the study and of the theatre. Every national prejudice, every vulgar superstition, every remnant of pedantic system, every sentimental like or dislike, must be left behind you, for the induction of the world problem. You must empty yourself before God will fill you.'

'Of what can I strip myself more? I know nothing; I can do nothing; I hope nothing; I fear nothing; I am nothing.'

'And you would gain something. But for what purpose?—for on that depends your whole success. To be famous, great, glorious, powerful, beneficent?'

'As I live, the height of my ambition, small though it be, is only to find my place, though it were but as a sweeper of chimneys. If I dare wish—if I dare choose, it would be only this—to regenerate one little parish in the whole world . . . To do that, and die, for aught I care, without ever being recognised as the author of my own deeds . . . to hear them, if need be, imputed to another, and myself accursed as a fool, if I can but atone for the sins of . . .'

He paused; but his teacher understood him.

'It is enough,' he said. 'Come with me; Tregarva waits for us near. Again I warn you; you will hear nothing new; you shall only see what you, and all around you, have known and not done, known and done. We have no peculiar doctrines or systems; the old creeds are enough for us. But we have obeyed the teaching which we received in each and every age, and allowed ourselves to be built up, generation by generation—as the rest of Christendom might have done—into a living temple, on the foundation which is laid already, and other than which no man can lay.'

'And what is that?'

'Jesus Christ—THE MAN.'

He took Lancelot by the hand. A peaceful warmth diffused itself over his limbs; the droning of the organ sounded fainter and more faint; the marble monuments grew dim and distant; and, half unconsciously, he followed like a child through the cathedral door.

EPILOGUE

I can foresee many criticisms, and those not unreasonable ones, on this little book—let it be some excuse at least for me, that I have foreseen them. Readers will complain, I doubt not, of the very mythical and mysterious dénouement of a story which began by things so gross and palpable as field-sports and pauperism. But is it not true that, sooner or later, 'omnia exeunt in mysterium'? Out of mystery we all came at our birth, fox-hunters and paupers, sages and saints; into mystery we shall all return . . . at all events, when we die; probably, as it seems to me, some of us will return thither before we die. For if the signs of the times mean anything, they portend, I humbly submit, a somewhat mysterious and mythical dénouement to this very age, and to those struggles of it which I have herein attempted, clumsily enough, to sketch. We are entering fast, I both hope and fear, into the region of prodigy, true and false; and our great-grandchildren will look back on the latter half of this century, and ask, if it were possible that such things could happen in an organised planet? The Benthamites will receive this announcement, if it ever meets their eyes, with shouts of laughter. Be it so . . . nous verrons . . . In the year 1847, if they will recollect, they were congratulating themselves on the nations having grown too wise to go to war any more . . . and in 1848? So it has been from the beginning. What did philosophers expect in 1792? What did they see in 1793? Popery was to be eternal: but the Reformation came nevertheless. Rome was to be eternal: but Alaric came. Jerusalem was to be eternal: but Titus came. Gomorrha was to be eternal, I doubt not; but the fire-floods came. . . . 'As it was in the days of Noah, so shall it be in the days of the Son of Man. They were eating, drinking, marrying, and giving in marriage; and the flood came and swept them all away.' Of course they did not expect it. They went on saying, 'Where is the promise of his coming? For all things continue as they were from the beginning.' Most true; but what if they were from the beginning—over a volcano's mouth? What if the method whereon things have proceeded since the creation were, as geology as well as history proclaims, a *cataclysmic* method? What then? Why should not this age, as all others like it have done, end in a cataclysm, and a prodigy, and a mystery? And why should not my little book do likewise?

Again—Readers will probably complain of the fragmentary and unconnected form of the book. Let them first be sure that that is not an integral feature of the subject itself, and therefore the very form the book should take. Do not young men think, speak, act, just now, in this very incoherent, fragmentary way; without methodic education or habits of thought; with the various stereotyped systems which they have received by tradition, breaking up under them like ice in a thaw; with a thousand facts and notions, which they know not how to classify, pouring in on them like a flood?—a very Yeasty state of mind altogether, like a mountain burn in a spring rain, carrying down with it stones, sticks, peat-water, addle grouse-eggs and drowned kingfishers, fertilising salts and vegetable poisons—not, alas! without a large crust, here and there, of sheer froth. Yet no heterogeneous confused flood-deposit, no fertile meadows below. And no high water, no fishing. It is in the long black droughts, when the water is foul from lowness, and not from height, that Hydras and Desmidiæ, and Rotifers, and all uncouth pseud-organisms, bred of putridity, begin to multiply, and the fish are sick for want of a fresh, and the cunningest artificial fly is of no avail, and the shrewdest angler will do nothing—except with a gross fleshly gilt-tailed worm, or the cannibal bait of roe, whereby parent fishes, like competitive barbarisms, devour each other's flesh and blood—perhaps their own. It is when the stream is clearing after a flood, that the fish will rise. . . . When will the flood clear, and the fish come on the feed again?

Next; I shall be blamed for having left untold the fate of those characters who have acted throughout as Lancelot's satellites. But indeed their only purpose consisted in their influence on his development, and that of Tregarva; I do not see that we have any need to follow them farther. The reader can surely conjecture their history for himself. . . . He may be pretty certain that they have gone the way of the world . . . abierunt ad plures . . . for this life or for the next. They have done—very much what he or I might have done in their place—nothing. Nature brings very few of her children to perfection, in these days or any other. . . . And for Grace, which does bring its children to perfection, the quantity and quality of the perfection must depend on the quantity and quality of the grace, and that again, to an awful extent—The Giver only knows to how great an extent—on the will of the recipients, and therefore in exact proportion to their lowness in the human scale, on the circumstances which environ them. So my characters are now—very much what the reader might expect them to be. I confess them to be unsatisfactory; so are most things: but how can I solve problems which fact has not yet solved for me? How am I to extricate my antitypal characters, when their living types have not yet extricated themselves? When the age moves on, my story shall move on with it. Let it be enough, that my puppets have retreated in good order, and that I am willing to give to those readers who have conceived something of human interest for them, the latest accounts of their doings.

With the exception, that is, of Mellot and Sabina. Them I confess to be an utterly mysterious, fragmentary little couple. Why not? Do you not meet with twenty such in the course of your life?—Charming people, who for aught you know may be opera folk from Paris, or emissaries from the Czar, or disguised Jesuits, or disguised Angels . . . who evidently 'have a history,' and a strange one, which you never expect or attempt to fathom; who interest you intensely for a while, and then are whirled away again in the great world-waltz, and lost in the crowd for ever? Why should you wish my story to be more complete than theirs is, or less romantic than theirs may be? There are more things in London, as well as in heaven and earth, than are dreamt of in our philosophy. If you but knew the secret history of that dull gentleman opposite whom you sat at dinner yesterday!—the real thoughts of that chattering girl whom you took down!—'Omnia exeunt in mysterium,' I say again. Every human being is a romance, a miracle to himself now; and will appear as one to all the world in That Day.

But now for the rest; and Squire Lavington first. He is a very fair sample of the fate of the British public; for he is dead and buried: and readers would not have me extricate him out of that situation. If you ask news of the reason and manner of his end, I can only answer, that like many others, he went out—as candles do. I believe he expressed general repentance for all his sins—all, at least, of which he was aware. To confess and repent of the state of the Whitford Priors estate, and of the poor thereon, was of course more than any minister, of any denomination whatsoever, could be required to demand of him; seeing that would have involved a recognition of those duties of property, of which the good old gentleman was to the last a staunch denier; and which are as yet seldom supposed to be included in any Christian creed, Catholic or other. Two sermons were preached in Whitford on the day of his funeral; one by Mr. O'Blareaway, on the text from Job, provided for such occasions; 'When the ear heard him, then it blessed him,' etc. etc.: the other by the Baptist preacher, on two verses of the forty-ninth Psalm—

'They fancy that their houses shall endure for ever, and call the lands after their own names.

'Yet man being in honour hath no understanding, but is compared to the beasts that perish.'

Waiving the good taste, which was probably on a par in both cases, the reader is left to decide which of the two texts was most applicable.

Mrs. Lavington is Mrs. Lavington no longer. She has married, to the astonishment of the world in general, that 'excellent man,' Mr. O'Blareaway, who has been discovered not to be quite as young as he appeared, his graces being principally owing to a Brutus wig, which he has now wisely discarded. Mrs. Lavington now sits in state under her husband's ministry, as the leader of the religious world in the fashionable watering-place of Steamingbath, and derives her notions of the past, present, and future state of the universe principally from those two meek and unbiased periodicals, the *Protestant Hue-and-Cry* and the *Christian Satirist*, to both of which O'Blareaway is a constant contributor. She has taken such an aversion to Whitford since Argemone's death, that she has ceased to have any connection with that unhealthy locality, beyond the popular and easy one of rent-receiving. O'Blareaway has never entered the parish to his knowledge since Mr. Lavington's funeral; and was much pleased, the last time I rode with him, at my informing him that a certain picturesque moorland which he had been greatly admiring, was his own possession. . . . After all, he is 'an excellent man;' and when I met a large party at his house the other day, and beheld dory and surmullet, champagne and lachryma Christi, amid all the glory of the Whitford plate . . . (some of it said to have belonged to the altar of the Priory Church four hundred years ago), I was deeply moved by the impressive tone in which, at the end of a long grace, he prayed 'that the daily bread of our less favoured brethren might be mercifully vouchsafed to them.' . . . My dear readers, would you have me, even if I could, extricate him from such an Elysium by any denouement whatsoever?

Poor dear Luke, again, is said to be painting lean frescoes for the Something-or-other-Kirche at Munich; and the vicar, under the name of Father Stylites, of the order of St. Philumena, is preaching impassioned sermons to crowded congregations at St. George's, Bedlam. How can I extricate them from that? No one has come forth of it yet, to my knowledge, except by paths whereof I shall use Lessing's saying, 'I may have my whole hand full of truth, and yet find good to open only my little finger.' But who cares for their coming out? They are but two more added to the five hundred, at whose moral suicide, and dive into the Roman Avernus, a quasi-Protestant public looks on with a sort of savage satisfaction, crying only, 'Didn't we tell you so?'—and more than half hopes that they will not come back again, lest they should be discovered to have learnt anything while they were there. What are two among that five hundred? much more among the five thousand who seem destined shortly to follow them?

The banker, thanks to Barnakill's assistance, is rapidly getting rich again—who would wish to stop him? However, he is wiser, on some points at least, than he was of yore. He has taken up the flax movement violently of late—perhaps owing to some hint of Barnakill's—talks of nothing but Chevalier Claussen and Mr. Donellan, and is very anxious to advance capital to any landlord who will grow flax on Mr. Warnes's method, either in England or Ireland. . . . John Bull, however, has not yet awakened sufficiently to listen to his overtures, but sits up in bed, dolefully rubbing his eyes, and bemoaning the evanishment of his protectionist dream—altogether realising tolerably, he and his land, Dr. Watts' well-known moral song concerning the sluggard and his garden.

Lord Minchampstead again prospers. Either the nuns of Minchampstead have left no Nemesis behind them, like those of Whitford, or a certain wisdom and righteousness of his, however dim and imperfect, averts it for a time. So, as I said, he prospers, and is hated; especially by his farmers, to whom he has just offered long leases, and a sliding corn-rent. They would have hated him just the same if he had kept them at rack-rents; and he has not forgotten that; but they have. They looked shy at the leases, because they bind them to farm high, which they do not know how to do; and at the corn-rent, because they think that he expects wheat to rise again—which, being a sensible man, he very probably does. But for my story—I certainly do not see how to extricate him or any one else from farmers' stupidity, greed, and ill-will. . . . That question must have seven years' more free-trade to settle it, before I can say anything thereon. Still less can I foreshadow the fate of his eldest son, who has just been rusticated from Christ Church for riding one of Simmon's hacks through a china-shop window; especially as the youth is reported to be given to piquette and strong liquors, and, like many noblemen's eldest sons, is considered 'not to have the talent of his father.' As for the old lord himself, I have no wish to change or develop him in any way—except to cut slips off him, as you do off a willow, and plant two or three in every county in England. Let him alone to work out his own plot . . . we have not seen the end of it yet; but whatever it will be, England has need of him as a transition-stage between feudalism and * * * * ; for many a day to come. If he be not the ideal landlord, he is nearer it than any we are like yet to see. . . .

Except one; and that, after all, is Lord Vieuxbois. Let him go on, like a gallant gentleman as he is, and prosper. And he will prosper, for he fears God, and God is with him. He has much to learn; and a little to unlearn. He has to learn that God is a living God now, as well as in the middle ages; to learn to trust not in antique precedents, but in eternal laws: to learn that his tenants, just because they are children of God, are not to be kept children, but developed and educated into sons; to learn that God's grace, like His love, is free, and that His spirit bloweth where it listeth, and vindicates its own free-will against our narrow systems, by revealing, at times, even to nominal Heretics and Infidels, truths which the Catholic Church must humbly receive, as the message of Him who is wider, deeper, more tolerant, than even she can be. . . And he is in the way to learn all this. Let him go on. At what conclusions he will attain, he knows not, nor do I. But this I know, that he is on the path to great and true conclusions. . . . And he is just about to be married, too. That surely should teach him something. The papers inform me that his bride elect is Lord Minchampstead's youngest daughter. That should be a noble mixture; there should be stalwart offspring, spiritual as well as physical, born of that intermarriage of the old and the new. We will hope it: perhaps some of my readers, who enter into my inner meaning, may also pray for it.

Whom have I to account for besides? Crawy—though some of my readers may consider the mention of him superfluous. But to those who do not, I may impart the news, that last month, in the union workhouse—he died; and may, for aught we know, have ere this met Squire Lavington . . . He is supposed, or at least said, to have had a soul to be saved . . . as I think, a body to be saved also. But what is one more among so many? And in an over-peopled country like this, too. . . . One must learn to look at things—and paupers—in the mass.

The poor of Whitford also? My dear readers, I trust you will not ask me just now to draw the horoscope of the Whitford poor, or of any others. Really that depends principally on yourselves. . . . But for the present, the poor of Whitford, owing, as it seems to them and me, to quite other causes than an 'overstocked labour-market,' or too rapid 'multiplication of their species,' are growing more profligate, reckless, pauperised, year by year. O'Blareaway complained sadly to me the other day that the poor-rates were becoming 'heavier and heavier'—had nearly reached, indeed, what they were under the old law....

But there is one who does not complain, but gives and gives, and stints herself to give, and weeps in silence and unseen over the evils which she has yearly less and less power to stem.

For in a darkened chamber of the fine house at Steamingbath, lies on a sofa Honoria Lavington—beautiful no more; the victim of some mysterious and agonising disease, about which the physicians agree on one point only—that it is hopeless. The 'curse of the Lavingtons' is on her; and she bears it. There she lies, and prays, and reads, and arranges her charities, and writes little books for children, full of the Beloved Name which is for ever on her lips. She suffers—none but herself knows how much, or how strangely—yet she is never heard to sigh. She weeps in secret—she has long ceased to plead—for others, not for herself; and prays for them too—perhaps some day her prayers will yet he answered. But she greets all visitors with a smile fresh from heaven; and all who enter that room leave it saddened, and yet happy, like those who have lingered a moment at the gates of paradise, and seen angels ascending and descending upon earth. There she lies—who could wish her otherwise? Even Doctor Autotheus Maresnest, the celebrated mesmeriser, who, though he laughs at the Resurrection of the Lord, is confidently reported to have raised more than one corpse to life himself, was heard to say, after having attended her professionally, that her waking bliss and peace, although unfortunately unattributable even to autocatalepsy, much less to somnambulist exaltation, was on the whole, however unscientific, almost as enviable.

There she lies—and will lie till she dies—the type of thousands more, 'the martyrs by the pang without the palm,' who find no mates in this life . . . and yet may find them in the life to come.,.. Poor Paul Tregarva! Little he fancies how her days run by! . . .

At least, there has been no news since that last scene in St. Paul's Cathedral, either of him or Lancelot. How their strange teacher has fulfilled his promise of guiding their education; whether they have yet reached the country of Prester John; whether, indeed, that Caucasian Utopia has a local and bodily existence, or was only used by Barnakill to shadow out that Ideal which is, as he said of the Garden of Eden, always near us, underlying the Actual, as the spirit does its body, exhibiting itself step by step through all the falsehoods and confusions of history and society, giving life to all in it which is not falsehood and decay; on all these questions I can give my readers no sort of answer; perhaps I may as yet have no answer to give; perhaps I may be afraid of giving one; perhaps the times themselves are giving, at once cheerfully and sadly, in strange destructions and strange births, a better answer than I can give. I have set forth, as far as in me lay, the data of my problem: and surely, if the premises be given, wise men will not have to look far for the conclusion. In homely English I have given my readers Yeast; if they be what I take them for, they will be able to bake with it themselves.

And yet I have brought Lancelot, at least—perhaps Tregarva too—to a conclusion, and an all-important one, which whoso reads may find fairly printed in these pages. Henceforth his life must begin anew. Were I to carry on the thread of his story continuously he would still seem to have overleaped as vast a gulf as if I had re-introduced him as a gray-haired man. Strange! that the death of one of the lovers should seem no complete termination to their history, when their marriage would have been accepted by all as the legitimate dénouement, beyond which no information was to be expected. As if the history of love always ended at the altar! Oftener it only begins there; and all before it is but a mere longing to love. Why should readers complain of being refused the future history of one life, when they are in most novels cut short by the marriage finale from the biography of two?

But if, over and above this, any reader should be wroth at my having left Lancelot's history unfinished on questions in his opinion more important than that of love, let me entreat him to set manfully about finishing his own history—a far more important one to him than Lancelot's. If he shall complain that doubts are raised for which no solution is given, that my hero is brought into contradictory beliefs without present means of bringing them to accord, into passive acquiescence in vast truths without seeing any possibility of practically applying them—let him consider well whether such be not his own case; let him, if he be as most are, thank God when he finds out that such is his case, when he knows at last that those are most blind who say they see, when he becomes at last conscious how little he believes, how little he acts up to that small belief. Let him try to right somewhat of the doubt, confusion, custom-worship, inconsistency, idolatry, within him—some of the greed, bigotry, recklessness, respectably superstitious atheism around him; and perhaps before his new task is finished, Lancelot and Tregarva may have returned with a message, if not for him—for that depends upon him having ears to hear it—yet possibly for strong Lord Minchampstead, probably for good Lord Vieuxbois, and surely for the sinners and the slaves of Whitford Priors. What it will be, I know not altogether; but this I know, that if my heroes go on as they have set forth, looking with single mind for some one ground of human light and love, some everlasting rock whereon to build, utterly careless what the building may be, howsoever contrary to precedent and prejudice, and the idols of the day, provided God, and nature, and the accumulated lessons of all the ages, help them in its construction—then they will find in time the thing they seek, and see how the will of God may at last be done on earth, even as it is done in heaven. But, alas! between them and it are waste raging waters, foul mud banks, thick with dragons and sirens; and many a bitter day and blinding night, in cold and hunger, spiritual and perhaps physical, await them. For it was a true vision which John Bunyan saw, and one which, as the visions of wise men are wont to do, meant far more than the seer fancied, when he beheld in his dream that there was indeed a land of Beulah, and Arcadian Shepherd Paradise, on whose mountain tops the everlasting sunshine lay; but that the way to it, as these last three years are preaching to us, went past the mouth of Hell, and through the valley of the Shadow of Death.